D1521672

A MARRIAGE MANUAL

A PRACTICAL GUIDE-BOOK TO SEX AND MARRIAGE

by

HANNAH M. STONE, M. D.

Medical Director of the Birth Control Clinical Research Bureau and of the Marriage Consultation Center at the Community Church, New York

and

ABRAHAM STONE, M. D.

Associate Attending Urologist at the Sydenham Hospital. Co-Director of the Marriage Consultation Center at the Community Church, New York

REVISED EDITION

SIMON AND SCHUSTER • NEW YORK

1230 SIXTH AVENUE
ROCKEFELLER CENTER, NEW YORK 20, N. Y.

TWENTY-FOURTH PRINTING

MANUFACTURED IN THE UNITED STATES OF AMERICA
BY THE HADDON CRAFTSMEN, INC., SCRANTON, PA.

TO

OUR DAUGHTER

GLORIA

FOREWORD

In writing this book it has been our object to present in a realistic and concrete manner and in simple, non-technical language the essential facts of mating and reproduction. For many years we have had the opportunity in lectures and consultations to discuss with men and women their problems of sex and marriage. During the course of our work, we have become familiar with the practical and intimate sexual and marital problems which confront the average individual. This book is based largely upon the results of these experiences, and is an attempt to meet the general need for more adequate information concerning the factors of human sex and reproduction.

A Marriage Manual *is written in the form of hypothetical consultations between a physician and a young couple about to be married. In reality it does represent a composite record of many thousands of pre- and post-marital consultations—at the Marriage Consultation Centers of the Labor Temple and the Community Church, at the Birth Control Clinical Research Bureau of New York, and elsewhere. We have adopted the dialogue style because we felt that it lent itself more readily to a vivid presentation of the questions and discussions, and because it appeared to be most suitable for a graphic portrayal of the subject matter.*

Our aim has been to deal mainly with the individual aspects of sex contact rather than with the social, ethical or moral problems of sex conduct. As such, this volume is offered primarily as a practical guide to sex and marriage. We have dealt at some length and detail with the structure and functions of the human sex organs because we feel that an intelligent union should be based on an understanding of the biological processes involved. We have also emphasized particularly the technique of the sexual relation and the problems of birth control because it has been our experience that an appreciation of the sex factors in marriage and reliable contraceptive information are essential for a well-adjusted and satisfactory marital union.

Though it may appear from the contents that some parts were written by one or the other of us, we have, as a matter of fact, made no attempt to divide the subject between us, but have written all of it jointly. It has been our custom for many years to exchange our medical experiences, impressions and observations and to discuss and analyze the various problems that have come to our attention. Hence all the material included represents the result of the experiences and viewpoints of both of us.

Dr. Hannah M. Stone
Dr. Abraham Stone

TABLE OF CONTENTS

ILLUSTRATIONS

CHAPTER I

FITNESS FOR MARRIAGE

"*We are about to be married, doctor, and we have come to you for a general consultation. We feel that we ought to obtain some information and advice before our marriage, and we have many questions we'd like to discuss with you.*"

"I shall be glad to give you whatever information I can. An understanding of the basic physical and psychological facts of sex and marriage certainly helps to lay a sounder foundation for the marital union. Are there any special problems about which you are concerned?"

"*No, we have no particular problems, but we would appreciate any information or advice that you think we ought to have.*"

"I presume you have already read some books on the subject."

"*Very few. In fact, we were going to ask you to recommend some to us.*"

"As we go along I shall mention many books that might be of interest to you. Before we proceed, however, have you had a physical examination lately?"

"*No, not for some time, doctor. That is really one of the reasons for our visit. We'd like to find out whether we are fit for marriage.*"

"Very well, I shall arrange for both of you to be examined later. However, if you were seriously interested in the question of your fitness for marriage, you should not have delayed finding out about it until this late date. By now, I presume, all your plans and arrangements have already been made, and it would probably be almost impossible to change them. To determine fitness for marriage it is really necessary to make a rather thorough study of the eugenic background, the past and present health record, and the general physical condition of the individual, and this should preferably be undertaken some time before the final decisions and plans for the marriage are made."

"*We realize that it is rather late for us to inquire about our fitness now. We come from pretty good stock, and neither of us has had any serious illness, so we somehow assumed that we were well. Are there any special standards of fitness for marriage, doctor?*"

"There really are no absolute norms or tests of suitability for the marital union. In marriage, as in other fields, fitness implies the ability to meet the necessary requirements or purposes. The standards of fitness for marriage, therefore, depend upon what we consider the objects or purposes of marriage to be.

THE OBJECTS OF MARRIAGE

"Fundamentally, marriage is a personal association between a man and a woman and a biological relationship for mating and reproduction. As a social, legal, and religious institution, marriage has undergone any number of modifications and changes—nevertheless its basic realities remain the same. The permanent, indissoluble, sacramental union of the Orthodox differs strikingly from the free, easily severed, and often not even officially registered marriage, let us say, of a modern Russian, and yet both of these marriages have certain underlying elements in common. In both instances the couple seek to make their union stable, they assume the freedom and privilege of a sexual relationship, and normally have as their ultimate aim the establishment of a family."

"*In our own case, too, we have decided to get married because we have come to feel that only marriage will give us a sense of stability and of completely 'belonging to each other.'*"

COMPANIONSHIP

"Quite so. A man and a woman who love each other, who feel a deep mutual attraction, who have many interests, tastes, and ideals in common will after a while want to make their association stable and permanent. They will want to live together, to build a home together, to be assured of lasting companionship. Under present social and legal conditions this permanency can be achieved only through marriage.

"Furthermore, they will also want to live together in a physical sense. Love is a mixture of sensuality and sentiment, and the sexual relation is a fundamental factor in marriage. Where a strong attraction exists there will also be the desire for a close physical intimacy. Under our present code of moral standards sexual relations outside of wedlock are socially and legally forbidden, and marriage therefore serves the purpose of sanctioning the freedom and privilege of a sexual relationship.

MATING

"Biologically, again, the object of marriage is not to legalize a sexual union, but rather to insure the survival of the species and of the race. From this point of view, marriage is not merely a sexual relationship, but a parental association. It is the union of a male and a female for the production and care of offspring, and reproduction is therefore another fundamental object or purpose of marriage."

REPRODUCTION

"*Would you say, then, that marriage should be postponed until a couple are in a position to have children and support a family?*"

"No, not necessarily. It is true that economic ability on the part of the man has always been regarded as one of the most important social standards of fitness for marriage. Even in primitive days, strength, endurance, and the ability to provide for the family were the essential marital qualifications. Westermarck, in his *History of Human Marriage,* reports that among many early tribes a young man had first to prove his courage and endurance before he was allowed to choose a wife. Among certain natives of South America, for example, no young man was permitted to marry before he had killed some big game, such as a jaguar; and if he killed five jaguars, he had a right to more than one wife. Among certain Eskimo tribes, a young man could have the young lady of his choice only after he had proved by his skill in hunting that he could support not only a wife and children but his parents-in-law as well.

ECONOMIC FITNESS

"At present, of course, no such feats of valor are expected of the young man, nor do parents-in-law expect to be supported by their prospective son-in-law. Today the combined economic skill of both husband and wife are sometimes necessary to insure their own support. While economic fitness still constitutes a very important social factor in marriage, it is being realized more and more, I believe, that it is not always advisable to postpone marriage until the man will be able to provide fully for the family. Young people reach physiological maturity long before they can attain economic security; the gap seems to be constantly widening and it is not always wise to wait for complete financial independence. It is better, it seems to me, for a couple to marry even though both may have to contribute to the family budget, rather than to wait until the husband's income alone will be sufficient for the needs of the home. This whole question, however, lies outside of our present discussion, and perhaps we shall return to it later on."

"*But wouldn't a marriage on such a basis necessitate a delay in the raising of a family? This really applies to our own case, doctor. We are both looking forward to the time when we shall be able to have children but we'd rather not have any until we are in a position to provide for their care and their needs, and this may not be possible for us for at least a year or two.*"

"This is a problem which confronts most young couples today. Our present social and economic conditions frequently compel the postponement of childbearing or the limitation of the size of the family. A large number of young people can marry only on the understanding that the coming of children will be voluntarily delayed until they are ready to plan for a family. Nevertheless, eventually, as you said yourself, you will want children, and this is true of every normal couple.

"While particular marriages may, of course, be entered into for any number of other reasons—family pressure, social convenience, financial considerations, and similar motives, basically the prime objects of marriage are companionship, sexual intimacy, and procreation. A man and a woman to be fit for marriage should therefore be emotionally companionable, they should be sexually normal, and they should be fit physically and eugenically to beget offspring."

"*I don't quite understand what you mean by being emotionally companionable. Isn't that mainly a question of an individual adjustment between two people? Some can get along well and some cannot.*"

"What I had in mind is the fact that certain people are unable to make a satisfactory adjustment in any marriage. I am not speaking of individuals who are incompatible with a certain mate, but rather of those who cannot adapt themselves to any marital relationship. Let me tell you, as an instance, about one couple I saw recently. It was the husband's third marriage. The first two had ended in divorce. In each case there were constant domestic disagreements and an adjustment seemed impossible. New difficulties and dissensions were beginning to develop in the third marriage. After several interviews it became quite evident that the basis of the maladjustment in this case was the man's exaggerated attachment to his mother, who had always dominated his life, an attachment from which he could not free himself sufficiently to enter fully into a new association. This is one form of emotional unsuitability for marriage; there are many others. There are men and women with psychopathic personalities, with serious emotional derangements, individuals with abnormal sexual tendencies, with conscious or subconscious homosexual inclinations, any of which may form a serious barrier to a harmonious marital adjustment. These are instances where the question of psychological fitness for marriage comes into consideration."

PSYCHOLOGICAL FITNESS

"*You mentioned the question of family attachment. Could this prove a hindrance to a satisfactory marriage?*"

"Normally, not at all. The case I mentioned involved, of course, a very exaggerated form of filial attachment. Ordinarily, family devotion should not interfere in the least with one's emotional adjustment in marriage. It is necessary, however, that after marriage a new understanding and a new sympathy should enter into the whole family relationship. The new couple should be emotionally free from parental domination and should be able to strike a wholesome balance between their allegiance and relation to each other and their loyalty to their respective families. When a man and a woman marry, they should be able to break away from the original unit and build up a new unit of themselves."

"*When you spoke of the need of being sexually normal in relation to fitness for marriage, doctor, were you referring to the question of sexual diseases?*"

"No, I had reference mainly to the question of sexual capacity, that is physical ability to enter into the sexual relationship. This is a problem which applies primarily to the man. Sexual disabilities of women are not often related to fitness for marriage, and we shall discuss these at some other time. Lack of sufficient potency on the part of men, however, is not an infrequent condition, and those suffering from this disorder may be unable to consummate the physical union in marriage. It is a serious mistake for anyone who is sexually inadequate to marry without first having his disability corrected, or at least without receiving competent medical advice. As a matter of fact, Hindu lawmakers decreed over a thousand years ago that before marriage 'a man must undergo an examination with regard to his virility.' Only after the fact of his virility had been established beyond doubt was he privileged to marry."

SEXUAL FITNESS

"*Is there any way of determining whether a man is potent or not before he has had sexual experiences?*"

"To some extent, yes. Normally, a man, even though he has never had any actual sexual relations, has probably had some kind of sexual manifestations. He has been stimulated sexually, has reacted in a definite manner, and he is, therefore, as a rule, conscious of his sexual capacities. Every now and then, however, it does happen that a man's sexual incapacity does not manifest itself until after marriage, or appears only at that time, but this is a chapter in the story of marriage that we shall consider more fully later on.

"Now, aside from the question of sexual capacity, fitness for marriage, as I mentioned before, implies also the ability to beget healthy children. The couple should be free from any infirmity which would prevent reproduction. In other words, neither the husband nor the wife should be sterile, or afflicted with any disease which would make procreation physically or eugenically inadvisable."

REPRODUCTIVE FITNESS

"*But suppose one can't or shouldn't have children for one reason or another, should that person never marry?*"

"No, not necessarily. I have known couples who have married in spite of the fact that they knew beforehand that they could never have children, and such marriages are sometimes quite successful. There are other factors which may decide a man or a woman to marry

—factors which even outweigh the inability to beget children. In all such circumstances, however, it is quite necessary that both should know of the condition beforehand and enter the marriage with such knowledge and understanding in mind."

"*Is it possible to know in advance whether a man or a woman will be able to have children?*"

FERTILITY AND STERILITY

"Well, it has been calculated that approximately ten per cent of all marriages remain sterile. Of every ten couples, in other words, one couple will not be able to beget offspring. In these instances either the wife, the husband or both may be responsible for the sterility. While it is now possible to determine fairly accurately the fertility of the male, there are no certain means available as yet to establish definitely the fertility of the woman, or whether the two will be fertile with each other. Except, therefore, in those cases where it can be demonstrated that the male is sterile, it is very difficult to tell with any degree of accuracy whether a particular couple will be able to bear children or not."

"*Can it be determined before the marriage whether a man is sterile or not?*"

"Yes, by a comparatively simple test. All that is necessary is to obtain a fairly fresh specimen of the man's seminal fluid, and this can then be examined microscopically for the degree of fertility. As a matter of fact, I would say that whenever there is any doubt concerning a man's fertility, as in the case where there is some congenital abnormality of the reproductive organs, or where there has been some sexual injury or disease, particularly an inflammation of the sex glands following a venereal infection, an examination for fertility should be made prior to marriage.

EUGENIC FITNESS

"The other question that comes up in connection with reproduction, is that of eugenics. The man and woman who marry naturally expect that their children will have every chance of being well born, sound in mind and in body. If one suffers from any disease which might be transmitted to the offspring, or if there is any hereditary taint in one's family, the possibilities should be carefully considered and competent advice obtained before marriage. Among some of the conditions which might be mentioned in this connection are the venereal diseases, certain forms of mental abnormalities or deficiencies, insanity, epilepsy, deaf-mutism. One in whose family, for instance, there are several cases of insanity should not marry without considering seriously the possibility of the hereditary transmission of the mental defect, nor should a man who has had syphilis marry without being definitely certain that he can no longer pass on the disease to his wife and to his offspring."

"*Has one's general health or physical condition any relation to fitness for marriage?*"

HEALTH OF THE HUSBAND

"Good health is naturally a desirable asset under all circumstances, and a bad liver may spoil even an ideal romance. Yet, generally speaking, perfect health is not an essential for marriage. Suppose a man had, let us say, scarlet fever in his childhood and this happened to leave him with a chronic kidney condition; or he had rheumatism at one time which had affected his heart—that does not necessarily bear upon his fitness for marriage. It may influence his earning capacities, his prospects for the future, the duration of his life, or even his general disposition and reactions, but it does not make him ineligible for marriage or incapable of making a fine husband. We have seen any number of marriages that were entirely happy and satisfactory in spite of the fact that one or the other of the couple was not in perfect physical condition. The thing to be remembered in this connection, however, is that when a chronic physical handicap does exist, it is well that both the man and his future wife should learn of it beforehand, so that the situation may be clearly understood and voluntarily accepted by both. Every now and then serious marital difficulties result from the fact that either the husband or the wife had failed to disclose before the marriage the existence of some chronic disability.

HEALTH OF THE WIFE

"Perhaps this is even more important where the woman is the one who is not well, because then the additional factor of childbearing comes into consideration. Certain chronic disorders make childbearing hazardous for the woman. To a woman with a bad heart, for instance, a pregnancy may constitute a considerable risk to her health and even to her life. It is best, therefore, that the presence of such conditions be known in advance of the marriage, so that there may be a mutual understanding of the possibilities involved and an opportunity for the needed physical and mental adjustments."

"*If the father or mother suffer from some chronic ailment, are they apt to transmit a similar condition to their children?*"

PARENTAL HEALTH AND HEREDITARY DISEASES

"This will depend entirely upon the particular disorder. We must distinguish clearly between ailments which are inherited and those which are acquired. Acquired disabilities are not transmissible. One may, for instance, develop a certain deformity as a result of an attack of infantile paralysis, but a deformity of this type would not be hereditary and would in no manner be transmitted to the children. Or one may become deaf because of an injury or infection of the ear, but this form of deafness is not transmissible. There is, however, a form of deafness which does run in families and which is definitely inherited. It is therefore necessary to study each case individually."

"*Is it ever safe for one who has had a venereal disease to marry?*"

VENEREAL DISEASES AND MARRIAGE

"Yes, but each case must be decided individually. Certainly no one who has had a venereal infection should marry without being assured by a competent physician that he can no longer transmit the disease. Because of their prevalence and far-reaching consequences, the venereal diseases constitute a real problem in relation to fitness for marriage. A number of factors have to be considered—the possibility of infecting the mate, the hazard to the future offspring, the ultimate effects upon the individual himself.

THE NEW YORK MARRIAGE LAW

"As a matter of fact, in a number of States the presence of a venereal disease is a legal barrier to marriage. In New York, for instance, a law which came into effect in July, 1938, requires a premarital medical examination for syphilis, including a blood test, from all applicants for a marriage license. The law provides that before the issuance of a marriage license each applicant must submit a statement signed by a physician to the effect that he or she was found to be free from syphilis in a stage which may become communicable. The statement must include a laboratory report showing that a blood test had been made. This test has to be taken within twenty days of the application for the marriage license; if more than twenty days elapse, another blood test is required. The license, when granted, is valid for only sixty days, and if the couple do not marry within that period, a new license must be obtained.

"Similar laws requiring premarital examinations for the presence of venereal disease, including a blood test, have also been enacted in several other States—in Connecticut, Illinois, Michigan, New Hampshire, New Jersey, Rhode Island, Wisconsin, and are under consideration in many other parts of the country. Aside from actually preventing the marriage of individuals who may transmit the disease, these laws generally tend to create a greater consciousness and sense of responsibility with respect to the problem of venereal infections."

"*Can a venereal disease really be cured completely?*"

GONORRHEA

"There are two different venereal diseases to be considered, gonorrhea and syphilis, and each presents its own special problems. In the case of gonorrhea, for instance, the course of the disease may vary from a comparatively mild inflammation lasting but a few weeks, to a severe and prolonged ailment. At times the infection may even lead to serious complications which require extensive operations and result in permanent sterility or chronic invalidism. Many of the operations performed on women and a great many sterile marriages are due directly or indirectly to the effects of gonorrhea. In the majority of instances, however, the disease is curable, and one may eventually marry without the danger of transmitting the infection."

"*If one had a gonorrheal infection, would there not be some effect upon the children later on?*"

GONORRHEA AND HEREDITY

"No. Gonorrhea is not a hereditary disease. Primarily, it is a local infection of the sex and urinary organs. Only rarely do the germs of gonorrhea enter the blood stream and spread to other parts of the body. In any event the hereditary qualities of the individual are not affected by the disease and it is not transmitted to the offspring as an inherited infection."

"*But people are always saying that if the parents have gonorrhea, the children may be born diseased.*"

"Yes, it is quite true that a new-born child may develop gonorrhea, but that is not because the disease is inherited. The child contracts it by being infected with the germs at the time of its birth. If the gonorrhea germs are present in the birth-canal of the mother, the child may come in contact with them there and acquire the infection. Usually they lodge in the eyes of the infant and produce a very serious inflammation which may actually result in blindness. That is the reason why the eyes of every baby are treated by the doctor soon after birth with a strong antiseptic solution as a routine measure. This application has proved to be an effective prophylactic against the transmission of the disease to the new-born, and has greatly reduced the amount of infant blindness."

"*What about syphilis? Can that be cured, too?*"

SYPHILIS

"Syphilis presents an entirely different problem. First of all, it is not a local disease like gonorrhea, but a generalized blood infection. It usually starts as a local sore or ulceration on the genitals or other part of the body, but from there the germs soon enter the blood stream and are carried through the entire system. They may lodge in any organ and produce serious consequences, sometimes many years after the first appearance of the infection. It is not easy to rid the body of a syphilitic infection, and it may take many years of active and intensive treatment before a patient can be rendered free from all evidence of the disease. Nevertheless it is the opinion of most authorities, I believe, that this can be accomplished in the majority of cases. Stokes, for instance, in a recent volume on the subject, maintains that a 'clinical cure,' by which he means complete relief from the symptoms and signs of the disease and ultimate non-infectiousness, can be brought about in from 80 to 85 per cent of patients who will coöperate in treatment and observation. The sooner treatment is begun after the onset of the disease, the better the chances of a permanent cure. If the disease is allowed to progress for some time without proper medical treatment and care, it may not be possible to effect even a so-called 'clinical cure.'"

"*Is one who has been infected with syphilis ever really fit to marry?*"

"Yes, provided sufficient and adequate treatment was received. The consensus of opinion is that if a patient has been treated actively for about three years, and has been entirely free from any evidence of the disease for two more years, he may marry without fear of transmitting the infection to his wife or offspring. This rule, however, is only a general one, and has to be modified according to the individual circumstances."

"*How is syphilis passed on from parents to their children?*"

SYPHILIS AND HEREDITY

"Modern medical opinion holds that syphilis is really not inherited, that is, that the disease is not transmitted to the offspring as a hereditary defect. What happens is that during the early months of pregnancy, the germs of the disease, if they are present in the mother, pass from her to the developing child and the latter becomes infected. The embryo may either soon die as a result of the infection; or it may continue to live for several months and die just before birth, the pregnancy ending in a miscarriage or still-birth; or else, if the fetus is strong enough to survive the initial attack, the infant is born with the infection present in its body."

"*But if the child is born with the disease, why isn't it considered hereditary?*"

"The fact that a child is born with a certain disease or defect does not necessarily imply that the condition is inherited. It may have been acquired accidentally during the period of the baby's growth in the mother's womb. A child may, for instance, develop typhoid fever before birth if the mother happens to become infected with typhoid germs during her pregnancy. Clearly, this is not an inherited disease. The same, it is now assumed, is true of syphilis. The germs of this disease infect the child sometime during its prenatal life, and it must therefore be considered in the light of an acquired rather than an inborn condition. A hereditary quality is one which is inherent in the reproductive cells of the parents and which is therefore transmitted to the child as a very part of its constitutional make-up."

"*How are the qualities of parents passed on to children?*"

"Well, many problems in the mechanism of heredity still remain obscure, although enormous progress has been made in this field since the discoveries of the principles of heredity by the Austrian monk, Mendel, and the more recent researches of the American biologists, Morgan, Bridges and others. The whole subject, however, still remains very complex, and I can give you now only a very sketchy explanation. As you may know, every human being arises out of the union of two microscopic cells, the sperm of the male and the egg of the female. In these minute cells are present certain bodies called chromosomes, which are made up of a very large number of individual units, technically known as genes. These genes are now considered to be the physical carriers of heredity, and are the elements which determine the innate characteristics of the child—the shape of his head, the color of his eyes, the size of his heart, and according to some, also the type of his intelligence and the nature of his personality and character. In other words, the genes constitute the biological basis of heredity and control the inherent physical, mental and emotional make-up of the individual."

HOW HEREDITY WORKS

CHROMOSOMES AND GENES

"*You mentioned the color of the eyes. Why is it that there is often a difference in the same family? My father's eyes are brown, and my mother's blue, but the eyes of the children vary. Some of them have blue eyes, and some have brown.*"

"This difference in color distribution is a good illustration of the mechanism of heredity. Each child, as we saw, inherits two sets of genes, one from the father and one from the mother, and in its own body these genes are mingled and combined in a rather unpredictable manner. The characteristics of the child will depend therefore not only upon the types of genes he inherits but also upon their particular combination. In the matter of the color of the eyes, for instance, if the child happens to inherit a gene for brown eyes from the father and another for brown from the mother, his eyes will be brown and he will be able to transmit genes only for brown eyes to his children. If he inherits a gene for blue eyes from both parents, his eyes will be blue and he will be able to transmit blue eyes only. Should he, however, receive a gene for brown from the father and one for blue from the mother, his own eyes will be brown, because it happens that brown dominates or masks the blue, but he will carry also a gene for blue in his chromosomes and he will be able to transmit to his offspring genes either for brown or for blue. Your father, then, presumably has genes both for brown and for blue and hence the color of the children's eyes are not similar. Please understand, however, that this is a rather simplified explanation, for even the color of the eyes is determined in a much more complex manner. It serves, however, to illustrate the general mode of inheritance."

"*Are mental traits also inherited in the same manner? Doesn't environment play a large part?*"

HEREDITY AND ENVIRONMENT

"The subject of the relative importance of heredity and environment will probably continue to be debated for years and years to come. There is no unanimity of opinion about it. The inheritance of mental and temperamental qualities has particularly been a source of controversy. Some maintain that a child's character is entirely the result of his surroundings, his education, his training, his early experiences and conditionings. Watson, for instance, in his book on *Behaviorism*, takes the very definite stand that 'there is no such thing as inheritance of capacity, talent, temperament, mental constitution and characteristics.' These things depend on training that goes on mainly in the cradle, he says; that is, in the early years of life. He goes even a step further and says that if he were given a dozen healthy, well-formed infants and his own world to bring them up in, he could train any one of them to be a doctor, a lawyer, an artist or a thief, regardless of the child's talents, abilities or racial ancestry. On the other hand, many eugenists and biologists maintain that a child's mental characteristics are determined almost entirely by heredity. In *The Child's Heredity*, Popenoe lists a very large number of physical, mental and personality traits, both good and bad, which he ascribes largely to hereditary influences, and he claims that the difference in the mental endowments and achievements of individuals are due in from 90-97% to inborn and inherited peculiarities. A more moderate and balanced viewpoint is taken by the biologist, Jennings. In his very stimulating volume on *The Biological Basis of Human Nature*, he ably analyzes the relative influence of environment and heredity, and concludes that mentality, behavior, temperament and disposition can be modified by either of these. Given two individuals with an identical heredity, differences in environment will produce marked variations in their personality and character; on the other hand, given two absolutely similar environments, if that were possible, no two individuals would react alike because of inborn differences, and hence they, too, will vary greatly in their personality and character. In other words, the same kind of differences between individuals can be produced by varying either the environment or the heredity.

"The relation of heredity to environment is perhaps most simply expressed as the relation of the seed to the soil, a comparison which has frequently been made. The seed has potentialities to develop into a certain type of plant, but whether these potentialities will be realized will depend to a very large degree upon the kind of soil into which it is planted; in a poor soil it will be stunted, in a good soil it will develop to its fullest capacities. On the other hand, no matter how good the soil is, it can only bring out the qualities which were already present in the seed at the time it was sown. Nature and nurture constantly interact and they are perhaps equally important in determining the character of an individual."

"*What about hereditary diseases, doctor? What kinds of abnormalities may be passed on from parents to children?*"

INHERITANCE OF DISEASE

"The question of the hereditary transmissibility of disease is still a subject of much difference of opinion among medical authorities. That certain physical and mental abnormalities are inherited is fairly definitely established. Last year, for example, I saw a child with six fingers on each hand. The child's father and grandmother had a similar abnormality and it was obviously a case of an inherited condition. The same is true of certain types of disorders of the eyes and ears, of bleeding tendencies, and other defects which definitely 'run in families' and are caused by defective genes. Of greater importance, however, is the question of the extent to which one may inherit or transmit a constitutional weakness which may make the individual more susceptible to a particular disease. It is assumed that in many instances a predisposition to some particular physical or mental disorder is transmitted by the parents, though whether the condition will actually develop in the offspring or not will depend upon later environmental factors."

"*Is tuberculosis inherited? Are parents who suffer from this disease apt to transmit it to their children?*"

TUBERCULOSIS AND HEREDITY

"Until the last century it was widely held that tuberculosis was hereditary. Since then, however, newer discoveries and researches have shown fairly definitely that the disease itself is not inherited. It has been found, for instance, that when children of tuberculous parents are removed from direct contact with infected individuals, they usually escape the infection. There is considerable evidence, however, that children from tuberculous families do inherit an increased susceptibility or predisposition to tuberculosis and are more liable to contract the disease if exposed to it. It must also be remembered that such children are of necessity in constant proximity to infected individuals from their earliest days, and are consequently in greater danger of becoming infected themselves. It is wisest, therefore, for tuberculous people to postpone having children as long as they are in the active or infectious stages of the disease."

"*Should one who had or has tuberculosis marry?*"

TUBERCULOSIS

"The question of marriage would depend upon the extent of the infection and the individual circumstances. In early or arrested cases marriage is not contra-indicated; with proper care the disease can be kept permanently in check. In the more advanced cases the situation is much more serious and each instance must be decided separately. There are several factors which have to be taken into consideration: the chance of early incapacity and invalidism; the psychic reactions and adjustments; the possibility of infecting the partner; and, in the case of the woman, the question of child-bearing, for a pregnancy may seriously aggravate an existing tuberculosis and endanger the patient's life. These factors must be carefully weighed in each instance. From a eugenic point of view, furthermore, it may not be desirable for one who comes from a family where there are many cases of tuberculosis to marry into another tuberculous family, for the danger of transmission and infection is so much the greater under such circumstances."

"*Is cancer hereditary? Is one more apt to develop cancer if there have been cases of cancer in the family?*"

CANCER AND HEREDITY

"Cancer is not considered to be a hereditary or transmissible disease, and we do not even know whether a susceptibility to cancer may be inherited. At any rate, it is a disease which does not develop until rather late in life, and even if it should be proven that it involves some hereditary factor, I do not see why the presence of cancer in any member of the family should restrain anyone from marrying or having children."

"*You spoke before of the possibility of transmitting a susceptibility to a disease. To what extent would such a possibility influence one's fitness for marriage?*"

"That would depend largely upon the condition in question. In very many cases, even though a predisposition may be inherited, the development of the disease may be prevented by the necessary hygienic measures.

"I have already mentioned tuberculosis as an example of this type of heredity. Another instance is diabetes. It is claimed that it is possible to trace hereditary influence in about 25% of diabetics. Yet even with an inherited susceptibility one may never acquire diabetes if the necessary precautions with regard to diet and habits of life are taken. The same in an even more striking manner applies to hay-fever, a condition caused by sensitivity to certain pollens. Some maintain that a susceptibility to hay-fever may be inherited, but, obviously, if one happens to reside in a district free from the offending pollen, he will never develop hay-fever even if he does inherit a predisposition to it.

INHERITED MENTAL ABNORMALITIES

"Of far greater individual and social significance, however, as far as the inheritance of disease is concerned, is the problem of the transmissibility of mental disorders and deficiencies. There is still a great deal of controversy as to the relative importance of heredity and such environmental factors as early training, experiences, emotional shocks, glandular disturbances, infections and so on in the causation of mental disorders. Nevertheless, the consensus of medical opinion seems to be that at least in a certain percentage of some forms of insanity, of epilepsy, feeble-mindedness and other types of psychopathic disturbances, there is definite evidence of familial tendencies and of hereditary defects."

"I know a family, doctor, where both parents are apparently entirely normal, yet one of the sons recently developed epilepsy. Could there be a question of inheritance in such a case?"

"Epilepsy may be either acquired or inherited. Injuries to the brain during birth or at any other time, infectious diseases, glandular disturbances and other conditions may give rise to this disease, and under such circumstances it is not inherited, of course, and does not constitute a family taint. In about 50% of cases, however, epilepsy does appear to be inherited, and there is usually some family history of this disease. Each case must therefore be studied individually in order to determine its origin and the chances of its transmissibility."

"But if the parents are entirely well and have never had any sickness, is it still possible for them to transmit some family defect to their children?"

TRANSMISSION OF DEFECTIVE GENES

"Unfortunately it is, for an individual may be entirely normal himself and yet carry a defective gene within him. One may, for instance, have brown eyes, as we saw, and nevertheless carry within him a gene for blue eyes, and the same applies to other both normal and abnormal characteristics. A man may have a fairly high intelligence himself, and yet be a carrier of a gene for defective mentality if there are other cases of mental deficiency in the immediate family. As a matter of fact, the existence of defective genes in normal people and the possibility of their transmission constitute one of the basic problems of eugenics."

"How can one tell then whether one is fit to have normal and healthy children?"

"In a general way, I would say that if a couple have no serious abnormality and there is no record of any hereditary disease in their families, they may safely assume that they will have normal children. If both of them are well, and there is a history, let us say, of insanity in one of the families, the possible chances of transmission will depend upon the type of disease, the number and nearness of the relatives afflicted and other factors, and a determination of their eugenic fitness will require a study of the individual circumstances. Should there be a history of insanity in both families, then the question of marriage and particularly of procreation must be even more carefully considered. We must frankly admit, however, that there is no definite way of determining the presence of any hidden or potential defect in an individual who is normal himself. It is not yet possible, in fact, to predict with any degree of certainty the character of the future offspring, nor are there any positive standards of eugenic fitness for reproduction."

"*People are always saying that near relatives should not marry because their children are apt to be abnormal. Is there any scientific basis for this idea?*"

MARRIAGE BETWEEN RELATIVES

"The physical and mental qualities of offspring coming from first cousins or other near relatives are subject to the same laws of heredity which govern the children of non-relatives. If both the father and the mother belong to the same family, the chances of the child's inheriting the dominant traits of that family are very much increased. If these traits and qualities happen to be good, so much the better for the child; but if there happens to exist some physical or mental deficiency in the family, the child will be subject to inherit these undesirable traits. In some families close intermarriage has produced brilliant offspring, in others it has perpetuated defective traits. Recently I saw a young woman who was suffering from a hereditary form of deafness. Four of her brothers and one sister had a similar condition. Neither of the parents are deaf, but they were first cousins and there were several instances of hereditary deafness on both sides of the family. In this case, obviously, inbreeding tended to bring to the fore the family defect. Marriages between relatives must always be considered individually. In general, perhaps, the advice of Leonard Darwin that such marriages should be 'discouraged but not condemned' is the wisest that can be given for the present."

"*From a eugenic standpoint, doctor, what standards can one be guided by in the choice of a mate?*"

"If one were to select a mate on a purely eugenic basis, with the sole idea of insuring the begetting of healthy offspring, one would naturally marry only a person who is both physically and mentally healthy and whose family background is eugenically sound. Few people, however, are at present willing to permit eugenic considerations to guide entirely the affairs of the heart. Cupid will not easily be replaced by a eugenic board, and in view of our present limitation of eugenic knowledge, perhaps it is just as well that this is so. The best advice that one can give is first, to avoid marriage with someone who is afflicted with a serious transmissible defect, and secondly, to preferably refrain from marrying into a family that happens to possess the same kinds of bodily and mental hereditary weaknesses as one's own. When the maternal and paternal genes are shuffled together in the new-formed child, the deal for the child is apt to be much more favorable if the two sets come from different stocks and contain many divergent qualities and factors. In the choice of a mate it is well also, of course, to give preference to one who comes from a family with desirable traits and qualities. The inculcation of a positive eugenic consciousness is, in fact, one of the chief aims of the modern eugenic movement."

INDIVIDUAL EUGENICS

"*What specifically is the program of the eugenic movement?*"

"The purpose of the movement is to breed a better human race. Some human beings, the eugenists say, are physically and mentally superior, and others are inferior. The superior group, because of greater foresight and higher standards, are limiting the number of their offspring, while those of the inferior type continue to multiply at a more rapid rate. There is therefore a distinct danger of the deterioration of the human race by these 'legions of the ill-born.' What should be done, then, they say, is to encourage the superior people to have more children by developing in them a eugenic consciousness, by giving them special bonuses and other privileges, and to diminish the reproduction of the socially inadequate by general eugenic education and, where necessary, by restrictive measures."

RACIAL EUGENICS

"*Doesn't that bring us back, though, to the problem of heredity and environment? Is not social superiority or inferiority often as much a question of chance and opportunity as of hereditary qualities?*"

"You are quite right. As long as the eugenists distinguish merely between people who are biologically or medically sound or unsound, they are, I believe, well justified in their conclusions. Certainly individuals afflicted with serious hereditary deficiencies—the feeble-minded, the insane, the epileptic—should be restricted from reproduction, though even then there is the possible danger of ascribing too much to heredity and too little to environmental factors in the causation of these diseases. When the eugenists, however, attempt to classify mankind into superior and inferior groups, into the better and desirable classes and the 'socially inadequate' or the 'social problem' groups, their claims become subject to serious criticisms. It is very likely indeed that such a stratification of society rests more on economic and social grounds than on actual biological differences. It is hardly possible, after all, to tell whether the people who today occupy the higher positions in society have reached their stations because of superior native endowments or because of some favorable environmental factors—better education, better opportunities, better connections, and so on. There can hardly be any doubt, in fact, that among the socially inadequate there are any number of individuals who might have attained greater social heights and been considered among the superiors, had they had a different economic, social and environmental background from the start. The majority of us probably have native and inborn capacities and potentialities which are never brought to the surface because of a lack of opportunity, and it is very likely that an improvement or change in the economic and social conditions of humanity may result in a considerable regrouping of our social strata. Perhaps such an improvement may accomplish more for social advance that any system of strict eugenic selection which may be applicable at the present time.

"We have had a rather long session today, and perhaps we had better postpone our further conversations for another time. In the meantime both of you may have your physical examinations. Before you go, however, I should like to give you the names of several books which you might read in connection with some of the subjects we were considering today."

WESTERMARCK, EDWARD. "The History of Human Marriage." The Macmillan Co.

Gives a classic account of the evolution of human marriage. Recently revised.

WALKER, K. M. "Preparation for Marriage." W. W. Norton & Co. (1933).

A sound, concise and well-written book on marriage by a group of English physicians.

JENNINGS, H. S. "The Biological Basis of Human Nature." W. W. Norton & Co. (1930).

Contains a stimulating and scholarly discussion of heredity and eugenics.

GROVES, ERNEST R. "Marriage." Henry Holt & Co. (1933).

A frank and comprehensive text-book on the subject of marriage.

DARWIN, LEONARD MAJOR. "What Is Eugenics?" Galton Publishing Co. (1929).

A brief and readable outline of the problems of eugenics.

POPENOE, PAUL. "The Child's Heredity." Williams & Wilkins Co. (1929).

Presents a detailed discussion of hereditary qualities.

LANDMAN, J. H. "Human Sterilization." The Macmillan Co. (1932).

Includes a well-authenticated and critical analysis of modern eugenics.

HOLMES, J. S. "The Eugenic Predicament." Harcourt, Brace & Co. (1933).

An able defense of the eugenic viewpoint.

CHAPTER II

THE BIOLOGY OF MARRIAGE

THE MALE SEX ORGANS

"I am glad to let you know that the results of the examination and of the tests we took last time all proved to be satisfactory. Both of you seem to be in good physical condition."

"*Thank you, doctor. We've been well all along and didn't expect you to find anything wrong. Still we're glad to get a clean bill of health. Neither of us has had a medical examination for some time.*"

"Well, one really should have a physical examination about once a year. In view of your coming marriage, I naturally paid special attention this time to the question of your marital fitness.

"And now let us proceed with our discussion. Perhaps we had better devote the time today to the question of the structure and function of the sexual organs. Are you at all informed on this subject?"

"*We had some courses in school on the human body, but we don't remember very much of it now. I think you'd better assume that we know very little or nothing at all.*"

"Very well, but if anything I may say seems too elementary, please don't hesitate to interrupt me. Naturally I shall not attempt to discuss with you the whole of human anatomy, but will limit myself to a brief review of the structure and functions of the male and female reproductive system. An acquaintance with these is really essential to an adequate preparation for marriage. Everyone contemplating marriage ought to have a clear understanding of the generative organs, not only of his own, but those of the opposite sex as well.

"The basis of sexual reproduction in nature is the union of the male and female sex cells, the sperms and the eggs. The primary function of the sexes, therefore, as far as procreation is concerned, is the production of the respective sex cells. The role of the male, however, is not limited merely to the production of the sperms; he must, in addition, deposit them in a place where they will have the best chance of coming in contact with the female cells. In some of the lower forms of life no special provisions are made for this latter purpose. Among certain marine animals, for instance, both the male and the female when ready for reproduction deposit their sex cells in the waters of the sea. There is no direct contact between the two sexes, and the sperms and eggs are left to meet by chance. In all the higher forms of life, however, special adaptations and organs are present in the male which serve to bring his spermatozoa, or sperms, close to or into the body of the female so that the union of the two cells may be more fully assured. This is the case with the human species where this meeting takes place within the genital tract of the female. In considering, therefore, the male sex organs we may distinguish between those which are concerned primarily with the production of the sperms, as the testes and related organs, and those which serve to carry the sperms into the female, that is, the penis and its adjacent structures.

THE ROLE OF THE MALE IN REPRODUCTION

"To get a clearer picture of this mechanism, let us look at this diagram of the male reproductive system (Fig. 1). It represents a side view of the organs which lie in the lower part of the abdomen below the waistline, that is, in the pelvis. The external genitals, too, are shown on this diagram.

MALE PELVIS

"To the right you can see the spinal column gradually tapering down. In front of it lies the lower part of the intestinal tract, the rectum, which communicates with the outside through the anus. In front of the rectum lies the bladder, a distensible, bag-like organ which serves as a reservoir for the urine. Below the bladder and between it and the rectum are the several organs which form a part of the reproductive system."

"*May I ask you a question, doctor? I understand that the urine is formed by the kidneys. What is the relation of the kidneys to the bladder?*"

"They are all a part of the urinary system. The urine is produced by the kidneys, but these lie higher up, one on each side of the abdomen, and are not shown on this diagram. Each kidney is connected with the bladder by a slender, delicate tube, the ureter. The urine is produced in the kidneys almost continuously and passes along the ureter, a few drops at a time, into the bladder. There it is stored until it is emptied through another tube, called the urethra, which leads from the bladder to the outside."

KIDNEYS, URETERS AND BLADDER

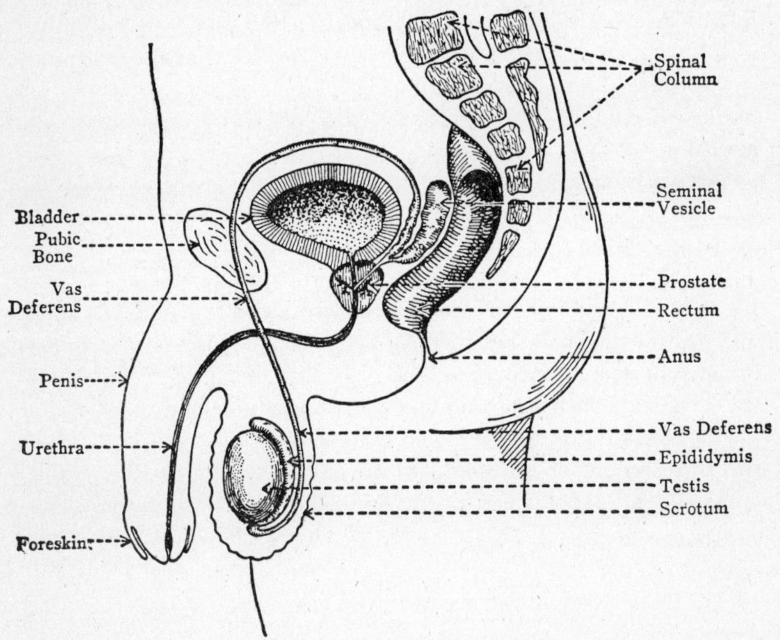

FIGURE 1. *Male Genital Organs (Side View)*

"Is there any special connection between the urinary system and the sexual organs?"

"Yes, indeed, particularly in the man. Anatomically, the urinary and the sexual apparatus are intimately related. For one thing, the urethra, which is really the outlet of the urinary system, lies through a great part of its length, as you see here, in the male copulative organ, the penis, and it serves not merely for the passage of urine but also for the transmission of the seminal fluid during an ejaculation. There are other organs, too, as we shall see later, which are closely related to both systems."

"*What is the seminal fluid, doctor? What does it consist of?*"

THE SEMINAL FLUID

"The term seminal fluid, or semen, is applied to the material discharged by the male during the ejaculation. The spermatozoa, of course, constitute its most important element, but the bulk of this fluid consists of the secretions from the accessory sex glands, the prostate and the seminal vesicles. During the ejaculation, all of these secretions are brought together and constitute the seminal discharge.

THE TESTES

"The spermatozoa, as I said, are formed in the testes, to which the term 'male sex glands' is usually applied. There is a right and a left testis, or testicle, each ovoid in shape and about the size of an ordinary plum. They measure about one and a half to two inches in length and about one inch in thickness, but there is a considerable individual variation in different men. The two testes are suspended in a special pouch called the scrotum, which hangs downward externally behind the penis.

"In addition to the sperm formation, the testes also produce a special secretion, or hormone, which has no relation to the seminal emission, and is not a part of the seminal fluid. This hormone is absorbed directly into the system and plays a very significant role in the development of the individual's physical and mental characteristics."

"*Do the testicles change in size? I have been under the impression that they become larger or smaller at different times.*"

THE SCROTUM

"The testes do not change in size, but the scrotum, or the pouch in which they lie, is subject to expansions and contractions. In warm weather, for instance, or after a hot bath, the scrotum becomes relaxed and the testicles are lower; in cold weather, on the other hand, the muscles of the scrotum contract and bring the testes higher up nearer to the body, so that it may seem as if the glands have actually grown smaller in size. The object of this mechanism is to maintain the testes in the most suitable temperature, for they are very sensitive to heat and cold and require protection from environmental changes."

"*Is the temperature in the scrotum different than in other parts of the body?*"

"Moore, who has done much work on the biology of the testis, claims that the temperature of the scrotum is a few degrees lower than that of the inside of the body, and that this lowered temperature is essential for the proper functioning of the testes. It has been shown, for instance, that the application of heat to the external surface of the scrotum of guinea pigs for only fifteen minutes will cause considerable injury to the sperm-producing function of the testes, and may even result in sterility."

"*I have sometimes noticed that the left testicle seems to be lower than the right. Is there anything abnormal about that?*"

"No, not at all. The left testicle is normally lower than the right, and is frequently somewhat larger in size also."

"*A friend of mine told me that he has only one testicle and he thinks he was born that way. Does that happen often?*"

"This is a condition which happens not infrequently, perhaps once in about 500 males. Sometimes one and sometimes both testes are missing from the scrotum. In the embryo the testes lie within the abdominal cavity, but before birth they descend through a canal in the groin and lodge in the scrotum. In certain instances one or both of the glands may fail to come down and they remain either in the abdomen or in the groin. This condition is known as 'undescended testicles.' Frequently the undescended testes come down of themselves around puberty due to their increased growth at this time, but sometimes it may become necessary to employ surgical means in order to lower them into the scrotum. Recent research tends to indicate that the descent of the testes is dependent upon the action of a certain hormone which comes from the pituitary gland. In the absence of this hormone the testes do not descend; on the other hand, in many cases of undescended testes it is now possible to bring them down into the scrotum during the early years of the child's life by the artificial administration of this pituitary hormone."

UNDESCENDED TESTES

"*When the testes do not descend into the scrotum, does it have any special effect upon the man? Would it affect his sex life or his fitness for marriage?*"

"If the testes remain undescended after puberty, they may atrophy and lose their ability to produce spermatozoa. Hence a man with undescended testes on both sides is very apt to be sterile. The internal secretions of the gland, however, do not seem to be affected by its failure to come down into the scrotum so that the development of the physical and mental characteristics which are controlled by the testicular hormones will proceed quite normally. I have seen many men with undescended testes who were quite normal physically and sexually, except that their seminal fluid did not contain any sperms. Furthermore, even if only one testicle descends, this will be quite sufficient for the reproductive functions of the individual, and the failure of the second testicle to come down into the scrotum will not affect his sexual or procreative abilities in any way."

"*How do the sperm cells get to the penis from the testes? Is there a direct communication between the two?*"

THE PATH OF THE SPERMS FROM THE TESTES

"No, the communication between the testes and the penis is quite indirect, and the course from one to the other is rather long and tortuous. The manner in which the spermatozoa pass from the testes through the genital tract is really a very interesting one. We can get a clearer understanding of this pathway by looking at the diagram of the male organs. The testes are made up of a very large number of fine hair-like tubules in which the spermatozoa are formed. These tubules gradually join together and then emerge at one side of the testes to form a special organ which carries the long name of epididymis.

THE EPIDIDYMIS

The epididymis lies at the base of the testes to which it is closely attached and consists of a very much coiled and convoluted duct. While the organ itself is only about two inches long and a quarter of an inch wide, the tube of which it is made up is really very extensive. It has been calculated that if this duct were unwound and stretched lengthwise it would extend for twenty feet."

"*Do you mean that a tube twenty feet long is compressed in so small a space?*"

"That is so. It indicates in a way some of the remarkable complexities in the structure of the body. The width of this tube is extremely small; it is only about 1/60 of an inch in diameter, which would correspond to the size of a coarse thread of cotton. At its lower end the epididymis is joined to and empties into a larger tube or duct, called the vas deferens.

THE VAS DEFERENS

"The vas deferens, sometimes called simply the vas, curves upward in the scrotum, passes through a canal in the groin and enters the lower part of the abdomen, or pelvis. Here it turns down again, passes over the bladder near its base, and finally opens into the back part of the urinary outlet, the urethra. Its length is about sixteen inches, and its diameter about one-tenth of an inch. The walls of the vas are fairly thick, so that it can be felt easily in the scrotum as it passes up into the groin."

"*Do all the sperm cells have to travel this rather roundabout way?*"

"Yes, indeed. And if for any reason this path is obstructed either in the epididymis or the vas, the spermatozoa from that particular side will be unable to pass through. If it happens on both sides, the man will be sterile."

"*How do these canals become blocked?*"

"Well, it might be caused by certain diseases or injuries. A rather frequent cause is a gonorrheal inflammation. If the inflammation happens to be bilateral, that is, if it occurs on both sides, it is very apt to result in a blockage of both ducts which may lead to sterility."

"*Then, there would be no seminal discharge at all under such conditions?*"

"No, the seminal discharge would still continue. As I mentioned before, the bulk of fluid which is ejaculated comes from the other sex glands—the seminal vesicles and the prostate, and these are not affected by the blocking of the vas."

"*What is the function of these other sex glands?*"

"The seminal vesicles—there are two of them—are sac-like organs which lie at the base of the bladder, and are connected through a special duct with the vas deferens. They appear to have a double function.

THE SEMINAL VESICLES

First, they serve as temporary reservoirs for the spermatozoa. As the sperm cells are formed in the testes and are carried along the vas, they pass into the vesicles through the connecting duct and are stored there until an ejaculation takes place. Secondly, they produce a gummy, yellowish secretion of their own which mixes with the spermatozoa and serves to thicken the seminal fluid and to give it greater volume.

"The prostate is another gland which takes part in the reproductive process.

THE PROSTATE

It is shaped somewhat like a horse-chestnut, and is located around the urethra, right below the bladder and in front of the rectum. During the ejaculation, the prostate contracts and helps to force out the seminal fluid, at the same time adding its own secretion to it, a thin, milky fluid which is alkaline in character and which forms a favorable medium for the spermatozoa. This fluid, it is believed, also contains some special activator, which increases the vitality and activity of the sperm cells."

"*With regard to the prostate, doctor, what connection has it with the urinary organs? I understand that prostate trouble is often accompanied by urinary disturbances.*"

"That is so. The prostate, while primarily a sex organ, lies in the very path of the urinary outlet so that disorders of this gland are apt to give rise both to sexual and to urinary symptoms. Because of its location and function it is subject to injury from both sources: it may be damaged by abnormalities or irregularities of sexual behavior or by inflammatory conditions of the urinary tract. A rather frequent cause of prostatic disease is the extension of a gonorrheal infection. The infection generally starts in the lower or front part of the urethra and may remain limited to this area, but in a high percentage of cases it passes upward and may involve the prostate too."

"*A relative of mine had some urinary trouble not long ago and his case was diagnosed as an enlargement of the prostate. Recently he was operated upon, and the prostate, I understand, was removed. What causes the prostate to enlarge?*"

"The reasons for the enlargement of the prostate are not clearly understood as yet, but it is quite generally assumed now that it is not due to any venereal or other infection. The prostate appears to have a general tendency to grow larger after middle age, that is after about the age of fifty, and in some people this increase in size may become quite pronounced in later life. Because of its anatomical position around the base of the bladder and the urethra, this enlargement may cause a serious obstruction to the passage of urine and lead to difficulty and frequency of urination and other distressing symptoms and constitutional disturbances. In advanced cases it sometimes becomes necessary to remove a part of or the entire prostate in order to alleviate the condition."

"*Where do the secretions from the several glands that make up the seminal fluid come together?*"

THE PENIS

"They are all brought together in the back part of the urethra, the channel which runs through the penis, and they are discharged through the latter during the ejaculation. The penis is the male copulatory organ, and serves primarily to bring the seminal fluid into the female genital tract. By its roots it is firmly attached to the bony parts of the pelvis. The external or visible part consists of a body, or shaft, and a head, or glans, at the tip of which is the opening of the urethra. The entire organ is covered with a rather loose, thin and elastic skin which extends as a double fold over the glans. The projecting portion of the skin is called the prepuce, or foreskin, and is the part which is removed when a circumcision is performed. The entire surface of the penis, and particularly the glans, is richly supplied with nerve endings and is very sensitive to contact.

THE ERECTION

"Ordinarily the penis is flaccid and limp and hangs down rather loosely in front of the scrotum. In this condition the foreskin projects over the glans so that the latter is almost completely covered. During sexual excitation and the process of erection the penis changes in size and direction; it becomes rigid, tense, enlarged and elevated. The foreskin is retracted so that the head, or glans, becomes exposed. This change is made possible by the peculiar sponge-like structure of the organ. All through the penis there are a large number of small spaces. When these spaces are empty and their walls collapsed, the organ is flaccid; when they become distended with an increased inflow of blood, the penis becomes firm and erect. Its blood vessels, the arteries and the veins, are so constructed that they can allow an increased inflow and a diminished outflow of blood at the same time, so that all the spaces become engorged and distended. In addition there is a great deal of elastic tissue in the penis which permits a considerable change in the dimensions of the organ. During an erection, it becomes both longer and wider."

"*What is considered the normal size of the penis?*"

"The average length of the flaccid penis, measuring from the back to the tip, is about three and three-quarters inches and its circumference around the shaft is approximately three and a half inches. During an erection, the length increases on an average to six inches and the circumference to four and a half. The size of the organ, however, is subject to marked individual variations."

"*Do the dimensions of the organ depend upon the general physique of the man?*"

"Not particularly. The dimensions of the penis seem to be controlled by factors other than those which determine the general build of the body, perhaps by the internal secretion of the sex glands. I have taken measurements of the organ in a large number of men, and I have not found any definite correlation between the size of the body and that of the penis."

"*Has the size of the penis any relation to the man's sexual power?*"

"Only insofar as the dimensions of the organ may be an index to the general character of his glandular functions and of his internal secretions. There is, however, little relation between the size of the penis and sexual capacity. I have seen many men who were sexually very active in spite of a comparatively small sized organ, and also many men who had a low degree of potency although their penile dimensions were far above the average."

"*Does circumcision have any particular value? How did this practice originate?*"

"There is a considerable difference of opinion concerning the origin of circumcision. Some maintain that the removal of the foreskin was in the nature of a sacrificial offer which was gradually substituted for more deforming and incapacitating practices of this type. Others claim that it originated as a tribal custom and was regarded as a tribal badge, or else that it was an initiation ceremony and a preparation for the marital act, although among some peoples the practice was later transferred to early infancy. It may also have arisen as a hygienic measure which gradually assumed the character of a religious rite.

CIRCUM-CISION

"The main value of the operation is that it permits greater cleanliness of the organ. Under the foreskin there is usually an accumulation of a whitish, pasty material, called smegma, which has to be removed at frequent intervals to avoid local irritation and inflammation. The amputation of the foreskin removes this overhanging tissue, exposes the parts and prevents smegma formation. Hence, circumcision is often indicated as a useful and a valuable sanitary measure."

"*Would you advise circumcision as a routine practice?*"

"Not necessarily. If the foreskin happens to be especially long or so tight that it cannot be easily retracted, circumcision is advisable. Ordinarily, however, there is no special indication for it. As far as we know there seems to be no difference either in the degree of sexual desire or sexual capacity between the circumcised and uncircumcised."

"*During an erection it happens sometimes that a few drops of moisture appear at the tip of the penis. Is this a part of the semen?*"

"No, this fluid is not a part of the seminal secretion. You will recall that the canal which runs through the penis, the urethra, serves a double purpose: it is the passage through which the urine comes out from the bladder and it is also the canal for the transmission of the seminal fluid. Now, urine is generally acid in character, and acids have a harmful effect upon the spermatozoa. To counteract any possible ill effect from this source, certain glands along the urethra pour out an alkaline secretion into this canal during sexual excitement. This presumably neutralizes any acids which may remain in the urethra so that the seminal fluid will not be impaired during its passage.

PRE-COITAL SECRE-TION

This secretion may appear at the opening of the penis, or meatus, as a drop of sticky moisture. Some believe that this moisture may also serve to lubricate the canal for the passage of the seminal fluid."

"*Does this secretion contain any sperm cells?*"

"Not as a rule. Ordinarily this fluid appears as a white, transparent, somewhat sticky secretion and is free from any spermatozoa. Under certain circumstances, however, it is possible for a slight leakage of the seminal fluid to take place during sexual excitement even before the actual ejaculation, and this, too, will appear as a slight discharge at the meatus. I happen to have made a special study of this particular question and I found that in a certain percentage of cases this discharge did contain either active or inactive spermatozoa. Their presence can be determined by a microscopic examination of this precoital secretion."

"*Is the seminal fluid being formed at all times, or only at the time of sexual stimulation?*"

THE EJACULATION

"The various secretions which go to make up the seminal fluid are being produced continuously, but the actual blending of these fluids into semen occurs only during the height of sexual stimulation and practically at the moment of ejaculation. It is at this time that muscular contractions of the genital tract force the spermatozoa which have been present in the epididymis and vas into the back part of the urinary canal. In the lower part of the vas they are joined by the secretions from the seminal vesicles. At the same time the contractions of the prostate force its own fluid out through a number of small openings into the urinary canal very near to the place where the sperm-fluid enters. There all the secretions are mixed together and are ejaculated in several jets through the penis."

"*If the seminal fluid and the urine pass through the same canal, how is it that the two do not mix during the ejaculation?*"

"This involves a rather interesting point. The two do not mix because of a fine adaptation of the nervous and muscular mechanism of the urinary and genital systems. When a seminal emission takes place, the opening between the bladder and urethra is automatically shut off by a reflex contraction of the appropriate muscles, and no urine can pass into the urethra during this process. It is another illustration of the delicate adjustments which we find so often in the human mechanism."

"*About how many sperm cells are present in one ejaculation?*"

THE SPERMATOZOA

"An amazing number indeed. In the average ejaculation, which consists of about a teaspoonful of fluid, there are probably from two to five hundred million spermatozoa. When it comes to the question of the propagation of the race, nature appears to have been extremely liberal in the supply of reproductive material."

"*Can the sperms ever be seen without a microscope?*"

"No. They cannot possibly be seen with the naked eye because of their minute size, each sperm measuring only about 1/600 of an inch in length. With an ordinary microscope, however, they can be seen very plainly. It is a very interesting sight to examine a drop of seminal fluid. In a fresh specimen every drop swarms with spermatozoa, and they can be seen moving actively and rapidly about. It has been calculated that the sperm cell can move about one-eighth of an inch in a minute, or, in other words, an inch in approximately eight minutes."

"*What does a sperm cell look like under the microscope?*"

"A spermatozoon resembles somewhat a minute, elongated tadpole. It consists of a rounded head, a small middle piece and a long, slender tail. The head and middle piece contain the important elements which take part in reproduction and heredity. It is here that the chromosomes and genes of which we spoke last time are located. The tail lashes rapidly from side to side and causes the movement of the cell, although the mechanism of the motion seems to reside in the middle piece. After a time the movements become slower and slower, until they cease altogether; the sperm remains immobile and soon dies. You can see a drawing of a sperm on another diagram (Fig. 5; Page 70)."

"*How long can the sperm cells remain alive after the ejaculation?*"

"That depends upon the environment into which they are placed after emission. I shall discuss with you later the life of the sperms in the genital tract of the female. Outside of the body, their length of life, when kept away from injurious chemical substances, depends largely upon the temperature. I have often had occasion to keep specimens of seminal fluid in glass vials under ordinary room temperature for varying periods of time, and I have seen sperms alive forty-eight hours and longer after emission. Under refrigeration they can be kept alive for several days. The cold temperature inactivates them temporarily, and when they are later warmed, their activity reappears. Heat, again, speeds up their motion; their energy is quickly used up and their life shortened."

"*Are spermatozoa being produced in the testes continuously?*"

"Well, in many of the lower animals the production of sperm cells is seasonal, and is limited to only a few months of the year; during the remaining months, the testes are inactive as far as spermatogenesis, that is sperm production, is concerned. In the higher animals the spermatozoa are generated all through the year. Man belongs to this latter group, and his sperm production is presumably continuous."

"*Suppose a man had one ejaculation and then an hour later, let us say, he had another. Would this second discharge contain as many sperms as the first?*"

"Probably not, though this will depend upon the degree to which the several glands empty their contents during the first emission. A second ejaculation soon after the first will most likely contain less fluid and fewer sperms. It may take some time, perhaps twenty-four hours, for the vas and the vesicles to fill up to their normal capacity after a complete emptying. If ejaculations follow in rapid succession, the fluid discharged later will be very thin and will contain very few cells. It is also claimed that the spermatozoa of later ejaculations are less vigorous and less efficient. Excessive copulation prevents the sperms from reaching their full maturity and physiological capacity."

"*If a man refrains from sexual relations and has few seminal discharges, does the retained semen have any beneficial effect upon him?*"

"This is a question about which there has been a great deal of discussion. In the Oneida Community, for instance, an American community which was organized during the middle of the last century, the men consciously abstained from discharging their seminal fluid during intercourse partly as a contraceptive measure and partly in the belief that this practice would benefit their health and increase their vigor. They called this form of sexual union—'male continence.' The practice was later abandoned, but whether it proved to be of any particular value to their health or not appears to be doubtful."

"*What happens to the sperms if no ejaculation takes place?*"

"The assumption is that the spermatozoa present in the vas and vesicles gradually die and are broken down. In animals, for instance, who are kept from any sexual contact, degenerated masses of spermatozoa may be found in the seminal ducts and passages. It has also been shown that the first ejaculation after a long period of abstinence contains less active or vigorous sperms than those which appear in ejaculations after moderately frequent intercourse, indicating that the sperms in the canals tend to lose their vitality if they remain there for a long time."

"*You mentioned before that in addition to the sperms, the testes also produce some other kind of substance, or hormone, which has an effect upon the body. What is really the nature of a hormone?*"

GLANDULAR HORMONES

"The term hormone is applied to chemical substances which are produced by certain glands, and which are carried by the blood from one part of the body to another. Because these secretions are not emptied through any ducts or channels but enter directly into the blood, hormones are also called 'internal secretions.' There are many hormone-producing glands located in various parts of the body. The more important ones are: the pituitary at the base of the brain, the thyroid in the neck, the adrenals near the kidneys, and the sex glands or gonads. Most of the hormones, as a matter of fact, play an important role in sex and reproduction, and we shall probably refer to them at various times as we go along."

"*What effect do hormones have upon the body?*"

"Hormones have the power of initiating and stimulating the activities of different organs and tissues. It is believed that each hormone has a specific role in the mechanism of the body. There is also considerable evidence that the various glands have a reciprocal action upon each other, and that if one does not function properly the others, too, may become affected.

PRIMARY AND SECONDARY SEXUAL CHARACTERS

"As far as the testes are concerned, the specific function of their hormones is to control the development of the so-called secondary sexual characters, that is of the qualities which distinguish the male from the female. There are certain features, as you know, both structural and functional, which are found in one sex and not in the other, and which differentiate the male from the female. The sex organs themselves constitute the primary sexual characters. When a child is born, the only way one can tell its sex is by looking at the genitals. As it grows older, however, other characteristics appear which serve to differentiate the sexes. At puberty, the boy develops a growth of hair on his face, his larynx enlarges so that his voice becomes deeper, the build of his body becomes distinctly masculine, while the girl gradually develops a feminine appearance, the rounded contour, the fuller breasts, the broader hips, the different hair distribution. These are called the secondary sexual characters. They are present in many animal species too. The cock, for example, develops a comb and spurs; the male deer develops antlers, male sheep grow horns, and the plumage of many birds varies with their sex—all these are secondary sexual characteristics."

"*How are these secondary sexual characters related to the function of the sex glands?*"

CASTRATION

"Their development is dependent to a very large extent upon the action of the hormones produced by the sex glands, or gonads. If the testes of an animal are removed soon after its birth, that animal will not develop the features or traits of his sex. The castrated cock, for instance, does not grow a comb and wattles, he does not crow, he lacks pugnacity and pays no attention to the females of his species. In the stag and in sheep this operation prevents the development of antlers and horns. The difference between the bull and the ox, the stallion and the gelding are due primarily to the effects of the removal of the sex glands. Such operations have been performed from the earliest times on horses, bulls, dogs, cats and other domestic animals for experimental or, more usually for economic purposes. Castrated animals are more valuable because they are more docile, more easily managed, they fatten faster and lose their sexual desire and drive."

"*What happens if the sex glands are removed in man?*"

"The removal of the glands before puberty in a boy markedly influences his later development, appearance and personality. This operation has not infrequently been performed on boys for a number of different reasons. In Oriental countries, for instance, it was and is still being done in order to produce an unsexed type of individual, or eunuch, who could serve as an attendant in harems. In Italy, castration of boys was a common practice at one time for the purpose of providing 'sopranos' for church choirs. Hirschfeld tells that during the middle ages one could see signs in the windows of most barbers and male nurses in Rome reading: 'Here castrations are done cheaply.' Among a certain religious group of Russia, known as the Skoptzi, the removal of the sex organs was practiced as a part of their rituals. Thus a considerable amount of information concerning the effects of castration in the male has been accumulated. In general it has been found that a boy deprived of his gonads does not develop the masculine secondary sexual characters, and tends to resemble more a neuter type of individual. His face remains beardless, his larynx does not enlarge so that he retains a high-pitched or soprano voice, he tends to deposit fat on special parts of his body, he undergoes marked mental changes, while his sexual organs remain undeveloped and his sexual impulses never awaken."

"*Do similar changes take place if a man's glands are removed later in life, after his masculine characters have already developed?*"

"Not exactly. The changes that follow castration after puberty are much less marked. Once the secondary sexual characters have appeared, they do not recede completely after castration, although various changes in growth, in deposition of fat, in psychological and emotional attitudes do take place. Sexual desire and sexual potency may be retained for a long time after the operation, although in some cases these soon become greatly diminished or even entirely lost.

"Incidentally, some very interesting work has been done with gland transplantation. It has been found possible to remove the glands from one animal and transplant them into another of the same or of a different species. Frequently these transplants 'take' and continue to grow in the body of the host. Such transplantations were first performed by Berthold in the middle of the last century, but they have been continued more recently and on a wider scale by Steinach, Voronoff, Moore and others. Steinach, working with rats and guinea pigs, found that if a young animal was deprived of his gonads, it was possible to cause the development of his secondary male sexual characters by implanting in him a testis from another animal. Later he went even a step further—he removed the sex glands from female animals and transplanted into them the testis of a male, and he reported that the females became masculinized—they increased in size, their genital organs changed somewhat to the male type, and they adopted a male sexual behavior toward the females. Similar results have been obtained with birds. Female birds whose sex glands were removed, were found to develop male characters when a male gland was implanted in them. The female developed the comb and wattles, the spurs, the plumage and even the sexual behavior of the males."

GLAND TRANS-PLANTA-TION

"*Have gland transplantations ever been performed on men?*"

"Yes, they have, although, as far as I know, this has never been carried to the point of implanting a male gland into a female. One of the first to transplant a testis was, I believe, the American surgeon, Lydston. In 1914, he obtained the testicle of a man who had committed suicide and transplanted it into his own scrotum in order to observe the effects. He claimed then that the operation benefited him greatly and that it improved his health and increased his vigor. Similar operations were later performed by Voronoff, Thorek and others. Voronoff employed the testes of simians—the famous 'monkey glands' —for the purpose, and he gave a glowing account of the results. To what extent these benefits were actually due to the effect of the internal secretions of the transplanted glands, and to what extent they were the result of the psychic stimulation of the individual is still a debatable question."

"*Some years ago, I remember, there was some discussion about the Steinach operation for rejuvenation. Is that also a form of gland transplantation?*"

REJUVENATION OPERATION

"No. Steinach's operation is altogether different. Steinach maintains that the part of the testicle which produces the internal secretion or hormone is distinct from the part which produces the sperms, and that if sperm production can be artificially stopped, a greater amount of hormone will be produced, which in turn will have an invigorating effect upon the individual. This result, he claims, can be accomplished by obstructing the passage of the sperms from the testes through closing the vas deferens. Accordingly, his operation consists of exposing the vas on one or both sides and dividing or tying these tubes in such a manner that no sperms will be able to pass through. After a while, he says, the testes cease to produce spermatozoa, and the amount of internal secretion is accordingly increased. Steinach reported some very excellent rejuvenating effects both upon the general physical functions and the sexual powers of the individual as a result of this operation, but his claims have been seriously questioned by other investigators. Moore, particularly, has been critical of these findings and he maintains that the obstruction of the vas does not stop sperm production or increase the secretion of testicular hormones, and that the rejuvenating effects of this operation have not been reliably proven."

"*Is there any value in the various gland products one sees displayed in drug store windows?*"

TESTICULAR EXTRACTS; THE MALE HORMONE

"The use of extracts from the male glands for the purpose of bringing about physical and sexual rejuvenation dates back to the famous physiologist, Brown-Séquard. At the age of seventy-one, Brown-Séquard injected himself with extracts from the testicles of a dog, and in 1889, he made a very glowing report of the results. He claimed that his general health, his muscular power and his mental activity became amazing stimulated. He felt, he said, like a youth with all the youth's vigor. Since then testicular extracts have been employed very widely but Brown-Séquard's claims have not been substantiated. There is little evidence that any beneficial effect could be obtained from the testicular gland extracts available heretofore.

"In the last few years, however, successful attempts have been made to produce an effective extract of the male hormone. These extracts have been obtained from the testes, from the urine of males, and from other sources. More recently they have also been isolated in pure form and produced synthetically from various chemical substances. These products have been reported to induce the development of the secondary sexual characters in animals whose testes had previously been removed, and to have had favorable effects in men suffering from various sexual deficiencies. It is still too soon, however, to pass final judgment on this matter. Men and women are subject to so many psychic and emotional influences that it is often very difficult to evaluate the results of therapeutic measures.

"We have covered many phases of the sexual physiology of the male today, and we still have to consider the female reproductive organs. Shall we leave that for tomorrow?"

CHAPTER III

THE BIOLOGY OF MARRIAGE

THE FEMALE SEX ORGANS

"We are to continue today with our discussion of sexual anatomy and physiology, and I intend to go on with a description of the female reproductive system.

THE ROLE OF THE FEMALE IN REPRODUCTION

"The role of the female in reproduction is very much more complicated than that of the male. In the begetting of offspring, as we have seen, the man's part consists merely in the production of sperms and their transmission to the female. With the deposit of his spermatozoa, his role, as far as the physiological processes of procreation are concerned, is completed. The female, too, has to produce her sex cells, the eggs, but, in addition, it is within her body that all the manifold steps of the development and growth of the embryo take place. It is within her that the male and female sex cells meet and unite, and that the fertilized egg nests and develops into its mature form; and it is with the secretions of her body that she nourishes and nurtures the new-born during the early period of its life.

"All the processes of procreation go on within the body of the woman, and naturally her reproductive organs and functions are considerably more diversified and complicated than those of the male and play a greater role in her general biological activities.

"In the male, as we have seen, the sex organs, which in the main lie outside of his body, include first, the glands which are concerned with the production of the sperms and the seminal fluid, and secondly, the passages and organs which serve to carry the fluid and to convey it into the female. In the female, similarly, there are first, the sex glands which produce the female sex cells or eggs, and secondly, the tubes and canals for the passage of the egg cells and reception of the sperms. In addition, however, there are also the organs which are concerned with the development and nutrition of the embryo. All of these structures are located inside of the body of the woman and are known as the internal sex organs. The external genitals are not directly concerned in the process of reproduction, and I shall speak of them separately later."

"*Our knowledge of female anatomy is very vague indeed. Can you show us a diagram of the organs?*"

THE FEMALE PELVIS

"Yes, this diagram (Fig. 2; Page 45) may make the relations of the female reproductive system clearer to you. It represents a side view of the pelvis, similar to the diagram of the male pelvis which we saw last time, and it shows the several organs which lie in this region between the lower part of the spine in the back and the abdominal wall in the front. I shall point them out first, and we can then discuss each one more fully. Here is the rectum close to the spinal column, and here is the bladder, near the abdominal wall in front, the same as in the male. Between the two, you will notice another canal or passage, the vagina. Projecting into the vagina from above is a pear-shaped body, the uterus or womb. Extending from the uterus on each side are two narrow ducts, the tubes, and at the outer end of each tube is a small glandular body, the ovary."

"*Are the ovaries the sex glands of the woman?*"

"Yes, the ovaries are the female sex glands and correspond to the testes of the male. Other glands, especially the pituitary at the base of the brain, also play a very important role in the sex physiology of the woman, but the term 'sex glands' refers to the ovaries. These are located inside of the body, in the lower part of the abdomen. Each ovary is oval in form, about an inch and a half long, an inch wide, and half an inch thick, and is often compared in size and shape to a large unshelled almond. Their primary function is to develop the female germ cells which are called ova, or eggs, but like the testes, they also produce internal secretions or hormones which influence greatly many of the woman's bodily functions.

"At birth each ovary contains several hundred thousand potential egg cells. They are potential because they are only in a very immature and primitive state at this time, and they still have to undergo a very complicated process of growth and development before they become fully ripened. As a matter of fact very few of the eggs ever reach the complete state of development. Out of the hundreds of thousands

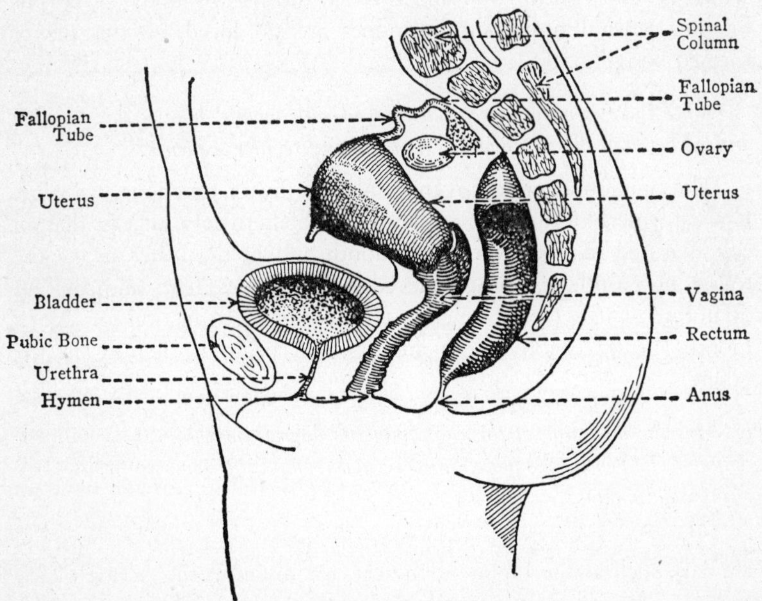

FIGURE 2. *Female Genital Organs (Side View)*

of primitive eggs, only a few hundred at most ever become fully mature human ova."

"*Do the eggs develop within the ovary?*"

OVULATION

"Yes. The ripening process goes on in the ovary and begins with the onset of puberty. It is from this time on that the primitive eggs commence to develop and mature at periodic intervals. About every twenty-eight days one of these cells increases in size and undergoes a series of very complex changes. Soon it becomes surrounded by a little sac of fluid, called a follicle. This little sac gradually makes its way to the surface of the ovary where it looks and feels like a small blister. After a while the wall of the sac breaks, and the ripe egg, or ovum, is extruded or pushed out from the gland. This process of the discharge of the mature ovum from the ovary is technically called ovulation.

"After ovulation has taken place, the follicle fills up with new tissue which is yellowish in color and is called the 'yellow body' or corpus luteum. Several important hormones are produced by this newly formed body."

"*Since there is only one egg discharged each month, how is this function divided between the two ovaries? Is there any regular sequence?*"

"The opinion at present is that only one ovary functions at a time. It was formerly assumed that they worked alternately, that is, that an egg matured in one ovary one month and in the other ovary the following month. It is now believed that such periodicity and rotation do not necessarily exist. Sometimes one ovary may function for several months in succession before an egg will begin to mature in the other."

"*Has the discharge of the eggs from the ovaries anything to do with the sexual act? Does it take place during sexual relations the same as the discharge of the male sperms?*"

"No, at least not so far as the human female is concerned. In certain animals, such as the rabbit or the cat, for instance, the release of the egg does depend upon the stimulus of the sexual relation, and occurs only during mating. In the woman, however, the cells mature and come out of the ovary entirely irrespective of sexual contact. It is possible that when an egg is fully ripened and ready to be expelled, the act of intercourse might hasten the process and bring about ovulation, but this is still a debatable point.

"Furthermore, the manner of development and release of the germ cells differs greatly in the male and the female. The sperms presumably mature continuously in the testes and are discharged in large numbers during the ejaculation. The eggs, on the other hand, ripen in the ovaries, as I said, only periodically and then, as a rule, only one egg at a time, and they are released from the ovaries at regular monthly intervals. This release has no relation to sexual contact."

"*As compared to the lavishness in the production of the sperms, the formation of eggs seems to be rather meagre.*"

"Yes, the difference is striking. Under ordinary circumstances only one egg is released every 28 days, and the number of eggs which may develop during a year would be only about twelve or thirteen. As her reproductive life lasts approximately 30 years, the total number of eggs which may mature in a woman would range between three to four hundred. This is in marked contrast to the male, where each ejaculation contains millions of sperms."

"*Is there any relation between the discharge of the egg cell and the menstrual flow of the woman?*"

OVULATION AND MENSTRUATION

"Yes, indeed. There is a very close physiological connection between the two processes. It is very generally accepted now that the structural and functional changes which lead to the appearance of the menstrual flow are dependent to a large extent upon the activities of the ovary. Certain chemical substances, or hormones, which are produced in the follicle of the ripening egg before, during and after the discharge of the ovum, are presumed to be the agents which initiate the physiological processes of menstruation.

"Both ovulation and menstruation begin at the time of puberty, and from then on both processes continue periodically until the woman reaches her 'change of life,' known as the menopause. At this time the maturing and discharge of the eggs gradually cease, and there is a consequent cessation of the menstrual flow."

"*Do the two occur at the same time? Does a woman menstruate at the time that an egg is being discharged?*"

"No, the two phenomena are not simultaneous. For a long time there was a considerable divergence of medical opinion as to when during the menstrual month ovulation took place. At present we believe that ovulation generally occurs about midway between two periods, and that it is the release of the egg from the ovary and the subsequent changes in the follicle which really initiate the next menstrual cycle. In other words, according to the modern view, menstruation occurs about twelve to seventeen days following ovulation."

"*Can a woman tell when an egg has ripened and is being discharged from the ovary? Does she feel anything at the time?*"

"Not as a rule. Some women claim that if they watch themselves carefully, they can observe a cramp-like feeling in the lower part of the abdomen or else a slight blood staining sometime during the middle of the menstrual month, and it is possible that this may correspond to the time when the egg is being expelled from the ovary. Ordinarily, however, a woman is not at all aware of the process, and cannot tell when ovulation occurs."

"*What does a human egg look like? How does it compare with a sperm cell?*"

THE EGG CELL (OVUM)

"The egg cell is quite different in structure and in form. Instead of being elongated, it is spheroidal or rounded in shape. It has no power of locomotion, and is stationary and passive. It is much larger than a sperm, being 1/200 of an inch in diameter, and just visible to the naked eye. Even so, however, it is extremely small—less than the size of an ordinary period on a printed page. The outside of the egg is surrounded by a jelly-like wall or shell, and the inside is filled with a large number of minute fat droplets, referred to as yolk matter. In the center of the cell, or somewhat to one side of it, lies the nucleus which holds the chromosomes with their genes, the carriers of the maternal hereditary qualities."

"*You mentioned the yolk as a part of the human egg. Does this egg have any resemblance to that of a bird?*"

"In its essential structure, the human egg is quite analogous to a bird's egg, except that it is, of course, much smaller and is not surrounded by a hard shell. The difference in size, however, is due primarily to a difference in the quantity of stored nutritive material. The fertilized egg of the bird does not remain in the body of the female, but is passed out to be incubated outside. The development of the offspring goes on within the egg quite independently of the mother, and hence the egg must possess a large quantity of food material to supply the need of the growing embryo until it is ready to hatch, and it needs a shell for protection. In the human species, the method of development is quite different. After fertilization, that is, after the union of the egg with a sperm, the egg remains in the body of the mother and for many months continues to obtain its nourishment directly from her. There is no need, therefore, for storing up much food material in the egg itself, and its size is consequently small."

"*What happens to the egg after it leaves the ovary?*"

THE FALLOPIAN TUBES

"If you will look at the diagram you will notice a narrow tube or duct extending from the ovary to the womb, or uterus. There are two tubes, one on each side, and they are known as the fallopian tubes, after the anatomist, Fallopius, who first described them. Each tube is about five inches long, with a very narrow canal running through it. Near the ovary, the end of the tube is somewhat expanded and has fringe-like projections which adhere closely to the gland. As the egg is extruded from the ovary, it is drawn into or caught up by the tube. Here it slowly makes its way inwards until it finally reaches the uterus."

"*Does the egg cell move of its own accord?*"

"No. The egg cell has no means of self-motion. As I said before, it is entirely immobile. Its movement along the tube is caused partly by the muscular contractions of the tube itself which forces it onward, and partly by the aid of very fine hair-like projections which line the tubal canal. These projections, known as cilia, constantly wave in an inward direction, and it is held that the motion of these cilia aids in propelling the egg towards the uterus."

"*Do the tubes open directly into the womb?*"

THE UTERUS

"Yes, both tubes enter the uterus, or womb, one on each side, as you can see clearly on this diagram (Fig. 3; Page 50). The uterus in size and shape appears somewhat like a pear. Its wider part, the body, is at the top and the narrower part, the neck, or cervix, at the bottom. The average size of the uterus is from two and a half to three and a half inches in length and from two to two and a half inches in width, being larger in a woman who has borne children. Its walls are very thick and made up largely of muscle. In the center of the uterus is a cavity with three openings leading from it, two on top, which communicate with the fallopian tubes on each side, and one at the bottom which opens into the vagina. The cavity is lined with a special membrane which is very richly supplied with blood vessels and which undergoes many complex structural changes every month, as a part of the process of menstruation. It is into this cavity that the egg first passes from the tube."

"*How long does the egg remain in the uterus?*"

"Well, it may stay there for a few days, or for many months, depending upon whether during its journey through the tube it had

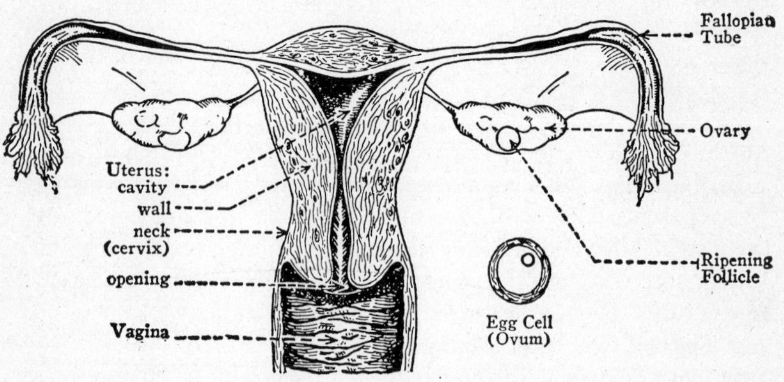

FIGURE 3. *Internal Female Genital Organs (Front View)*

been fertilized by a sperm cell or not. An unfertilized egg soon either disintegrates and is absorbed, or else it passes out through the lower opening of the uterus into the vagina and from there to the outside.

"A fertilized egg, however, attaches itself to the wall of the uterus, nests there for about nine months and during this period it slowly undergoes a series of remarkable transformations and differentiations until it emerges as the new-born baby. The uterus serves as an incubator and feeding place for the fetus. It is a nest in which the embryo finds not only protection and warmth but also its necessary nourishment. The egg, as we saw, contains a certain quantity of nutritive material which carries it through the initial stages of its growth. Then, however, it must obtain nourishment from some other source.

This it gets, as we shall see later, from the mother's body through a special apparatus which develops at the site of its attachment to the womb. At the end of the period of pregnancy, when the baby is ready to be delivered, the strong muscular walls of the womb contract and force the child out of the mother's body."

"*If an egg is not fertilized, does the woman know when it is passing out from her body?*"

"No. The passage of the egg through the uterus and vagina is not accompanied by any sensation, and the woman is not aware of its occurrence. In fact, the egg may even disintegrate completely before it comes out, or else it may pass out together with the menstrual flow. The egg, as I mentioned, is so small that it can hardly be seen with the naked eye, and, as far as I know, it has never been found in the discharges from the vagina.

"Strangely enough it is only within recent years that a mature human egg has ever been observed. The fact that the ovaries of mammals form eggs was demonstrated only about a hundred years ago by von Baer, and it was not until 1928 that the first ripe human ova were seen. Allen and his co-workers, after an extensive and intensive search, succeeded in finding and observing several human egg cells in the tubes. In three instances, single cells were found, and in one case a pair of twin eggs, making a total of five eggs. Incidentally, you may find a fascinating account of the long search for a solution to the mysteries of human reproduction in Guttmacher's *Life in the Making*."

"*You mentioned before that menstruation is dependent upon the ripening of the egg. What is really the purpose of the menstrual flow?*"

THE PHYSIOLOGY OF MENSTRUATION

"Every mature egg as it is released from the ovary is a potential embryo. If fertilized by a sperm cell it will develop into a new life. This development, as we just saw, goes on largely in the womb or uterus, and the lining of the latter has to undergo certain changes in order to accommodate the fertilized egg cell. Every time an egg cell matures, chemical hormones are sent to the uterus which initiate structural changes in its lining and prepare it for the coming of the egg. The lining receives an increased blood supply and becomes congested and thickened. If the egg is fertilized, this thickened wall continues its growth and forms a nesting place for the embryo. If, however, the egg has not been fertilized, there is no need for this newly formed tissue and, through the action of other hormones, it is broken down and shed from the body. Together with an accompanying discharge of blood from the uterus, this constitutes the menstrual flow. In other words, menstruation signifies that a mature egg cell has not been fertilized."

"*Why is menstruation generally accompanied by so much pain? Several friends of mine are so uncomfortable during the period that they have to give up their regular activities for a day or more each month.*"

PAINFUL MENSTRUATION

"Under normal conditions a healthy woman should have no pain during menstruation. It is a fact, nevertheless, that only a small percentage of women are entirely free from any unpleasant sensations at this time. The discomfort may vary from a slight feeling of heaviness in the pelvic region, and perhaps a general indisposition and irritability, to quite severe abdominal cramps, backache, intestinal disturbances and so on. The cause of these manifestations is not as yet clearly understood in all instances. Underdevelopment of the genital organs, displacements of the uterus, inflammatory conditions in the pelvic region, improper functioning of the glandular hormones, general debilitating conditions, marked constipation, and many other factors may cause painful menses. Psychiatrists often ascribe menstrual discomforts to emotional and psycho-neurotic disturbances. To some degree, the present widespread prevalence of painful menstruation may be due to our accelerated mode of life, to faulty dietary habits, to the neglect of personal hygiene, to neurotic tendencies and similar factors. The menstrual phenomenon is still often regarded with traditional tabus, and even women themselves tend to view this process as a hereditary feminine affliction rather than as a normal physiological function. Such an attitude often leads to neglect and indiscretions, and to an emotional state which contributes considerably to the pain and discomfort."

"*If a girl suffers painful menstruation, is the pain likely to be diminished or relieved after marriage?*"

"That would depend, of course, upon the underlying cause of the discomfort. It sometimes happens, it is true, that the physical and emotional changes brought about by the marriage relationship may indirectly influence the menstrual function and the menstrual pain, but this is not invariably the case. Quite frequently, however, a woman will be free from subsequent menstrual discomforts once she has gone through a pregnancy and childbirth, due to the local and systemic changes which accompany the processes of reproduction."

"*Is bathing permissible during the menstrual period? I have heard many different opinions about it.*"

HYGIENE OF MENSTRUATION

"There seems to be no sufficient reason for the restrictions put upon the use of water and cleansing during the menses. On the contrary, cleanliness is particularly indicated at this time. It is advisable, in fact, to thoroughly bathe and cleanse the external genitals several times daily during the days of the menstrual flow. Nor is there any objection to tub bathing, providing the water is kept at a comfortable temperature. Extremes of heat or cold are inadvisable, and that is why lake or sea swimming is not to be recommended. The most convenient form of bathing during the menstrual period is probably the shower or sponge bath."

"*What about athletic activities during the menstrual period? Is it advisable to participate in any sports or exercises at this time?*"

"It is generally accepted now that moderate physical activity during the menstrual period is not harmful. As a rule, a girl may indulge in any form of activity to which she is usually accustomed, unless the flow happens to be profuse or the accompanying discomfort rather marked. Severe exertion, however, and particularly competitive sports, should be avoided in order not to cause undue bodily fatigue at this time or any increased congestion of the pelvic organs."

"*Does the menstrual discharge come from the uterus only?*"

"As I mentioned before, the menstrual flow consists of the broken-down tissues of the uterine lining together with an admixture of blood. This is discharged by the uterus through its lower opening into the vagina, and from there it passes to the outside.

"The vagina constitutes a path of communication between the

uterus and the exterior. It is the receptive sex organ and genital passage of the woman, receiving the male organ and the seminal discharge during sexual contact, and carrying the menstrual flow and other uterine secretions to the outside. The vagina also serves as a channel for the passage of the new-born child on its way from the uterus and hence is often called the 'birth-canal.'

THE VAGINA

"As you see on the diagram (Fig. 2), the vagina opens below to the outside. This opening is called the vaginal orifice, or mouth of the vagina, and in the virgin it is partially covered by a special membrane, called the hymen. Above, the vagina is closed all around, with the neck of the womb indenting it and projecting into it. To the examining finger the neck feels like a small, firm knob in the center of which is a small depression, the entrance into the womb. The only openings of the vagina, then, are the one below to the outside, and the one above into the uterus. The walls of the vagina are pinkish in color and are thrown into numerous folds so that the canal has a somewhat corrugated appearance."

"*Is there any possibility of any object being pushed up into the uterus, or into the inside of the body through the vagina?*"

"The only communication between the vagina and the uterus is through the tiny opening in the neck of the womb. Ordinarily this orifice is only about 1/6 of an inch in diameter, and the cavity of the neck is also very narrow. Larger objects, therefore, cannot possibly be introduced into the uterus unless the uterine opening and canal is forcibly or surgically dilated. Hence, under ordinary circumstances, an object placed into the vagina cannot enter the uterus. Nor can it get into the inside of the body, because the upper part of the vagina is closed all around and there is no other communication between it and the abdomen, except through the uterus and tubes. If anything were to reach the abdomen from the vagina, it would first have to go through the uterus and this, as we have seen, is not possible under ordinary circumstances. There is therefore no basis for the fear which some women have that medical substances or appliances introduced into the vagina might 'get lost' inside."

"*How wide is the opening to the vagina?*"

"The vaginal orifice varies greatly in size. Before defloration, that is before the hymen is dilated, the orifice may measure about half an inch in diameter. In the married woman the diameter increases to one and a half and even two inches, depending upon the length of marriage, the extent of sexual experience, the number of childbirths and other factors. The tissues around the orifice are very elastic, so that during childbirth it can stretch to a width of nearly four inches in order to permit the passage of the head of the new-born child. After delivery however, the opening returns to nearly its previous size."

"*Is there much difference in the dimensions of the vagina between one woman and another?*"

"The depth of the vaginal passage measures on an average from three to three and a half inches. This size, however, is subject to many individual variations as well as to changes in accordance with the woman's sexual life and reproductive history. The important fact, perhaps, is that the walls of the vaginal canal are very elastic and the canal can be easily dilated and distended. Normally, the vaginal walls are practically in apposition and almost touch each other so that there is very little if any actual vaginal cavity. When an object is introduced into the canal, however, the walls separate and can be stretched apart to a considerable distance. In other words, the vagina in the natural state may be compared to a collapsed balloon which can be dilated by the introduction of air, liquid, or a solid body."

"*Is there much difference in the size of the canal in a woman who has had sexual relations and one who has not? Does the vagina change in size after marriage?*"

"The marital relation in itself does not affect the size of the vaginal canal to any very marked degree. The variations in size probably depend more upon natural anatomical differences than upon the extent of a woman's sexual experience. I have encountered unusually deep vaginae in virgins, and very shallow ones in women who had been married for many years. The changes in the depth and width of the canal after marriage are due largely to the anatomical changes incident to the process of pregnancy and childbirth."

"*There is one thing that is not quite clear to me, doctor. You said last time that during an erection the male organ may attain a size of about six inches. If the length of the vagina is only about three inches, isn't there a great disproportion between the male and female parts?*"

"I expect to discuss with you the mechanism of coitus in some detail later on. As far as your question is concerned, however, I might point out to you now that the coital canal, that is the path which the male organ takes during coitus, involves more than the mere length of the vagina. It includes also a certain part of the external genitals, which form what Dickinson, in his source book on *Human Sex Anatomy*, calls a 'funnel of entry' into the vagina. This funnel is about an inch long. In addition, the tissues around the genitals as well as the vaginal walls themselves are distensible and compressible, so that in spite of

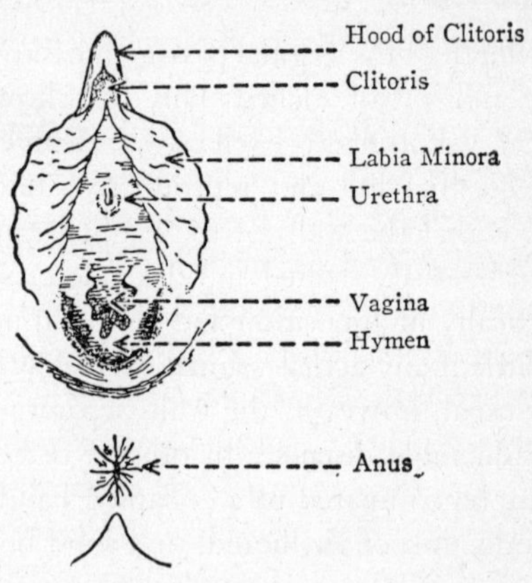

FIGURE 4. *External Female Genital Organs* (*Front View*)

the fact that the depth of the vagina is only a little over three inches, the total length of the coital passage of the female ordinarily averages from five and a half to six inches.

"So much, then, for the internal sex organs, which include the ovaries, tubes, uterus and vagina. I should also like to consider with you briefly the external female genitals, that is those sex organs which lie externally and are more or less exposed. Collectively these are known as the vulva, and consist of the outer lips, the inner lips, the clitoris and the hymen. You may perhaps get a clearer understanding of the relation of these organs from this diagram (Fig. 4).

THE EXTERNAL GENITALS

"The external genitals present numerous variations in contour, general appearance, size, shape and location of the component parts.

The outer lips may be thick or thin, the inner lips small or elongated, the clitoris may be long or short, hooded or exposed, the hymen may be absent or complete and the orifice of the vagina closed or gaping. Thus the vulvar features of women present a wide range of individual differences."

"*What is the particular function of the external genitals, doctor?*"

"Generally speaking, they are sensory and protective in character. They serve as the seat of erotic sensations and protect the internal structures. On top they merge over the pubic region into a cushioned area called the mons veneris. This area is covered with short, coarse hair, the pubic hair. The pubic hair is closely associated both anatomically and physiologically with the reproductive organs. It is one of the secondary sex characters both in the male and in the female, and its appearance is considered one of the first signs of the onset of puberty. In fact, the term puberty comes from the word pubescent which means hairy.

MONS VENERIS

"Incidentally, there is a definite difference in the distribution of the hair in the two sexes. In the male, the pubic hair covers the region over the pubis and then tapers upwards towards the umbilicus or navel, forming somewhat of a triangle with its apex pointing upwards. In the female the upper margin of the hairy surface forms a horizontal line above the mons veneris, and hence is shaped more like a triangle, with the apex pointing downward.

"The outer lips, also called the larger lips, or labia majora, are two elongated cushions or folds which surround and enclose the other external genital organs. They are covered by an extension of the pubic hair, and serve in the main to protect the more delicate parts of the vulva which lie on the inside. In young women, especially those who have small inner lips and who have borne no children, the two outer lips almost meet in the center, and cover all the other structures, so that these cannot be seen until the outer lips are separated and held apart. During childbearing and childbirth and with advancing age, changes occur in the contour of the outer lips so that they no longer come together, and the other parts of the vulva become more readily visible.

OUTER LABIA

"When the outer lips are drawn apart the inner or smaller lips, called the labia minora, come into view. These are parallel to the outer lips and begin near the upper point of the vulva diverging on each side like an inverted V. In size, in shape, in form, in position, in texture, the inner lips present very wide differences. They vary from two small ridges which are hardly visible, to two projecting flaps of tissue which may cover up all the underlying parts and actually have to be held apart before the vaginal orifice and other structures can be seen. I have often seen labia barely a quarter of an inch wide and I have examined women whose inner labia measured two and a half inches in width. Between these two extremes all kinds of variations in the form and size of these structures may be found.

INNER LABIA

"On the outer side the two inner lips have a firm skin-like texture, but their inner surface is lined with a more delicate type of tissue. The lips are richly supplied with blood vessels, nerves and elastic tissue, so that they are sensitive to stimuli and are subject to engorgements and changes in size. Under proper excitation they may become firmer and more erect.

"At the upper angle of the vulva where the two inner lips meet is located the clitoris, a small but sexually important organ. In structure the clitoris is analogous to the penis of the male except that it is diminutive in size, being only about one-fifth of an inch long. Its tip is generally rounded, resembling somewhat a small pea. It is composed largely of erectile tissue richly supplied with nerves and is very sensitive to contact and erotic stimulation.

THE CLITORIS

"It may be of interest to mention the fact, which Havelock Ellis points out, that the importance of the clitoris as a sexual organ has only been recognized within the last century. Previously its existence was so little known that in 1593 a man by the name of Columbus first claimed to have 'discovered' this organ, although it was later shown that other anatomists had described it before."

"*Can a woman tell where her clitoris is located? Can she see it?*"

"Like the other external genital organs, the clitoris varies widely in size and form. Sometimes it is so small and so completely covered over by extensions from the inner lips, which form a sort of hood over it, called the prepuce, that it is rather difficult for the average woman to see and find it herself. In many women, however, this organ is well developed and may be easily defined. The size of the clitoris, incidentally, does not seem to bear any relation to the general size of the woman's body or to the degree or strength of her sexual impulses."

"*What is the function of the clitoris, doctor?*"

"The clitoris is perhaps the main seat of the woman's sensuous feelings, and is very responsive both to physical and psychic erotic stimuli. Because of its location in the vulva and nearness to the vagina, it is subject to contact and pressure during sex play and sexual relations, and in many women the sexual response can only be evoked by direct stimulation of the clitoris. During sexual excitation the clitoris becomes firm and erect, but because of its small size the erection is not very distinctive or easily perceptible.

"The opening to the vagina is situated about an inch or so below the clitoris, between the lower edges of the inner labia. In the virgin this orifice is partially covered by the hymen, or maidenhead."

"*Is the hymen located in front of the opening of the vagina or behind it?*"

THE HYMEN

"The hymen is a membrane which extends across the very entrance to the vagina. It lies across the orifice somewhat like a perforated drum, varying greatly in shape, size and the extent of its perforation. In some cases the hymen is shaped like a semi-circle or crescent projecting across the lower half of the vaginal orifice and leaving a fairly large opening above. In others, the membrane surrounds the vaginal entrance almost completely, like a diaphragm, with but a small aperture at some point. Usually the opening in the hymen permits the passage of only the tip of an examining finger. I have, however, come across a number of young women in whom the opening was almost pin point in size, and then, again, I have seen very many others in whom the orifice was large enough, even before defloration, to permit the introduction of an examining instrument, an inch or more in diameter."

"*Then the entrance to the vagina is not entirely closed by the hymen even in the virgin?*"

"No, for even in the virgin there must be an opening for the menstrual and other uterine discharges to come through. In the rare cases where there is no opening—cases of so-called 'imperforate hymen'—the condition requires surgical interference at puberty, as soon as menstruation begins, in order to release the accumulated blood behind the hymen. Several such cases have come under my observation, and in each instance the hymen had to be opened artificially to provide relief."

"*What is the purpose or function of the hymen, doctor?*"

"The hymen seems to be a special acquisition of the human female, for it is not found in any of even the higher animal species, except in a very rudimentary form. Its biological function, however, is still not definitely understood. It certainly plays a much more important role as a social and moral symbol than as a useful sexual organ. Metchnikoff, in fact, regarded the hymen as one of the anatomical disharmonies in the human body. He suggested that in the primitive history of the human race when sexual relations were begun at a very early age, the hymen, by narrowing the entrance into the vagina, may have served to make sexual congress more satisfactory for the immature male organ, but that at present when sexual relations do not as a rule occur before maturity, the hymen has lost its purpose and function. More plausible, perhaps, is the hypothesis of Havelock Ellis that the hymen serves as an obstacle to impregnation of the young female by immature, aged or feeble males, and it is therefore an anatomical expression of the admiration for force which marks the female in her choice of a mate. Even so, however, the hymen has lost any such biological function in civilized human life, where forcible impregnation of the female is a rather rare occurrence."

"*Is it true that the hymen is often accidentally torn as a result of athletic activities?*"

"There is a common belief that the hymen may be injured from exercise, accidents or careless manipulation. While the membrane is often quite thin, it is rarely so thin that it could be torn during the usual athletic activities or ordinary cleansing of the genitals. It takes a certain amount of direct force and pressure to cause an actual tear in the membrane. The hymen may, however, be gradually stretched or dilated by long continued manipulation of the vaginal orifice."

"*Is it really possible to tell from the condition of the hymen whether a woman has or has not had sexual relations?*"

"Generally speaking, I would say that it is possible to determine the presence or absence of virginity with a fair degree of accuracy from a careful examination of the vaginal orifice. There are instances, however, where this cannot be told with certainty. The opening in the hymen, as I said before, is subject to many variations and there are occasions when it is not possible to determine definitely whether an enlarged or dilated orifice is a natural condition, or the result of sexual contact or of some other manipulation. On the other hand, I have also seen a large number of women in whom the hymen was still present months or even years after marriage, a condition that we shall perhaps discuss fully at some other time."

"*Does the breaking of the hymen always cause pain and bleeding?*"

"That would depend largely upon the texture, the consistency and the position of the hymen as well as upon the size of its orifice. The hymen normally varies considerably in all these respects. It may be thick or thin, soft or fibrous, elastic or firm. It may dilate easily under pressure without much pain or bleeding, or it may be so resistant that it will require a surgical dilatation.

BARTHOLIN'S GLANDS

"Near the opening of the vagina are two small glandular bodies, one on each side. Technically these are known as Bartholin's glands, and they produce a clear, viscous fluid. This secretion becomes rather profuse under sexual stimulation, and it serves primarily to lubricate the entrance of the vaginal canal. Bartholin's glands are not visible because they lie underneath the skin, but their secretion comes to the surface through two minute openings located in the groove between the hymen and the inner labia."

"*Should there normally be any discharge from the vagina? What are vaginal discharges due to?*"

"A discharge around the external genitals may come from the vulva, the vagina, or the uterus. Under perfectly healthy conditions of the genital organs there should be no vaginal discharge, except near the time of the menstrual period. The presence of a persistent and appreciable discharge at other times may indicate some local disturbance, the nature of which can be determined only by a gynecological examination."

"Last time, doctor, you mentioned that in the male there is a close relation between the urinary and sexual organs. Is there any similar connection in the female?"

THE FEMALE URETHRA

"If you will look at the diagram of the external genitals again (Fig. 4), you will notice that between the clitoris and the entrance of the vagina there is another rather small orifice. This is the opening of the urinary canal, the urethra, through which the urine passes from the bladder. There is a marked difference in shape and function of the urethra in the two sexes. In the male, the urethra is long, curved, passes through the length of the penis, and serves not only as a channel for the urine, but also as a passage for the seminal fluid during the ejaculation. In the female, the urethra is much shorter, only a little over two inches in length, is rather straight in its course, and has no direct connection with the sexual or reproductive apparatus, except that it is located in the region of the external genitals.

"As a matter of fact, as you see on the diagram, there are three orifices in this area, all rather close to each other. The upper one is that of the urethra, or urinary canal. This opening is very small and sometimes can hardly be distinguished as it lies among the folds of the external genitals. A little below it, in a straight line, is the orifice of the vagina, and about two inches below that is a third opening, that of the anus which leads into the rectum and the intestinal tract."

"Then there is no direct connection between the urinary passage and the vagina?"

"No, there is no communication between the bladder and the vagina. The opening of the urethra is located above the vagina, between it and the clitoris, although in some instances it is situated close to the vaginal orifice, but even then the urinary passage is distinct from the vaginal canal. The bladder empties itself through the urethra directly to the outside so that the urine does not come in contact with the inside of the vagina.

"We have now considered the important internal and external female sex organs. There is one other organ, however, which might well be included in any discussion of the female reproductive system. I am referring to the breasts or mammary glands, as they are technically called."

"*Is there any direct relation between the breasts and the sexual system of the woman?*"

THE BREASTS (MAMMARY GLANDS)

"The breasts are the most important of the secondary sexual characteristics of the female, and their development is influenced largely by the internal secretions, or hormones, of the female sex glands. During childhood there is very little difference between the breasts of the boy and the girl; it is only at the onset of puberty that the breasts of the girl begin to grow and enlarge, and gradually assume the characteristic feminine form.

"The primary function of the breasts is, of course, to supply the nutrient fluid, or milk, for the new-born. In addition to their secretory function, however, the breasts also serve as a center for erotic sensations in the woman and play an important part in her sexual responses and reactions. The nipples, particularly, and the surrounding area are supplied with muscles and elastic tissue, and are somewhat erectile in character. Under contact and sexual stimulation they contract and become erect, and may serve as a zone of erotic gratification."

"*What are the hormones of the female glands? Is their effect upon the woman similar to that of the testicular hormone upon the man?*"

OVARIAN HORMONES

"In a general way it is, although the problem of hormone production of the ovary is very much more involved than that of the male because of the greater complexity of the female reproductive functions. The main ovarian hormone, usually referred to as the female sex hormone, seems to control the development of the other genital organs and of the secondary sexual characters of the female, but there are also other ovarian secretions which appear to be directly concerned with the processes of menstruation, pregnancy and lactation. In all of these, however, there is a very marked interaction between the ovary and other glands of the body, particularly the pituitary. Recent discoveries have emphasized the importance of the pituitary gland as the activator or 'motor' of the entire sexual apparatus."

"*What happens if the ovaries of the female are removed?*"

"The effects of the removal of the ovaries are somewhat similar to those which follow castration in the male. The spayed female does not develop the characteristics of her sex. When performed upon immature animals, the genital organs fail to develop normally. The uterus remains infantile, the mammary glands are small, and there is a general tendency toward a more or less neuter type of appearance. In the adult animal the removal of the ovaries is often followed by a gradual atrophy of the genitals, an increased deposition of fat, the development of a lethargic disposition and a loss of the sexual drive.

CASTRATION OF THE FEMALE

"In many birds, incidentally, a female deprived of her ovaries assumes a plumage which is characteristic of the male. This fact, according to Marshall, is often taken advantage of by South African Ostrich breeders. They castrate the females in order to induce a masculine type of plumage, as the tail feathers of the male are the more valuable. In mammals, however, the removal of the ovaries is not followed by the development of any distinctive masculine characters. The result is merely a loss of the female characters and a reversal to a neuter type."

"*What effect has the removal of the ovaries upon the woman?*"

"The effect would depend largely upon the age of the woman at the time of the operation—the earlier it is performed, the more marked the results. I do not know of any authentic records of cases where the ovaries were removed from girls before puberty, but judging from analogy, such a girl would never menstruate, her genitals, including her breasts, would remain undeveloped or infantile, and she would probably not develop the normal feminine physical characteristics.

"When the operation is performed atter puberty the changes are less marked. Among some of the effects are sterility, cessation of the menstrual periods, a decrease in the size of the genital organs, and a tendency to a deposition of fat. The general emotional and psychic manifestations which frequently accompany the menopause period may also ensue. It is interesting to note, however, that the sexual desire is but little affected by the removal of the ovaries, especially when this is performed after maturity."

"*Have any attempts been made to transplant the ovaries from one female to another?*"

"Yes, operations of this kind are often performed on animals for experimental purposes, and they have served to establish definitely the relation of the ovary to the development of the sexual characters. If a young female is deprived of her ovaries and another ovary implanted later, the animal will go on to normal sexual growth and maturity. Steinach, Moore, Sand and others have also shown that it is even possible to feminize certain male animals by substituting their testes with an ovary. A feminized guinea pig or rat shows the physical appearance and sexual behavior and reactions of a female. A particularly striking effect is the marked enlargement of the breasts, the feminized male guinea pig yielding milk and actually suckling young ones. Sexually he reacts like a female, and shows definite maternal instincts toward young animals placed in his cage. A somewhat similar effect has recently been obtained by injecting certain pituitary and ovarian hormones into male animals. It would almost seem as if maternal instinct and behavior were largely the result of certain chemical stimuli.

TRANSPLANTATION OF OVARIES

"A very interesting phenomenon of abnormal lactation is the occasional appearance of milk in the breasts of both male and female new-born children. This is ascribed to the influence of the female sex hormone which circulates in large quantities in the blood of the mother during pregnancy and is absorbed by the growing fetus."

"*Have transplantations of the ovary ever been performed on women?*"

"Yes, transplantations of ovaries from one woman to another have been performed, but I don't believe that attempts have ever been made to feminize a human male and to render him maternally inclined. In women, ovarian transplantations have been carried out either for therapeutic purposes or for rejuvenation effects. On occasions when it is necessary to remove the ovaries of a woman because of some disease or abnormality, surgeons have transplanted into such patients a part or an entire ovary from another female, with apparently beneficial results. Voronoff has also engrafted ovaries from female chimpanzees into a number of aging women and has reported successful rejuvenating effects. There is a great deal of scepticism, however, concerning his work and the possibility of rejuvenating senile tissues by glandular implantations."

"Have the hormones of the ovary ever been extracted from these glands?"

THE FEMALE SEX HORMONE

"Yes, some ten years ago Allen and Doisy succeeded in extracting and isolating the ovarian hormone, and remarkable progress has since been made in this field. It is very interesting that this hormone can be obtained most readily from the urine of pregnant women, for during pregnancy there is a greatly increased production of this substance and much of it passes out in the urine. The effects of these hormones have been established by injections into animals whose ovaries had previously been removed. Such treatment seems to replace the function of the ovary as far as the development of the sexual characters and behavior is concerned. Both in lower and higher animals these injections cause a growth of the uterus, tubes, vagina and breasts, and the appearance of normal sexual activity. What their effects are when used upon the human female have not as yet been clearly determined. Much experimental work is being carried on now, and it will probably take some time before the value and limitations, as well as the possible dangers, of these newer products are definitely established.

"Shall we finish our session now and continue with our discussion next time? Let me give you the names of a few books which deal with the physiology of sex and reproduction."

PARSHLEY, H. M. "The Science of Human Reproduction." W. W. Norton & Co. (1933).

Clear, comprehensive, authentic and modern.

MARSHALL, F. H. A. "An Introduction to Sexual Physiology." Longmans, Green & Co. (1925).

A concise and authoritative account of the physiology of reproduction.

GUTTMACHER, ALAN F. "Life in the Making." The Viking Press (1933).

An accurate, scientific story of human procreation, charmingly written.

ALLEN, EDGAR (Editor). "Sex and Internal Secretions." Williams & Wilkins Co. (1932).

This is a technical book, but it presents a most scholarly survey of the subject by a group of outstanding American biologists.

CHAPTER IV

THE MECHANISM OF REPRODUCTION

"Today I should like to outline to you briefly the mechanism of reproduction—the processes of conception, childbearing and childbirth.

ASEXUAL REPRODUCTION

"Among the primitive forms of life, such as bacteria and single-celled organisms, there is no differentiation into sexes; there are no males or females, and the methods of reproduction are correspondingly simple. When an amoeba, a common one-celled animal, for instance, reaches a certain size, it merely divides into two, and each half proceeds to grow and mature until it in turn is ready to divide. The hydra, a minute fresh water animal, sends out small buds which soon break away from the parent and develop into mature organisms. Even a flatworm may break up into several parts, each part becoming a separate organism. These methods of multiplication do not involve any sexual mechanism, and are known as asexual modes of reproduction.

"Nevertheless, even in primitive life, certain sexual processes have been observed. One-celled organisms, for instance, may continue to multiply asexually for many generations, but after a while they show signs of fatigue and aging. It is then that two cells will come together, fuse for a time, and separate again. During this process of fusion or 'conjugation,' as it is called, the two organisms exchange some of their cellular contents and this interchange appears to have a rejuvenating effect upon them, permitting them to resume once more their asexual form of multiplication. In one form or another, sex is probably a fundamental phenomenon in all living organisms.

"In the more highly organized forms of life a method is evolved whereby only certain specialized parts of the animal take part in the process of reproduction. Special germ cells, the sperms and the eggs, are formed, and new organisms arise only from the union of these two elements. In some animals, as the earthworm or the snail, the parents are hermaphroditic, that is, both the sperms and the eggs are produced by the same organism. In most species, however, there is a differentiation into two distinct sexes—the sperm-producing male and the egg-producing female. Reproduction becomes dependent upon the meeting of the parents and the union of their sex cells, and this constitutes the sexual method of reproduction."

SEXUAL REPRODUCTION

"*Are there any particular advantages in the sexual method of reproduction?*"

"Yes, indeed. It is certainly greater economy for the parents to produce the sex cells than to separate themselves into halves, and it also permits the starting of many new lives at once. In the higher forms of life, sexual reproduction also allows a longer period of development and growth for the infant before birth and greater parental care later on. The most important biological advantage, however, would seem to lie in the fact that the union of two different cells from two distinct parents, each cell carrying its own genes and its own potentialities, offers a greater chance and possibility for new variations to arise and hence for the evolution of new forms and new types of life.

"The basis of sexual reproduction is the fusion of the sperm and the egg. The significance of this fact became known only within the last hundred years, and it is an illuminating example of the comparative recency of biological science. The spermatozoa were first seen under the microscope by Leeuwenhoek in 1677, and the egg cells of mammals were actually seen in the ovaries for the first time by von Baer in 1827. Yet it was not until the end of the 19th century that the role which each of these elements plays in the process of reproduction became recognized. And even today the full story is still not known.

"Sexual reproduction may occur either outside or inside the parental bodies. Among most aquatic animals, as I believe I have already mentioned, this process takes place outside, the sperms and the eggs meeting in the waters into which they have been discharged. In several rare instances the two cells meet in a special sac located on the outside of the body, called a brood-pouch. Oddly enough, as in the case of the sea-horse, it is the male who possesses this brood-pouch, and it is he who carries the eggs around with him until they hatch. Another example, incidentally, of paternal incubation is the so-called 'obstetrical toad,' where the male carries the fertilized eggs with him, wound around his legs, until the tadpoles are ready to emerge. But these are rather exceptional types of animal reproduction.

INSEMINATION

"In practically all higher forms of life, the meeting of the sperms and the eggs occurs within the body of the female, and for this purpose physical union, or copulation, is essential. During copulation, the male deposits his seminal fluid in the genital tract of the female, a process called insemination. In a few instances insemination occurs directly into the womb. According to Marshall, for example, the sheep, gazelle, giraffe and several other animals possess a mechanism by which the sperms are injected directly into the uterine canal, the male copulatory organ having a long thread-like appendage which enters the uterus during mating and carries the sperms into its cavity. In all other cases, however, the seminal fluid is deposited into the vaginal canal, and from there the spermatozoa ascend the female genital tract, passing into the uterus and tubes. Here is a diagram which indicates the path of the spermatozoa in the female genital tract (Fig. 5; Page 70)."

"*Does this apply to human reproduction, too? Are the sperms deposited into the vagina only?*"

VAGINAL INSEMINATION

"Presumably so. The male ejaculates his seminal fluid into the vagina at or near the entrance to the womb, and within a very few minutes, if not seconds, the spermatozoa enter the uterine canal. Sims, Hühner and others have found active sperm cells in the cervical canal, that is the canal of the neck of the womb, within a very few minutes after intercourse. I have also had occasion to examine women immediately after they had had sexual relations, and in a number of instances I found active sperms inside of the opening of the womb within three to five minutes after the ejaculation."

"*Do the spermatozoa reach the womb so quickly because of their own motion?*"

THE ENTRY OF THE SPERMS INTO THE UTERUS

"The motility of the spermatozoa is no doubt a very important factor. The sperms can travel, as you know, at the rate of about one-eighth of an inch in a minute, or an inch in about seven to eight minutes. As the distance from the point of ejaculation to the uterine orifice may be less than an inch, the sperms should be able to reach the uterine cavity within a very few minutes after the ejaculation. However, there are probably several additional factors involved. It is possible that during and following the ejaculation some of the seminal fluid is brought in

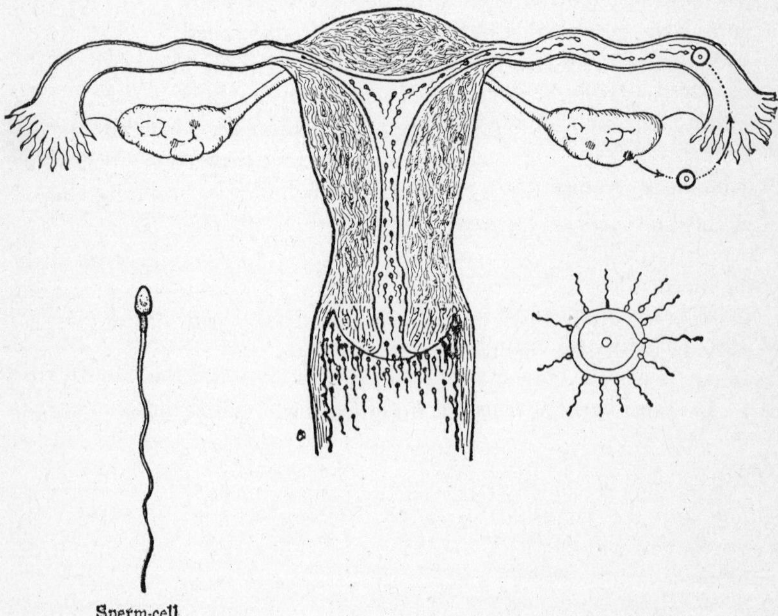

Sperm-cell

(Through the Courtesy of Dr. Julius Jarcho)

FIGURE 5. *Spermatozoa and Ovum in Female Genital Tract*

direct contact with the uterine opening by the copulatory movements, while a part of it may possibly even be injected directly into the opening of the womb. Furthermore, the contraction of the genital muscles at the time of the sexual climax may bring the walls of the vagina in closer contact with the uterus, thus facilitating and hastening the entry of the spermatozoa into the womb. The claim has also been made that during the sexual climax of the woman the uterus contracts and relaxes rhythmically a number of times exerting a suction-like action, so that some of the seminal fluid is actually drawn in. This point, however, is still uncertain, for very few authentic observations on the subject have been reported."

"*Do the spermatozoa in the vagina always move towards the womb?*"

"They probably move in every direction, but there is a biochemical reason why they should especially go in the direction of the uterus. The secretions in the vagina are normally acid, while those coming from the uterus are alkaline. The spermatozoa require an alkaline medium for their survival, consequently they will tend to go in the direction of the uterus and away from the vaginal environment. During sexual excitement the uterine secretions are increased in quantity, and coming out into the vagina they may form a path along which the spermatozoa travel up into the womb."

"*Is it possible for the sperms to enter the vagina while the hymen is still present? I mean, can pregnancy occur before the hymen has been broken?*"

"Cases of pregnancies in women with the hymen intact have been reported many times, and I have had occasion to see a number of such instances myself. However, this can occur only when the seminal fluid is ejaculated very close to the vaginal orifice, so that the spermatozoa can gain access to the vagina and from there proceed to the uterus."

"*Do all of the ejaculated spermatozoa enter the uterus?*"

"No, only comparatively few do. If you recall, each ejaculation contains several hundred million sperm cells. Of these, however, but a small number succeed in reaching and entering the uterine canal. The greater part of the sperm-bearing ejaculate does not pass beyond the vaginal canal."

"*What becomes of the fluid and the sperms that remain in the vagina?*"

"Most of the fluid gradually flows out of this canal and passes out of the woman's body, although some of it may adhere to the vaginal walls for many hours. As for the spermatozoa, they very soon become immobilized because of the hostile conditions within the vagina. It is very generally accepted now that the sperms cannot live in the vagina for any length of time, and that the majority of them probably die in this canal within a few hours or in an even shorter time.

"It is possible that some of the seminal fluid is absorbed through the vaginal walls. It has been shown definitely that drugs and chemicals can be absorbed in this manner, and it is not unlikely that the same applies to seminal fluid, or at least to certain elements of it. This question, however, has not yet been definitely settled, and there is a considerable difference of opinion on the subject."

"*Would the seminal fluid absorbed in this way have any special effect upon the woman?*"

"This, too, is still a debatable point. Some maintain that the absorption of the seminal fluid has a beneficial effect upon the woman's general condition. The fact that many women tend to improve in health and gain in weight after marriage is sometimes attributed to the stimulating action of the hormones from the absorbed seminal fluid. But then, men, too, at times show a similar effect after marriage, and there are so many other physical and psychological influences which accompany the change to the marital state that it is difficult to evaluate the factors involved in such an improvement. Thus far it has not been definitely shown that the absorption of the seminal fluid has any specific stimulating effect."

"*What happens to the sperms that enter the womb? Do they remain alive in there for any length of time?*"

"In the uterus the spermatozoa can survive for a much longer period than in the vagina, and motile cells are found in the canal of the neck of the womb many hours after intercourse. On several occasions I have recovered active sperms from this canal twenty-four hours after coitus, and others have reported their presence there for much longer periods. However, the extent of time that the sperms will survive in the upper genital passages of the female is not definitely known. It is now assumed that they cannot retain their fertilizing capacity for more than two or three days, but the evidence is not conclusive and the subject requires further research and observation.

"As for the progress of the sperms after they enter the uterus, they continue their upward migration until they reach the openings leading into the tubes. This ascent is probably aided by the contractions of the muscles of the uterus which propel the fluid upward toward the tubal passages. The sperms enter the tubes on each side and move on or are carried along toward the outer end. If an egg happens to be present in the tube at the time that the spermatozoa are passing through, some form of biochemical attraction is set up which causes them to swarm around the egg until one of the sperms unites with it. This union of the sperm and the egg is called fertilization, and marks the moment of conception. The process of fertilization is shown diagrammatically on this drawing (Fig. 6)."

PASSAGE OF SPERMS INTO THE TUBES

FERTILIZATION

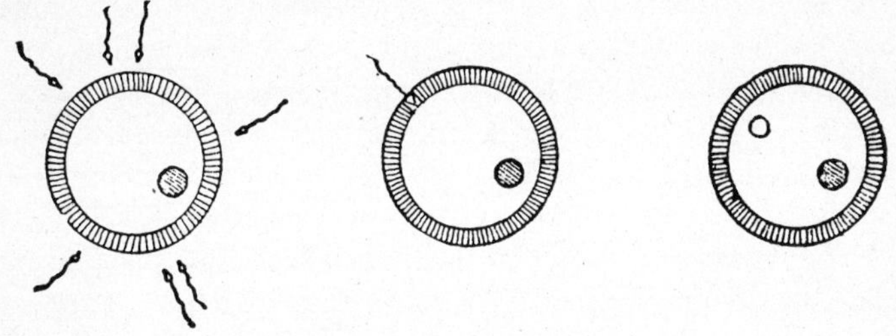

FIGURE 6. *Fertilization*

"*Does only one sperm unite with an egg? What becomes of the others which are in the tube at the time?*"

"There is a special biological mechanism which normally prevents the entry of more than one sperm into the egg cell. A large number crowd around the egg, but only one succeeds in uniting with it. As soon as the first one penetrates, the outside of the egg becomes surrounded by a thickened membrane which sets up a physico-chemical barrier to the entry of any other sperms. Those that remain in the tubes gradually disintegrate and are absorbed."

"*How long does it take the sperm to reach the egg cell? I mean how soon after intercourse can conception occur?*"

"The length of the uterus is about three inches and that of the tube five, making a total distance of eight inches between the opening into the uterus and the end of the tube. If the sperms travel inside of the body at the same rate that they have been known to do under the microscope, that is an inch in seven to eight minutes, it should take them about an hour, providing they travel in a straight line and meet with no obstacles, to reach the end of the tube, where fertilization generally occurs. Please understand, however, that this is a purely theoretical consideration, for the actual time has never been observed in human beings. Recent research on animals tends to indicate that the progress of the sperms through the womb and the tubes does not depend so much upon their own motility as upon the action of the muscles of these organs which propel them onward, so that they may possibly reach the tube in even a shorter period."

"*Does the union of the egg and sperm always take place in the tube? Suppose the two cells meet in the womb instead, won't fertilization occur there?*"

"No. It is generally accepted now that fertilization can only take place in the tube. The present opinion is that the life of the egg lasts for only a short time, certainly not more than forty-eight hours and probably much less. As it takes several days for the unfertilized egg to be transported through the tube into the uterus, it loses its vitality by the time it reaches the womb and can no longer be fertilized. The meeting of the sperm and the egg must therefore occur in the tube, not far from the ovary, if fertilization is to ensue."

"*What happens to the egg after it unites with the sperm?*"

PREGNANCY

"After fertilization, the egg continues its journey towards the uterus, but its progress is rather slow, the passage through the tube taking three to four days. While in the tube, however, it already begins to develop and to go through the initial stages of its growth. The uterus, in the meantime, is preparing itself for the reception of the newly formed embryo. The lining of its cavity becomes thickened with new tissues and an increased blood supply so as to provide a suitable nesting place for the developing egg. Within a few days after its entry into the womb, the egg which by now has already undergone some development, sinks deeply into this lining, and by a complicated process gradually attaches itself at some point. Here it continues to grow and develop until at the end of the period of pregnancy it emerges as the new-born child."

"*What are the steps in the development of the child from the fertilized egg?*"

"The growth and development of the embryo, or fetus, is an extremely fascinating phenomenon. It is, however, also a very complex one, and I shall give you now but a very brief outline of this

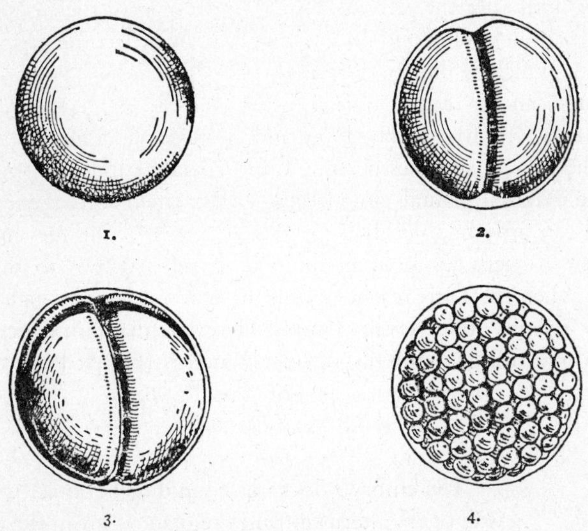

FIGURE 7. *Early Divisions of Fertilized Ovum*

DEVELOPMENT OF THE EMBRYO

process. The single cell which is formed in the tube from the fusion of the egg and the sperm soon divides into two cells which remain attached to each other. Each of the two rapidly divides again, so that soon a body of four cells appears, then of eight, sixteen, thirty-two and so on and on. By the time the embryo has entered the uterus from the tube it is composed of a small ball of cells, probably the size of a pin-head. Here is a schematic drawing of the early development of the fertilized cell (Fig. 7).

"The later changes consist of continuous divisions of the cells and their gradual rearrangement and evolution into various bodily structures and organs. At the end of four weeks the embryo is about two-fifths of an inch or even less in size. It is still in an unformed state, although the beginnings of facial features can now be discerned. At this time and even during the first half of the second month, the human embryo does not differ in appearance from that of other mammals. It possesses gills, in fact, and exists in a sac of fluid, indicating, perhaps, its aquatic origin. It even has a distinct tail which does not disappear until after the second month. By the end of the eighth week it is about an inch long, and now the fetal outlines become perceptible. The head, which is disproportionately large, the facial parts and the extremities can be readily distinguished. By the sixteenth week the embryo is about five inches long and possesses a definitely human form. The fingers and toes become fully separated and bear soft nails, while the external genitals are already well formed so that the sex of the child can now be told. This process of growth continues until the end of the fortieth week or tenth lunar month, that is to the time of birth, when the fetus reaches a length of about twenty inches, and generally weighs about seven pounds. Here is a diagrammatic representation of a full-grown fetus within the uterus (Fig. 8; Page 77)."

"*Is the embryo attached to the wall of the womb? How does it obtain its nourishment?*"

THE BAG OF WATERS

"The embryo does not lie in direct contact with the wall of the uterus during pregnancy. From the earliest stage it becomes surrounded by membranes which form a sac filled with fluid, commonly referred to as the 'bag of waters.' In this distended sac the embryo floats rather freely, and the fluid serves as an excellent protective mechanism as well as shock-absorber for the child.

THE PLACENTA

"At the point where this sac is attached to the uterine wall, there gradually develops an organ, called the placenta, through which contact is maintained between the embryo and the mother. Here the blood of the mother and the child come together, although they do not actually mix, and an exchange of nourishment and waste products takes place. During the nine months of its tenancy in the uterus the growing fetus thus obtains its oxygen and its nourishment from the mother's blood, and gives off all of its waste products into her circulation. The placenta, when fully developed, is a fairly large organ. It is flattened and oval, about seven inches in diameter, and weighs over a pound. Because it is expelled by the uterus after the birth of the child, it is generally called the 'afterbirth.'

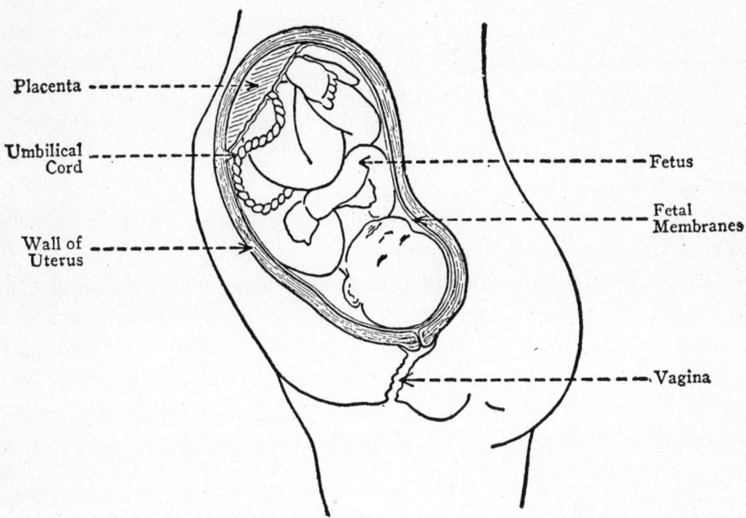

FIGURE 8. *Full-term Pregnancy. Position of fetus in uterus before birth*

THE UMBILICAL CORD

"The embryo is connected to the placenta by a tube-like structure, known as the umbilical cord. This cord, which is about two feet long, is attached to the navel of the fetus, and contains the blood vessels which transport the fetal blood to and from the placenta. After birth this cord has to be severed in order to free the new-born child completely from its maternal attachment."

"*How does the womb enlarge to such a degree that it can accommodate a full-grown infant?*"

"The increase in the size of the uterus during pregnancy is due largely to an actual growth of its muscle tissues, although toward the end there is also a stretching and thinning of its walls. The uterus grows in size so that by the sixth month of pregnancy it reaches the level of the mother's umbilicus, or navel, and by the ninth it comes up to nearly the top of the abdomen. At the same time its cavity enlarges so that instead of a normal capacity of a teaspoonful or two of fluid, it can now hold from eight to ten pints. There is a corresponding increase in the weight of the organ—from a normal weight of about one ounce it may weigh as much as two pounds at the end of pregnancy. After childbirth, however, the womb rapidly involutes, that is, it diminishes in size, and within a few weeks returns to nearly its original dimensions. This decrease is very striking, for within five or six weeks the uterus actually shrinks to one-twentieth of its size before childbirth."

"*How soon after a woman conceives, doctor, is it possible to tell that she is pregnant? Does she feel anything at the time the egg cell is being fertilized, that is at the moment when conception occurs?*"

SIGNS OF PREGNANCY

"The union of the egg and the sperm does not give rise to any feelings or sensations. Neither emotionally nor physically is the woman aware of its occurrence. It is a rather strange and often very disconcerting fact that even for the first few weeks after conception there may be neither symptoms nor signs to indicate the existence of a pregnancy. The woman may not feel any change, and a physical examination at this time may fail to disclose any evidence of conception. The physical signs of pregnancy develop gradually, and it is not until the fifth or sixth week that the enlargement of the uterus and the other genital changes have progressed sufficiently far to make a diagnosis possible. Puzzling cases are not infrequently encountered where it is very difficult to tell definitely even then whether a woman is or is not pregnant, and where one has to wait for several more weeks before a definite diagnosis can be made. However, by a special urine test the presence of a pregnancy may now be determined with a fair degree of accuracy as early as the third week after conception."

"*I heard about this urine test lately, doctor. Is it a recent discovery? How can one tell from the urine that a woman is pregnant?*"

"The urine test for pregnancy was developed by two German physicians, Aschheim and Zondek, in 1928. The test depends upon the fact that during pregnancy certain hormones of the pituitary gland are present in the urine in rather large quantities. These hormones are capable of stimulating sexual development and the ripening of the egg cells in immature animals. The test itself consists of the injection of a small quantity of the woman's urine into a young female mouse or rabbit. From one to four days later, depending upon the animal used, its abdomen is surgically opened and the ovaries examined. If the woman is pregnant, the hormones of the urine will have caused a rapid maturing of the animal's egg cells, and this fact can easily be determined by an inspection of its ovaries."

THE URINE TEST FOR PREGNANCY

"*Is the urine test for pregnancy reliable?*"

"Yes, it is. When carefully performed the results are considered to be accurate in over 95% of cases. It is not infallible, however, and every now and then the findings prove to be incorrect. The urine test in itself cannot, therefore, be taken as an absolute evidence of the presence or absence of a conception, but should be considered in connection with the other symptoms and signs of pregnancy."

"*What are these symptoms, doctor? How does a woman know whether she has conceived?*"

"Ordinarily, the first indication of a conception is the failure of the expected menstrual period to appear. While a temporary delay of the menses may be caused by many other physical or even emotional factors, the cessation of the menses in a woman whose periods have been regular and who has reason to believe that she might have conceived is a presumptive sign of a pregnancy. At about the fourth or fifth week after conception other symptoms begin to manifest themselves. There may be nausea and vomiting, called 'morning sickness' because it usually occurs during the early part of the day; the breasts and the nipples begin to enlarge and undergo changes in contour and coloration; there is an increased frequency of urination, and the woman may become more sensitive emotionally. Later, after the fourth month, there is a noticeable enlargement of the abdomen, and in the fifth month the woman may begin to feel 'life,' that is she may become conscious of the movements of the fetus within her.

"At the same time various physical changes suggestive of pregnancy develop in the uterus, vagina and other parts of the body and these can be determined by a medical examination. Some of the physical signs appear as early as the fifth or sixth week after conception, and others not until much later. Around the third month it is possible to determine the presence of a fetus in the uterus by means of an x-ray, and at about the fifth month the heart sounds of the baby can be heard. These are, of course, positive signs of pregnancy."

"*What particular sensation does a woman have when she feels 'life'?*"

"The feeling of 'life,' sometimes referred to as 'quickening,' is ordinarily first experienced by the woman toward the end of the fifth month of pregnancy. At first the sensations are as if there were a gentle fluttering or tapping inside of the abdomen, but gradually they become more frequent and more pronounced, although, curiously enough, they are not in the least painful or uncomfortable. The strength and frequency of these sensations depend upon the position of the baby, the thickness of the uterine wall, the amount of fluid in the sac which encloses the fetus and other factors. The feeling of 'life' can generally be taken as a definite evidence of pregnancy, although it is not an infallible symptom, for occasionally it is simulated by other internal sensations."

"*Can the pregnant woman hear her baby's heart beat?*"

"No, the sounds of the baby's heart can be heard only when the ear or an instrument is placed over the mother's abdomen. The beats are rather faint, and their rate varies from 120 to 140 per minute. This is nearly twice as fast as the mother's heart beat which normally ranges between 70 and 80 to the minute. It is a strange fact that it was not until only a little over one hundred years ago, in 1818 to be exact, that the fetal heart sounds were detected for the first time.

"I mentioned before that when the fetal heart beats are heard they can be regarded as an absolute evidence of pregnancy, for this is one of the few signs which cannot be duplicated by other conditions. The extent to which a woman may occasionally show most of the other signs of pregnancy without actually being pregnant is, at times, truly remarkable. The menses may cease, nausea and vomiting may occur, the breasts may increase in size, the abdomen may enlarge to considerable proportions, and the woman may even feel 'life'—and yet she may not be pregnant. All these symptoms may be simulated by psychic and emotional factors as well as by causes which are unrelated to pregnancy. The uterus, of course, does not enlarge, and the feeling of 'life' is caused by the movement of gas in the intestines. Such cases of 'false pregnancies' are said to occur mainly in elderly women who are very anxious to have a child, but instances have been reported in women of different ages and under many different conditions. When I was taking my obstetrical training in a New York hospital, I recall, I was once called out to examine a woman who was supposedly in the last month of pregnancy and was beginning to have labor pains. Her husband, who had called the hospital, thought, in fact, that she was on the verge of giving birth, and he was very much excited lest she do so before the doctor arrive. On reaching her bedside, I found a rather stout woman, appearing like one far advanced in pregnancy, and moaning as if she were having active labor pains. To my utter amazement, however, and to the great shock of the woman and her husband, I found upon examination that she was not even pregnant. This woman was 41 years old, had one child from a former marriage, but none with the second husband, to whom she had now been married for seven years, and both of them were very anxious for a child. Since then I have come across a few other cases of false pregnancies, but none that had gone for the full nine months without having been discovered. Instances of imaginary pregnancies are comparatively rare, although one physician has recently collected over 400 cases from the medical literature."

FALSE PREGNANCIES

"*What about prenatal influences? To what extent does the condition of the mother during the pregnancy influence the child within her?*"

"It is perhaps well to emphasize that the embryo in the mother's womb is in reality not a part of the mother. At the moment of the fusion of the sperm and the egg a new life comes into being. The mother provides the embryo with protection and nourishment but its development goes on quite independently. In fact, the entire evolution of the fertilized egg into the new-born infant proceeds without the addition of any materials from the parents except food and oxygen. In other words, within the fertilized egg are already packed all the innumerable physical and mental qualities and characteristics of the child-to-be, and these can be influenced to but a very small degree by the experiences of the mother during the period of pregnancy.

PRENATAL INFLUENCES

"Nevertheless, there is some physiological basis for prenatal influences. The physical growth and development of the fetus is dependent largely upon the supply of food materials which comes to it through the mother's blood, so that the state of the mother will naturally influence the condition of the baby. There is considerable evidence, for instance, that it is possible to control to a certain extent the weight and size of the child at birth by regulating the diet and the activities of the mother during pregnancy. Similarly, if during her pregnancy a woman is deprived of certain essential dietary elements, such as vitamins or mineral salts, this may have an adverse effect upon the child she is bearing. Then, again, many types of toxins or poisons, if they circulate in the mother's blood, may pass through the placenta and affect the fetus. Hence, the diet and physical condition of the mother during her pregnancy may have a definite influence upon the well-being of the coming offspring."

"*Does the mother's mental state at this time affect the child in any way?*"

"I doubt whether a categorical answer can be given to this question. Moods and temporary emotional strains of the mother probably have no influence at all upon the child. However, severe and lasting emotional disturbances of the mother, by throwing out of balance her glandular secretions, may, according to some endocrinologists, indirectly also affect the growing baby."

"*My niece has a red mark on her thigh, the size of a dime, and her mother attributes it to the fact that during her pregnancy with this child she was frightened by a fire. Can a scare or a shock during pregnancy leave a physical impression upon the child?*"

BIRTHMARKS

"Many women will connect the presence of certain black or red marks on the body of a child with some incident during the course of their pregnancy, but it has never been scientifically proven that there is any connection between the two. There is certainly no physiological basis for the assumption that any sudden experiences on the part of the mother will leave a physical mark upon the child."

"*How long does pregnancy actually last? How much time elapses from the day of conception until the birth of the child?*"

DURATION OF PREGNANCY

"The average duration of pregnancy is taken to be about 280 days, that is ten lunar months, or approximately nine calendar months. This includes the period from the first day of the last menstrual flow until the birth of the child. As conception, however, presumably occurs around the middle of the menstrual month, the actual duration of pregnancy is probably nearer to 270 days. There are of course many individual variations, and normal pregnancies have been known to last considerably less or more than the average time stated. Because of these uncertainties it is not always possible to predict accurately the date of an expected childbirth."

"*What causes the child to come out of the womb at a certain time?*"

CHILDBIRTH

"The factors which cause the child to emerge from the mother's body on a more or less definite day after conception have long been a puzzling medical problem. Primitive peoples usually regarded the onset of labor as a voluntary effort on the part of the child to come out from its close quarters. If childbirth was difficult, they frequently attempted to coax the child out by promises of food or threats of punishment. Even today, however, it is not clearly understood whether the onset of labor is due to changes in the life-processes of the fetus itself or in those of the mother. Many theories have been offered to account for this phenomenon but none of them have proven entirely adequate. The present opinion is that childbirth is initiated by the action of certain hormones secreted by the pituitary gland. At the end of the term of pregnancy these hormones set up stimuli which cause the muscles of the uterus to contract, giving rise to the so-called 'labor pains.' At first the contractions are rather feeble and of short duration, coming on about every half hour or so, but as labor advances they increase in strength and frequency. Gradually the opening of the womb stretches and dilates, until with a final effort the fetus is forced out of the uterus and is delivered through the vagina to the outside."

"*How long does the process of childbirth take?*"

"That depends upon a number of factors. The size of the child, the pelvic dimensions of the mother, the contractile powers of her uterine muscles, her general condition and other factors influence the duration of childbirth, and may either shorten or lengthen it. However, the average period of labor is about 18 hours for a first-born and about 12 hours for subsequent births. The process is generally divided into several stages. The first stage extends from the beginning of the uterine contractions which mark the onset of labor until the opening of the womb is dilated sufficiently to permit the passage of the child. This dilatation occurs in part as a result of the mechanics of the muscular action of the uterus itself, and in part through the pressure of the 'bag of waters' which surrounds the baby. As the uterus contracts above, this bag is forced downward and acts like a wedge which aids materially in dilating the opening of the uterus. When the dilatation is nearly complete, the bag breaks and the fluid runs out. The average duration of the first stage varies from eleven to sixteen hours.

"During the second stage, the child is expelled from the womb and is forced through the vagina to the outside. Usually the head comes out first and then the rest of the body soon follows. The pains are stronger, more violent and more frequent during this period, but this stage lasts only about two hours. Even after the child emerges, it is still attached to the mother by the umbilical cord which extends from its navel to the placenta in the uterus. As I have already mentioned, this cord has to be severed, and only then is the child completely freed from its maternal attachment.

"The third stage of labor consists of the expulsion of the placenta and the membranes which had surrounded the fetus. This occurs usually about half an hour or so after the birth of the child, hence the name 'after-birth.' The pains during this stage are comparatively mild and of short duration."

"*What is 'dry labor'? I have heard it mentioned on several occasions in connection with childbirth.*"

"As I mentioned, the sac of fluid, or 'bag of waters' in which the baby lies, usually breaks toward the end of the first stage of labor, that is, when the opening of the womb is almost fully dilated. It may happen, however, that the bag breaks much earlier, either at the very beginning of labor or even before its onset. As the fluid runs out at this time, the subsequent childbirth is called 'dry.' Because the dilating effect of the waterbag is thereby lost, the delivery may become a little more difficult and prolonged."

"*Does the baby always come out of the mother with its head first?*"

"No, not always, but in the majority of instances. Perhaps in about 95% of all cases, the head is the first part to appear during birth. The usual position of the fetus in the womb is with its head downward, and with its arms and legs bent or flexed, so as to occupy the least space. As the head points down, it will naturally be the first part to emerge during labor, and the child is therefore generally born in this position. Because of its rounded shape and its comparative firmness the head also serves as an excellent aid in dilating the uterine opening during childbirth. The child may, however, lie in a different position, and the part to appear first may be the face, the extremities, or the buttocks. Such positions usually make the delivery more difficult.

"The first instinctive act of the new-born baby is to cry. The transition from the protected and warm surroundings of the mother's womb to the exposed environment of the outside constitutes a profound change in the life of the infant. Upon birth its communication with the circulation of the mother is interrupted, and it is no longer able to obtain its food and oxygen from that source. The cry which the new-born infant emits appears to be but a reflex phenomenon. With the cry it expands its lungs and establishes its own respiration so that it may take in the oxygen directly from the outside air."

"*Is childbirth really so very painful? I have always had a dread of it.*"

PAINLESS CHILDBIRTH

"Childbirth need not necessarily be a very painful process. During the first hours of labor the pains are comparatively mild; it is only during the latter part of childbirth that the pain may become severe, but with present-day obstetrical care even this can be largely eliminated by the administration of anesthetics or sedatives."

"*Some time ago, I recall, there was much talk about 'twilight sleep' as a means of making childbirth less painful. Is it used at all now?*"

"Not to any extent. The drugs employed in 'twilight sleep' were found to be not altogether safe for the baby, and their use has therefore been largely discontinued."

"*What methods are being used at the present time to make childbirth easier?*"

"Ordinarily an anesthetic such as chloroform or gas is administered at short intervals during the final stages of labor. When this is done, the labor goes on uninterruptedly while the pains of the contractions are hardly felt. Another method which is being employed by many physicians today, called analgesia, consists of a rectal administration of an anesthetic, in conjunction with other drugs. This is intended to carry the woman through the entire period of labor in a semi-wakeful and comfortable state. Newer methods for making childbirth easier and less painful are constantly being developed and perfected."

"*Is it true that childbirth is much simpler for the primitive woman? I remember having read a description of the ease with which a peasant woman gives birth. Why have the hazards of childbearing increased with civilization?*"

"Many factors have probably contributed to the comparative ease of childbearing and childbirth among primitive peoples. The primitive woman, as Jarcho and others have pointed out, had ample sunshine on her exposed body, and her diet contained the essential, bone-building vitamins, so that her skeleton and pelvis were well developed. At the same time, her hard and active life tended to diminish the size of her child—all of which made labor so much the easier for her. There was also little mixture of racial types or cross breeding, and her bones and organs were well suited for the type of child she was to bear. The woman whose pelvis, for instance, was adapted for a long-headed baby was usually impregnated by a man of her own type, and not by one of a different race who might transmit to the offspring a wide head or larger body. Then, again, she was psychologically and emotionally much more placid and resigned to the hardships of childbearing. All this applies also to the peasant woman of today. With the coming of civilization, however, and the strains and stresses of urban life, many profound biological as well as social changes have taken place, and childbearing has become relatively more difficult for the modern woman.

"On the other hand, it is well to bear in mind that formerly whenever any abnormal complication arose during childbirth, both the mother and the child almost inevitably perished, and that numberless women died because of infections and unsanitary care. While the modern, civilized woman has greater difficulty in childbirth, the progress of obstetrical science and technique has served to save a very great number of women and children who would not have survived under more primitive conditions."

"*I understand that in some cases it actually becomes necessary to remove the child through the abdomen by means of an operation. Is such an operation very dangerous, doctor?*"

CESAREAN OPERATION

"The procedure you refer to is called a cesarean operation or section and consists of the opening of the abdomen and the uterus and the extraction of the child through the incision. This operation has been practiced from earliest times, but until the 14th or the 15th century it was performed only on women who had died in labor, in an attempt to save the child at least. In 715 B.C., a law was enacted in Rome that the child should be removed in this manner from any woman who died during the last few weeks of her pregnancy, and as the Roman laws later became known as the laws of Cæsar, it is assumed that the name cesarean operation originated in this manner.

"The modern type of operation was first described by the German physician, Sänger, in 1882, and since then it has been improved and perfected to a remarkable degree. It is usually performed wherever a safe delivery by any less radical manner is not possible. With the modern improved technique, the operation has lost practically all of its dangers, and is resorted to with increasing frequency in difficult labors for the purpose of saving the life and health of both mother and child."

"*An intimate friend of mine was married last year, and became pregnant soon after her marriage. At first there was some question about her pregnancy, but later the doctor said that the pregnancy was outside the womb, and she had to be operated on. How do such cases occur?*"

"Ordinarily, as we saw, the union of the egg and the sperm occurs in the outer part of the tube, and then the fertilized egg makes its way slowly down the tube until it finally reaches the uterus and lodges there. It may happen, however, that, for one reason or another, this journey to the uterus is interfered with, and the egg is stopped at some point of its route. Inflammations of the tube, constrictions along its walls, or anatomical abnormalities of its structure are among the more common causes of such a condition. At any rate, instead of entering the uterus, the fertilized egg attaches itself to the tubal wall and commences to grow and develop there. This is called an extra-uterine pregnancy, and usually requires operative interference."

EXTRA-UTERINE PREGNANCIES

"*Can a woman herself tell when a pregnancy occurs outside of the womb?*"

"The symptoms of an extra-uterine pregnancy are frequently vague and indefinite, and it may be difficult even for a physician to establish a diagnosis during the first few weeks. The usual history is that a woman who has missed a menstrual period and who shows the usual early manifestations of a pregnancy, begins to notice some irregular vaginal bleeding or staining, and perhaps also experiences cramp-like pains in the lower abdomen on one or the other side. A gynecological examination at this time may reveal indications of the abnormal location of the pregnancy. The urine test is also very helpful, although it is not as reliable as in cases of normal uterine pregnancies."

"*What would happen if the pregnancy were to go on? Would it be dangerous for the woman?*"

"It is extremely unlikely that a living child could result from an extra-uterine pregnancy. There is always the danger, on the other hand, that the wall of the tube may break at any moment, and cause a serious internal hemorrhage. When a definite diagnosis of a tubal pregnancy is made, it is always necessary to operate and remove the developing egg before complications arise."

"*After a woman has given birth, how long does it take before her organs return to their normal condition?*"

"Pregnancy influences profoundly not only the reproductive organs but the entire system of the woman, and the actual process of labor places a particularly severe strain upon the genital tract. The neck of the womb, the vagina and the vulva are stretched and distended to a very marked degree during the passage of the baby. All these changes, however, are only temporary, and the period of repair and involution is remarkably rapid. Within five to six weeks after a normal delivery the generative organs of the woman return to nearly their original condition. Difficult labors, however, may result in a more permanent stretching and relaxation of the muscles of the genital tract, a condition which may require surgical repair."

THE LYING-IN PERIOD

"*How long should a woman remain in bed after her confinement?*"

"The lying-in period, that is the period a woman should rest after her delivery, generally varies from one to two weeks, depending upon her general physical condition and the rapidity with which her organs are returning to normal. Peasant women are often at their work two or three days after confinement, and it is reported that primitive women are able to resume their usual occupations within a few hours after labor, but, if so, the civilized woman of today can hardly hope to emulate her savage sister in this respect."

"*Is there milk in the mother's breasts at the time the child is born?*"

"The woman's breasts enlarge early in pregnancy and about the third month they begin to secrete a slightly yellowish, thin fluid. This secretion continues until the third or fourth day after childbirth, when the breasts become much fuller and firmer rather suddenly, and the fluid is rapidly changed to milk. Recent research has shown that the function of milk secretion, or lactation, is controlled by certain hormones which come mainly from the pituitary gland and the ovaries. Ordinarily lactation continues for about eight or nine months. It has been definitely shown, incidentally, that mother's milk is the best type of food for the new-born baby. Infants brought up on breast milk are less subject to intestinal and other physical disturbances, and generally have a better chance of survival. Among certain primitive groups the women continue to nurse their babies for one, two and even more years, but such prolonged lactation does not seem to be physiologically desirable either for the mother or the child."

LACTATION

"*How soon after her confinement does a woman begin to menstruate again?*"

"That depends largely upon whether she is nursing her baby. If she is, the menses reappear in most instances in from three to six months after labor, otherwise they return within about eight weeks. The menses are also reëstablished sooner after the first than after subsequent deliveries."

"*In reference to twins, doctor,—how does it happen that a woman will sometimes give birth to more than one child at a time?*"

TWINS

"Twins or other multiple births may come about in two different ways. Ordinarily, only one egg ripens during the month. It is possible, however, for two or more eggs to ripen in the same month, either in one or both ovaries. All of these eggs may be fertilized at the same time, and the woman will then give birth to twins, triplets, quadruplets or even quintuplets, as the case may be. Each embryo in such instances develops quite independently within its own sac and with its own attachments to the womb. The children thus born come from different eggs and sperms, and resemble each other no more than other brothers and sisters do. They may be of different sexes, and may be quite unlike each other physically, mentally and temperamentally."

"*Why is it, then, that some twins look so much alike that they can hardly be told apart?*"

"I was just coming to that. There are twins which arise in a different manner. They come from but a single fertilized cell. Soon after fertilization, the egg ordinarily divides into two cells which remain attached to each other. Every now and then, however, it happens that these two cells fall apart, and each one continues to develop independently of the other. When both of them go on to complete maturity, twins are born, but such twins coming originally from the same fertilized cell are very much alike in every respect. They are always of the same sex, they possess similar physical and mental traits, and are known as identical twins."

"*Is it true that the bearing of twins is apt to run in families?*"

"Twinning often occurs in several members of the same family, and there is considerable evidence that the tendency is hereditary in nature. Some women, furthermore, tend to have multiple births at each pregnancy. There is the authenticated record, for instance, of a woman who had three different husbands, and with each one of them she had twins, triplets, and with one even a quadruplet; in 15 pregnancies she had given birth to 42 children. This woman's fertility obviously could not be ascribed to any particular quality on the part of her husbands. On the other hand, there is the story of the Russian peasant who had been married to two wives, and each one of them gave birth to twins and triplets with him, so that he had a total of 87 children to his credit. This would tend to indicate that the male, too, may possibly carry the quality of multiple births within him. Aside from the hereditary factor, however, it would appear that twinning is more apt to occur in older women, between the ages of 35 to 40 and also, for some reason, in blondes more frequently than in brunettes."

"Is it possible to tell during pregnancy whether a woman is carrying twins?"

"In the early months it may be difficult to determine the presence of twins. In the latter months, however, the more marked abdominal enlargement, and the detection of the outlines of two different bodies may serve to indicate the presence of more than one embryo. A definite diagnosis of twins can be made when two distinct fetal hearts can be heard on examination. The rate at which the two hearts beat is very rarely the same, and when the doctor hears, for instance, at one point a fetal heart beating at a rate of 120 times per minute, and at another point a heart beating 140 times a minute, it is certain that there are two different embryos in the uterus. At the present time, the diagnosis of twins can also be made by the use of x-rays, which would show the outline of two distinct fetal bodies."

"Can the sex of a child be told before its birth? Every now and then doctors seem to predict accurately the sex of the coming baby."

"Our professor of obstetrics at college gave us the good advice always to tell the parents that the coming child will be a girl. If you happen to be right, he used to say, you will get the credit for prognosticating correctly, and if it should happen to be a boy, the parents will be so pleased that they will soon forget and forgive your wrong prediction. I have since learned that this advice was not altogether original with our professor, for in a book written some 300 years ago, a famous doctor of the time gave a very similar counsel to his colleagues.

SEX PREDICTION

"As a matter of fact there is no means of ascertaining before the actual delivery what the sex of the child will be. From time to time various tests have been suggested for that purpose, but thus far not one has proven to be at all reliable. One rather common method is based on the fact that the heart beats of the male child in the uterus are slower than those of the female, and hence if the number of heart beats is below 125 per minute, the child is assumed to be a male, and if it is above 145, it is presumed to be a girl. This method, too, however, is unreliable because of the normal variations and differences in the fetal heart rate. It is very likely, though, that with the progress of scientific knowledge a chemical or biological test may soon be developed by which a correct diagnosis of the sex of the embryo will be possible. Many promising investigations in this field are being carried on at present.

"It is of interest in this connection that in the early months of pregnancy it is difficult to tell the sex of the child even from a direct physical examination of the fetus. If a woman miscarries, for instance, in the second or third month one cannot tell from a superficial inspection whether the child would have been a boy or a girl. It is only by the end of the third month of fetal life that the external genital organs are sufficiently well differentiated to identify the sex of the child."

"*Is it known now just what determines the sex of the offspring?*"

SEX DETERMINATION

"The theory generally accepted today is that there are two different kinds of sperm cells, one male-producing and the other female-producing, both types being formed in equal numbers. The egg cells, on the other hand, are all alike. If it happens, then, that the sperm which unites with the egg belongs to the male type, the child will be a male, and if it is of the female type, the offspring will be a girl."

"Then the mother really plays no part in the determination of the sex of the child?"

"Not as far as our present knowledge indicates. There was a theory at one time that the sex of the child was dependent entirely upon the character of the egg cell. It was assumed that the eggs from the right ovary could develop only into male children, while those of the left ovary could grow up only into female offspring. This theory, however, has long been proven to be without any foundation. It is a well known fact that women in whom one ovary has been removed may give birth to both girls and boys. Whitridge Williams, the noted obstetrician, made many observations on ovaries during Cesarean operations and he found no relation between the side from which the egg came and the sex of the child."

"Is there anything that can influence the sex of the child after a pregnancy has already started?"

"No, not at least as far as the higher animals and human beings are concerned. At one time it was suggested that the sex of the child depended upon the mother's nutrition during the pregnancy and that a change of her diet would affect the sex of the future offspring, but this theory, too, was shown to be a fallacy. It is generally accepted now that the sex of the child is established at the moment when the sperm and the egg unite, and that no subsequent influences can change the sex after conception has occurred."

"Not so long ago I read in a newspaper report that it was possible for a woman to control the sex of the future offspring by taking certain types of douches before the sexual relation. Is there any basis for this?"

"Several years ago, a doctor made the claim that an alkaline medium favors the male-producing, and an acid medium the female-producing sperms. Accordingly he advocated the use of sodium bicarbonate douches, which are alkaline, before intercourse, if a boy was wanted, and lactic acid douches if a girl was desired. As far as I know, however, the truth of this theory has not been proved, and there is much doubt whether it has any sound basis."

"Is there any known way, then, by which the sex of the child can be controlled?"

"Some 150 years ago, a scientist by the name of Drelincourt brought together some 262 different hypotheses concerning the causes which determine sex and how to control them. He proceeded to show that all of these were incorrect, but then he added another theory of his own, which in due time was, of course, also shown to be wrong. Since then hundreds of other suggestions have been made for the control of sex, but without any success. More recently, however, working on a newer hypothesis, several investigators claim to have actually succeeded in controlling the sex of the offspring in animals. The principle of this method is based upon the separation of the male-producing from the female-producing sperms in the seminal fluid and the artificial insemination of the animal with the desired cells. Even if this is theoretically possible, however, it would hardly be practical for human beings. Another method for controlling the sex of offspring which has recently been reported depends upon injecting the female with certain substances which would influence the egg cell in such a manner that it will unite only with the desired type of sperm. This, however, is still in the experimental stage and the success of the method is thus far doubtful. The possibility of any widely applicable method for the production of any desired sex at will still lies in the cradle of the future.

"There are many more problems of reproduction which I should like to discuss with you, but we have had a rather long session today, and perhaps we had better continue tomorrow. You will find very fine chapters on this subject in the books by Parshley, Marshall and Guttmacher, which I mentioned to you last time."

CHAPTER V

THE PREVENTION OF CONCEPTION

"Before we continue today, is there any phase of the mechanism of reproduction which you would like me to clarify further?"

"*Yes, there is one closely related subject which we'd very much like to discuss with you—the question of birth control. As we said to you once, doctor, we both want children, and eventually we hope, in fact, to have a fairly large family. Just now, however, we are not in a position to plan for a baby, at least not for the next year or two, and we should not want to have one until we can afford to give the child proper care and a decent upbringing. In the meantime, we shall, of course, have to consider the question of birth control, and we'd like to talk to you about it now.*"

"I shall be glad to discuss with you the subject of the prevention of conception, for it is clearly a very significant aspect of the marital relation. Birth control, of course, is still a controversial topic. It carries with it so many different social, economic, political, racial, religious, and moral implications that it naturally provokes a wide and sincere divergence of opinion. In our discussion, however, I should prefer to leave these controversial aspects aside, and consider the question primarily from a medical point of view. In my opinion, birth control constitutes an important health measure. It helps to conserve the well-being of the family and the home and is an essential factor in marriage."

"*In what way, doctor, is birth control related to the health of the family?*"

"The health and welfare of a family depend upon an intelligent planning of the coming of children. I shall not speak now of women who are ill and should not bear children because of their illness.

BIRTH CONTROL AND HEALTH

Obviously, if a woman is suffering from an ailment—whether of body or mind—which would make a pregnancy hazardous for her, she must be given adequate contraceptive information as a therapeutic measure. But even when she is in good health, she must be taught how to avoid untimely conceptions in order to preserve her future well-being. Not many women, under our present mode of life, can go on bearing children continually during all the years of their reproductive activity without detriment to their physical condition. Nor is it good for the child when it is born too close to its sister or brother. Too frequent and too numerous conceptions are to be avoided for the sake of both the mother and the child. The fear of an unexpected pregnancy, furthermore, is a source of recurrent anxiety in the home. This ever-present tension and fear make a satisfactory marital adjustment very difficult to attain. Adequate physical and mental health in marriage can indeed hardly be realized without an understanding and a knowledge of birth control."

"*What particular health conditions may make it necessary for a woman to avoid or postpone a pregnancy?*"

MEDICAL INDICATIONS FOR BIRTH CONTROL

"First of all there are a number of medical contra-indications to childbearing. The existence of a serious heart or kidney condition, of tuberculosis, diabetes, glandular disturbances, psychopathic disorders or other ailments and defects may render childbearing or childbirth dangerous to the woman. Certainly a woman suffering from any such condition should not undertake a pregnancy without due deliberation and competent medical advice. Similarly, the presence of a transmissible disease, whether of the wife or the husband, might also serve as a medical or eugenic contra-indication to the begetting of children. Under all these circumstances the use of contraceptive measures is essential in order to conserve the health or life of the wife and the welfare of the family, or to prevent the birth of defective offspring.

"Then, there is the question of the spacing of children. It is quite generally accepted that there should be a definite period of rest between successive childbearings. Lack of proper spacing of births has a deleterious effect both upon the mother and upon her offspring. This has been shown by a number of able statistical studies. Those of

Woodbury, of the Children's Bureau in Washington, are of particular interest. He showed that there was a very close correlation between the infant death rate and the interval between childbirths. If the interval between successive births, for instance, is three years, the death rate is 86.5 per 1000 births, that is out of every 1000 children born, 86.5 die in infancy; if the interval is two years, the rate is 98.6; and if the interval between births diminishes to only one year, the infant mortality rises to 146.7. Obviously, then, proper spacing of pregnancies is essential for family welfare, and serves to conserve both health and life."

THE SPACING OF CHILDREN

"*Then it really seems that every married couple should be given birth control information.*"

"Yes, I think that on purely medical grounds every couple should receive adequate information about the prevention of conception, preferably at the time of their marriage. They should be provided with whatever scientific knowledge is available on the subject, so that they may be able to plan their future family in an intelligent and rational manner. The fact is, furthermore, that the great majority of married couples today already resort to various contraceptive practices in an attempt to regulate child-bearing. It is well, then, from a medical point of view, that adequate information concerning the comparative value of the various means available for the control of conception should be given to them at the start, so that they may avoid practices that might prove either physically or psychologically harmful and unsatisfactory."

"*Recently I happened to be present at a meeting on birth control, and someone argued that any attempt to prevent conception is unnatural, saying that those who use birth control, 'conspire to cheat the laws of nature.'*"

"Most of the achievements of civilization have been made possible by man's learning how to control the forces of nature. The use of the lightning rod, of steam heat, of anesthesia during childbirth, are all unnatural in the sense that they tend to interfere with natural phenomena or 'to cheat the laws of nature,' yet we should hardly wish to do without them. The practice of birth control is but another step in the increase of our power to control human welfare

BIRTH CONTROL AND MORALITY

rationally. Few people nowadays deny the need of family planning and family limitation; it is only a question as to what particular method should be employed for the purpose of controlling conception."

"*But is it not against certain religious tenets to use measures for the avoidance of conception?*"

"There are some people, it is true, who sincerely believe that the sexual union should serve primarily the purpose of race propagation, and that it is sinful to avoid or prevent conception while continuing marital relations. Yet this, as far as I understand, is not the position of all ecclesiastic authorities. In the main, I should say, religious opinion today looks upon birth control as an approved social measure, entirely in harmony with ethical and moral beliefs. In a report on this subject by a Committee of the Federal Council of Churches, for instance, the following statement appears:

> A majority of the committee hold that the careful and restrained use of contraceptives by married people is valid and moral. They take this position because they believe that it is important to provide for the proper spacing of children, the control of the size of the family and the protection of mothers and children; and because intercourse between mates, when an expression of their spiritual union and affection, is right in itself.

"Similarly, Canon Valère J. Coucke, a Catholic Professor of Moral Theology, in a very lucid and well-written booklet on *The Sterile Period in Family Life,* says explicitly that 'married people may have intercourse and deliberately choose for it a time at which fecundation is improbable or even impossible.' In other words, according to this ecclesiastic opinion, sexual relations need not be limited only to the purpose of procreation, and a normal marital life may be morally continued even though conception is deliberately avoided. The controversial problem, it would seem, is only as to the particular birth control method to be employed. Some would avoid conception by limiting sexual relations to the presumably infertile period of the month, while others believe that measures which prevent the meeting of the sperm and egg also come within the limits of religious and moral approbation. However, as I said before, the question of the moral aspects of birth control lies outside of our immediate discussion."

"Has birth control been practiced by any of the primitive peoples or is it entirely a development of our modern civilization?"

PRIMITIVE BIRTH CONTROL

"From time immemorial man has been endeavoring consciously to control the number of his offspring. Briffault remarks that in primitive societies failure to exercise moderation in the size of one's family was commonly regarded as a manifestation of unpardonable improvidence. The means employed by these peoples to limit the number of their children were generally very much more drastic than our own, for they resorted chiefly to abortion and infanticide. Infanticide was indeed a very widespread practice among uncultured races. Various methods of contraception, however, were also employed although these were very crude and naive. The primitive woman relied mainly upon various kinds of weird potions and concoctions, or upon magical incantations and charms, which were supposed to render her sterile. Whether these measures ever worked is beside the question—the fact remains that in all ages people did attempt to control the number of their offspring."

"It seems though that it is only within the last few years that there has been so much discussion of birth control."

THE MODERN BIRTH CONTROL MOVEMENT

"Yes, the modern birth control movement is of comparatively recent origin, although references to the use of birth control measures can be found in the medical and lay literature of every period. A prescription for a contraceptive preparation was even discovered in an Egyptian papyrus which dates back some four thousand years. Malthus published his *Essay on Population,* a book which actually served as the impetus for the family limitation movement, in 1798, and a complete medical volume on contraception, *The Fruits of Philosophy,* was published by an American physician, Dr. Knowlton, in 1832—over a hundred years ago. It is quite true, however, that the widespread interest in birth control has arisen only within the last quarter of a century or so. In America, for instance, it was only a little over twenty years ago that Margaret Sanger first began to advocate a wider dissemination of birth control knowledge and initiated the birth control movement in this country, and it was not until even more recently that the significance of family regulation as a crucial factor in human relations has become generally recognized. The rapid social, economic and political changes of our age are making birth control an essential need in modern life."

"*Still some people think that if birth control knowledge were freely available many would avoid the responsibility of children altogether.*"

VOLUNTARY PARENTHOOD

"All normal married couples want to have children, and the practice of birth control does not in the least diminish this desire. It merely enables them to regulate the time of childbearing and the number of their offspring according to their particular circumstances. The use of contraceptive measures serves to render the occurrence of a conception a matter of deliberate planning on the part of the parents, rather than the mere accidental result of a casual sexual relation in marriage. Many couples will still go on planning for a large family. Even they, however, will find occasions when, for health or other reasons, a pregnancy should be postponed, and they will therefore require a knowledge of the means of preventing conception during these periods.

"Please let us understand quite clearly that sexual relations of married people cannot be restricted to those few occasions when conception is desired. In animal life, sexual contact is but a prelude to fertilization and reproduction. In human life, the sexual relationship, aside from reproduction, also serves the purpose of adding an essential physical and spiritual unity and balance to the association of the man and the woman, a balance which can be fully realized only when reproduction is dissociated from the other factors in the sex life of the couple, and when the birth of a child becomes a voluntary and deliberate choice on the part of the parents."

"*How long is it desirable to wait between one pregnancy and another?*"

"That would depend to a large degree upon the health of the individual woman, the character of her former pregnancies and labors, and many other personal factors. Even in the case of a perfectly healthy woman, however, there should be a definite interval between successive childbirths both for her own health and for the sake of her offspring.

Hegar, the distinguished gynecologist of the last century, said that there should be an interval of two and a half years between births. From an endocrinological point of view, Timme recently made the statement that in order to be fit to bear a healthy child, a woman should allow herself a period of two summers of sunshine between pregnancies so that her glands, particularly the thyroid and pituitary, may be restored to normal activity. It seems best, indeed, that after a woman has given birth she should not conceive again for at least eighteen months, and preferably longer."

"*How soon after childbirth can a woman become pregnant again, if no preventive measures are taken?*"

"There seems to be a considerable individual variation in this respect. Some women may go for a year or more after childbirth without becoming pregnant, while others will conceive within the first few months. I have seen women who have given birth one year and even ten months after a previous confinement. During pregnancy, ovulation, that is, the maturing and release of the egg from the ovary, ceases, but this function is reëstablished soon after childbirth, and conception becomes possible again. The menstrual cycles, as I have mentioned, usually reappear within two to six months after labor, depending to some extent upon the duration of the nursing period, and the return of the menses is as a rule an indication that the eggs are again ripening and that a pregnancy may occur once more. No reliance, however, can be placed on this as a sign of fertility, for some women conceive even before the menses are reëstablished, while others may remain sterile for several months in spite of the return of the menstrual cycle. For the present there are no means available of determining for the individual woman just how soon after childbirth she may be able to conceive again."

"*I once heard that as long as a woman continues to nurse her baby she cannot become pregnant. Is there any basis for this belief?*"

"The idea that a woman cannot conceive during the period of lactation is very generally held, both by primitive and civilized peoples, yet there seems to be but little scientific evidence for it. It is known, in fact, that women readily conceive during the period of nursing, and I have seen many such cases myself. Among primitive peoples, nursing is sometimes prolonged for many years, supposedly on the basis that it acts as a contraceptive measure, but if they find this method at all efficacious, it may very likely be due to other factors. Thus, for instance, Malinowski reports that among the inhabitants of the Trobriand Islands, where lactation is continued for two years or more, sexual intercourse is strictly tabu during this entire period. The freedom from conception, then, on the part of nursing Trobriand women can evidently be accounted for by more obvious causes. In my opinion it is not advisable for a woman to rely upon the possible existence of sterility during the nursing period, and if she has to avoid conception she should employ preventive measures as soon as sexual relations are resumed."

LACTATION AND BIRTH CONTROL

"*What about self-control? Do not some people abstain altogether from sexual relations when for one reason or another a pregnancy is not desired.*"

"Yes, continence is practiced by some married people for the purpose of preventing conception, and I have records of many couples who had been abstaining from sexual contact for months and even years at a time on that account. It is certainly the most effective method of avoiding a pregnancy, yet it is one which cannot be advocated or advised as a general practice."

CONTINENCE

"*But why not, doctor? Is continence harmful?*"

"Well, first of all, continence is not feasible. Normally-sexed individuals, living in the intimate daily contacts of married life, find it impossible as a rule to abstain completely from marital relations. Only people who have an unusually high degree of control over their instincts and desires, or, what is more generally the case, those who have a very low degree of sexual libido, are able to refrain from sexual contact with their mates for prolonged periods of time.

"Secondly, persistent continence in married life is physiologically and psychologically not desirable. When two people who love each other and live together in the close intimacies of marriage attempt to avoid sexual relations, it inevitably gives rise to marked stresses and strains, both physical and emotional, which may eventually lead to serious physical and sexual disharmonies. Prolonged continence in marriage may lead to psycho-sexual injuries, and may ultimately affect the individual's health and sexual capacities. I should very definitely say that a satisfactory sex life is essential for a satisfactory marital union, and that not many marriages can long survive the complete repression of the sexual instinct."

"*You mentioned before that there are certain days during the menstrual month when a woman is not likely to conceive. Do you mean that sexual intercourse during that time will not result in pregnancy?*"

THE 'SAFE PERIOD'

"It is assumed now that there is a rhythm of fertility and sterility in the woman's menstrual month and that impregnation can occur only on certain days. During the other days of the month she is supposedly infertile, and sexual relations may not result in conception. This constitutes the so-called 'safe period' which is presumed by some to provide a suitable method for the avoidance of conception."

"*Is the existence of the safe period a new discovery?*"

"The belief that there is a period in the menstrual cycle during which conception is not possible, is not at all of recent origin. It probably dates back to antiquity. Over two thousand years ago Hindu physicians spoke of a period of absolute sterility in the menstrual month. The Mosaic laws which prohibit sexual relations during the menstrual flow and for a week thereafter were possibly also based, in part at least, on the theory that certain days of the month were more likely to be fertile than others. Then, again, Soranus, a Greek physician who practiced in Rome during the second century, was in his days advising women who wanted to prevent conceptions to limit their sexual relations to certain periods of the month. In more recent times, Capellmann, in a book published in 1883, mentioned specific days as being free from the chance of conception and advocated this safe period as a means of birth control. Incidentally the days he mentioned have since been shown to be quite correct. The fact is that until lately the scientific data available on the subject have not been sufficient to establish with any degree of certainty the actual days, nor, in fact, even the existence of a sterile period during the month.

"Within the last few years, however, newer advances in sexual physiology have reawakened an interest in the safe period. The investigations, particularly, of Knaus of Austria and Ogino of Japan have given a new impetus to the study of the subject. Basing their conclusions on their respective scientific findings, these two physicians have actually charted the fertile and the sterile days of the menstrual month. In other words, they have indicated the days of the menstrual month on which conception is and is not possible, thus establishing the existence of the 'safe period' on a more certain basis. This method of family limitation has received the sanction and endorsement of many Catholic authorities, and within the last few years a number of popular books on the subject have been published with the full ecclesiastic approbation."

"*What is the theory of the safe period based on? Why should a woman be unable to conceive during a part of the month?*"

THE PHYSIOLOGICAL BASIS OF THE SAFE PERIOD

"The existence of a sterile period is based upon several physiological assumptions. It is very generally accepted now that in the human female only one egg ripens and is released each month, and investigations indicate that the egg retains its vitality, that is, its capacity of being fertilized, for a short time only, probably not longer than forty-eight hours, and perhaps even less. Consequently, if the egg is not fertilized at the time of its release, it soon deteriorates, and impregnation becomes impossible until the next ovulation, a month later. Then, again, it is now believed that after entry into the uterus or tubes the spermatozoa, too, do not survive for very long, but lose their fertilizing power within forty-eight hours or so. Hence, conception should only be possible when sexual relations take place just around the ovulation time. At other times intercourse presumably cannot lead to a pregnancy because there is no fertilizable egg present in the female genital tract, and because the spermatozoa will not live there long enough to wait for the egg which will be released the following month. In other words, according to this theory, there is a sterile period, or safe period, from a day or two after one ovulation until two or three days before the next one."

"*Is there any way of determining just when the egg is being released from the ovary in a woman, I mean the exact time that ovulation is taking place?*"

"No practical methods are available for this purpose as yet. In animals certain comparatively simple tests have been developed by which the exact time of ovulation can be determined. Two American investigators, Stockard and Papanicolaou, have found that in many animals the lining of the vagina undergoes periodic changes corresponding to their reproductive cycles. By examining a small quantity of the secretions of the animal's vagina, it is now possible to determine quite accurately, almost to the hour, the time when the egg is being discharged from the ovary. More recently Papanicolaou has found that the lining of the vagina of the human female also undergoes monthly changes in correlation with ovulation and the menstrual cycle. It is very likely that in the near future a suitable and practical test will be evolved by which the ovulation time of the individual woman may be definitely ascertained. The determination of a woman's safe period will then be established on a much firmer basis than it is at present."

"*Is it possible to tell what the days of the safe period are for an individual woman?*"

DETERMINATION OF SAFE PERIOD

"To calculate the safe period for a particular woman it is necessary first of all to determine her ovulation time, and this varies considerably in accordance with the length and regularity or irregularity of her menstrual cycles. Before the safe period of a woman can be established, therefore, it is necessary to have an exact record of her menstrual periods for the preceding six and preferably twelve months, so that her individual cycles can be studied and charted."

"*Suppose a woman menstruates regularly every twenty-eight days, what would her safe period be?*"

"The available data would seem to indicate that a woman with a regular twenty-eight day menstrual cycle usually ovulates around the middle of the month. It is not yet possible to tell the exact day of ovulation, but it presumably occurs between the eleventh and sixteenth days of the cycle, counting from the first day of menstruation. On any one of these days an egg may be present in the tubes and the woman will then be fertile. This period of fertility must be extended two days backward to include the survival time of the spermatozoa, and one or two days forward to include the possible survival time of the egg. Accordingly, the fertile period of the woman would extend from the ninth to the eighteenth day of her menstrual month. During the other part of the month, that is from the nineteenth day until the ninth day after the onset of the next menses, she would presumably be in her safe period."

"*But if a woman menstruates irregularly, is there any way of determining on what days she is sterile?*"

"If the menses are irregular, the safe period is subject to greater variations, and this incidentally is one of the serious complications of this theory. For the fact is that the menstrual cycles are usually irregular, as a great many women find when they actually note on a calendar the exact day of their menses. This factor makes the calculation of the ovulation time of a woman and of her sterile period rather uncertain. Perhaps a general statement which may apply to the average woman is that the last ten days of the month, that is, the ten days prior to the onset of the next menstrual period are now considered to be more or less safe from the likelihood of conception. In addition, it is possible that the days of the actual menstrual flow and one or two days thereafter may also be sterile, but this is much less certain."

"*If one could tell definitely the days of the safe period, would it not offer a very simple and satisfactory method of birth control?*"

THE SAFE PERIOD AS A BIRTH CONTROL MEASURE

"Yes, if the theory of the safe period were to be fully substantiated and a method developed to determine a woman's individual sterile days, it would prove an exceedingly important and valuable contribution to the conscious control of conception. Unfortunately, there are several factors which still remain in doubt, and we do not, as yet, I feel, have sufficient data to accept the safe period as an adequate contraceptive method. Our knowledge, for instance, concerning the duration of the life of the egg and the length of time that the spermatozoa retain their fertilizing capacity is based largely upon experimental studies of animals, and we do not know with certainty whether these findings apply equally to the human sex cells. If it should be found that the human egg or sperm cells can survive for a longer period, it will obviously alter our view of the safe period. Then, again, many variations in the ovulation time are apt to occur, even under normal conditions. There is a possibility, for example, that the act of intercourse might in itself hasten the discharge of the egg from the ovary, or, that a second ovulation might perhaps occur during the month. All these factors have to be definitely settled before the safe period can be depended upon for the prevention of conception.

"It is rather odd that centuries of observation and study have as yet not revealed the answer to such vital problems in human physiology and that today we should still be in doubt as to whether and when a safe period exists. However, the investigation of human fertility is being pursued more actively today than ever before, and we may expect many further advances in our knowledge of this subject."

"*Would you advise anyone at present to employ the safe period as a birth control measure?*"

"Not in instances where a pregnancy might prove detrimental. Our knowledge of the safe period has not, as yet, progressed to a point where one could advise a woman who is obliged to avoid a pregnancy, to rely upon this method. As a matter of fact, reports from women who had conceived after a single sexual relation during the month would indicate that impregnations have occurred on days which according to the present theories should have been sterile. I myself have had occasion to observe a number of instances of women who became pregnant from a single sexual exposure during their presumably safe periods. It is certainly altogether too premature, it seems to me, to depend upon the sterile period for the control of conception, and it is particularly inadvisable for the average woman, especially if her menstrual cycles are irregular, to rely upon any book or ready-made calendar in calculating her sterile days. It is best to obtain individual medical advice.

"Furthermore, in all animal life the days of ovulation coincide with the period of greatest sexual desire. In many species, in fact, the female will accept the male only during her fertile period. It is likely that in the human female, too, there is an increased sexual interest during her ovulation time, and the observance of the 'safe period' which bars sexual relations at this time is a practice which is not always desirable or advisable from a psycho-sexual point of view."

"*What measures, then, doctor, are available for the avoidance of conception?*"

"I should make it clear, perhaps, at the outset that an intelligent and satisfactory choice of a contraceptive measure can only be made by a physician after an individual examination. A method suitable for one couple may be quite inadequate for another. At present I shall merely consider with you the biological principles which underlie the practice of birth control. Please understand that I am not now prescribing for you or advising you to employ any of the measures I may discuss. At this time I merely wish to outline the theoretical basis of the practice of contraception.

THE BIOLOGY OF CONCEPTION AND CONTRACEPTION

"The principles of contraception are based upon the several steps in the mechanism of reproduction. These we have already discussed at some length, but for the sake of clarity let me review a few points briefly now. For a pregnancy to occur, the following sequence of events must take place:

"First, the testes of the male must produce normal and healthy sperm cells, and the ovaries of the female must produce normal and healthy eggs.

"Secondly, the sperms must pass through the various canals and ducts of the male, and be ejaculated into the female genital tract.

"Thirdly, the sperms must enter the uterus or womb, and from there pass into the tubes.

"Fourthly, one of the sperms must meet an egg in one of the tubes and fertilize it.

"And finally, the fertilized egg must be transported into the womb, imbed itself there, and develop into the future baby.

"These are the necessary steps in the mechanism of conception, and the practice of contraception is based upon the fact that by interfering with any one of these essential processes reproduction can be prevented."

"*Is it possible to prevent conception by affecting the production of the sperms or the eggs?*"

"Yes, it is. By means of x-rays, heat, or glandular hormones it is possible to affect the function of the testes and the ovaries. Exposure of the sex glands to x-rays, for instance, may either temporarily or permanently arrest their capacity to produce the sex cells, depending upon the dose of the x-rays and the length of exposure. Theoretically, then, the x-rays could be used as a contraceptive measure, but in practice they are not suitable for this purpose, for the present at least, because of certain potential dangers. First, there is the possibility that the effect of the rays may be too lasting and that the man or woman may become permanently sterile; and, secondly, there is some chance that even if the sperm or egg formation is subsequently resumed, the sex cells may not be entirely healthy and as a result the offspring may show certain abnormalities. Much more research has to be done before x-rays could be employed for contraceptive purposes. It is interesting to note, incidentally, that very brief exposure to small doses of the rays may produce an opposite effect, stimulating instead of suppressing the functions of the sex glands, and this method is sometimes employed as a therapeutic measure in cases of sterility."

EXPOSING SEX GLANDS TO X-RAYS

"*Does exposure of the glands to x-rays have any effect upon sexual desire or virility?*"

"Apparently not. The sexual response, it seems, is not influenced by the rays. The seminal discharges of the male also remain quite normal in character and amount but they do not, of course, contain any spermatozoa. The fluid of the emission, as we have seen, comes chiefly from the accessory sex glands, the prostate and the seminal vesicles, and these are not affected by the treatment."

"*Did I understand you to say that heat also affects the glands?*"

"Yes, but this applies only to the male glands. Exposure of the testes to high temperature may markedly influence their sperm-producing function. You will recall that when we spoke of the testes I mentioned their sensitiveness to changes in temperature. It has been shown that the application of heat in the form of hot water, hot air, electric light, and so on, to the outside of the scrotum of animals may arrest sperm production for several weeks. This procedure has thus far been applied to men in a few experimental

APPLYING HEAT TO TESTES

cases only, but it is possible that with further research it may be developed into a serviceable contraceptive measure.

"For the present, however, it is not practicable to prevent conception by affecting the formation of the sex cells. We must therefore consider the next step in the mechanism, namely, the passage of the sperms through the ducts, and see whether this can be hindered or prevented.

MALE STERILIZATION (VASECTOMY)

"You will remember that in order to reach the outside, the sperms have to pass from each testis through a long tube, the vas deferens. By a comparatively simple operation it is possible to cut or tie off this tube so that the sperms will not be able to pass through. When this is done on both sides, the man becomes sterile."

"*Can a woman's tubes be closed up in the same way so that the egg will be unable to pass through?*"

FEMALE STERILIZATION; CUTTING OF TUBES

"Yes, it is possible to cut or tie off the fallopian tubes of the woman, or block their canals in some other manner, so that the egg would be prevented from reaching the uterus and the sperms from reaching the egg.

"Neither the cutting of the vas nor of the fallopian tubes, however, can be considered as a practical contraceptive measure because in both instances the operation produces a permanent sterility. As a matter of fact, they belong more properly to a discussion of sterilization, a subject which we shall consider at some other time.

"While it is not feasible, then, to prevent conception by interfering with the passage of the sperms through the tubes, the next step in the process of reproduction can be forestalled quite easily. It is comparatively simple to avoid impregnation by preventing the entry of the sperms into the genital tract of the woman during sexual contact. Such measures are very widely used in almost every part of the world, and may be classed as male methods, because their practice depends entirely upon the man.

COITUS INTERRUPTUS

"One of these methods has a rather venerable history. It is described, in fact, in some detail in the Bible, in connection with the interesting story of Onan, although it had undoubtedly been in use long before biblical times, perhaps ever since man realized the relation between mating and conception. I have reference to the method which is technically known as 'coitus interruptus.'"

"*What is the story of Onan? I remember having read it in the Bible, but I can't recall the details now.*"

"Well, it seems that there was an ancient Hebrew law or custom to the effect that when a married man died without leaving a son, his unmarried brother, if he had one, was required to marry the widow, and the first-born son of this union was to be named after the deceased brother. It happened that a young man by the name of Onan found himself in such a situation. His elder brother had been killed, and it was now his duty to marry the widow. For one reason or another, however, Onan did not want 'to raise up seed' to his brother, and so, during intercourse, he, to use the biblical phrase, 'spilled his seed upon the ground.' In other words, Onan practiced a method of birth control which even today constitutes perhaps the most widespread practice for the prevention of conception."

"*Did the term 'onanism' arise from this story? I have always been under the impression that onanism meant the practice of masturbation.*"

"That is a rather common belief, but it is evident that the story of Onan applies not to the practice of masturbation, but rather to coitus interruptus, or withdrawal. This term implies the withdrawal of the male organ just prior to the ejaculation and the discharge of the seminal fluid outside of the female genital tract."

"*Is this a satisfactory method for preventing conception, doctor?*"

"No, I would say that it is considered quite unsatisfactory. It is not satisfactory, first because the practice is physiologically and psychologically unsound, and secondly, because it is not sufficiently reliable. It is unsound because the interruption of the sexual act at its very climax constitutes a considerable psychosexual strain on both the man and the woman. With this practice there is the recurrent tension and fear lest the withdrawal be unduly delayed, so that the natural coital cycle is of necessity disturbed. There is also the possibility that the long-continued practice of coitus interruptus may give rise to congestions of the various sex organs, which may lead to local or general disturbances. This does not mean that the occasional resort to the method will prove harmful, but rather that it is undesirable as a habitual and repeated practice.

"There is another point which might be mentioned in this connection. If, as some maintain, the absorption of the seminal fluid is in itself of any physiological value to the woman, then this benefit is naturally lost by the practice of withdrawal. As I said, however, further research is still necessary to determine the importance of this particular factor.

"Aside, however, from the possible psychosexual harm which may result from coitus interruptus, this practice, as I said, is also not sufficiently reliable as a contraceptive measure. Statistical studies have shown that the percentage of failures with this method is high and that it provides but an inadequate protection against conception."

"*But why does it fail? After all, if the sperms are not deposited within the vaginal canal how can conception occur?*"

"It fails most likely because it is not always possible to gauge exactly the moment of ejaculation, and a few drops of the fluid may possibly be emitted before the withdrawal. Furthermore, in a number of instances I have found that the so-called male pre-coital secretion, that is, the moisture which appears during sexual excitement before the actual ejaculation, does contain some sperm cells at times. I mentioned this fact when we spoke of the male genital organs. These factors are probably largely responsible for the many failures with this method.

COITUS RESERVATUS

"A practice which is somewhat similar to coitus interruptus is that in which the male abstains completely from an ejaculation during sexual contact. Technically this is called 'coitus reservatus,' and was the measure advocated at one time by Noyes of the Oneida Community, and also by Alice Stockham, for the prevention of conception. It requires, however, a degree of physical and emotional control which few people possess or could acquire, nor is it certain that the use of this method is not without ultimate harmful effects."

"*Do you mean that those who resort to this practice do not ejaculate at all?*"

"That is so. It seems, according to a report from the colony I mentioned, that by training themselves the men were able to continue the act of coitus with many intermissions for an hour or longer without reaching a climax. This practice was resorted to partly as a contraceptive measure and partly under the belief that the retention of the seminal fluid is of some particular benefit to the man. I do not know, however, of any scientific basis for this latter theory.

THE SHEATH

"Another male method to prevent the sperms from entering the vagina is the use of a mechanical cover which is placed over the male organ during intercourse. This cover is commonly known as the male sheath, or condom, and is supposed to have been first suggested by Fallopius some four hundred years ago. The sheath really serves a twofold purpose: by retaining the seminal discharge it prevents conception, and by covering the penis it prevents the transmission of sexual or venereal infections.

"There are two main types of sheaths: the so-called 'fish-skin' sheath, made of a special animal tissue, and the rubber sheath, which is prepared from natural or artificial rubber. The fishskins have to be moistened before application, and this is not always convenient or desirable. Although they are generally more expensive, I do not think that they have any special advantage over the rubber type."

"*What is your opinion of the sheath? Is it a reliable method?*"

"That depends largely upon the care taken in its application. The difficulty with the sheath, from the point of view of efficiency, is that it often breaks during use and hence the percentage of failures is rather high. I feel, however, that if the cover is of a good quality, is properly examined for any breaks or tears, tested beforehand by stretching and blowing-up with air, and applied with care, it can prove to be a fairly reliable method.

"To decrease the chances of its breaking, as well as to avoid irritation, sufficient lubrication should be present. If natural moisture is absent, an artificial lubricant, preferably an antiseptic one, should be applied to the outside of the sheath after it is adjusted. Some prefer to apply a little of the lubricant to the inside of the cover as well. The cover should not be applied too tightly over the head of the penis, and it is also advisable to have a douche available in the event that the sheath should break during use."

"*Is the use of the sheath in any way injurious; can it cause any harm to the man or to the woman?*"

"No, as far as we know the sheath does not produce any harmful effects, and many people find this method quite satisfactory. Some women, it is true, experience some local irritation when it is used, but this can be obviated to a large degree by proper lubrication. A more serious objection perhaps is the fact that the cover has to be applied after an erection has been attained and at the height of sexual excitement. This necessitates an interruption of the sexual act, which in some cases proves to be psychologically disturbing and affects the sexual responses. Other disadvantages are that it prevents direct contact of the organs during coitus, and that, as is the case with coitus interruptus, it keeps the seminal fluid from entering the vaginal canal. Nevertheless, I believe that the sheath can be classed as one of the better methods available for contraceptive purposes.

"The contraceptive value of the male methods we have just discussed depends upon the fact that they prevent the entry of the seminal fluid into the genital tract of the female. The mere deposition of active sperms in the vagina, however, is not sufficient to bring about conception. The sperms must first pass into the uterus and tubes before they can meet the egg, and if this can be prevented conception will not occur. This brings us to the next step in the mechanism of the control of conception."

"*You mean, then, that it is possible to prevent conception even after the seminal fluid has been discharged into the vagina?*"

"Yes, for just as a sheath may be applied over the male organ to prevent the seminal fluid from reaching the vagina, it is also possible to apply a sheath or veil over the entrance to the uterus, thus preventing the sperm from gaining access into the womb. I shall discuss this principle more fully later, but just now I want to mention several other ways by which conception may be prevented even after the discharge of the seminal fluid.

THE DOUCHE

"It is possible, for instance, to remove the seminal fluid from the vagina by means of a wash or douche. If all of the sperms should be removed or destroyed by the solution before they have a chance to get into the uterus, conception will not occur. The addition of antiseptics to the douche may serve to enhance somewhat its protective value, although plain or soapy water is probably as effective for this purpose as any of the highly advertised antiseptics."

"*How soon after intercourse should a douche be taken?*"

"You will recall that the sperms travel at the rate of about an inch in eight minutes or so. Hence even if they have not entered the uterus during intercourse they may still reach the uterine canal within a very few minutes, depending upon where they have been deposited. In order, therefore, to be at all effective, the douche should be taken as soon after sexual contact as possible, but even then it will prove ineffective if direct insemination into the uterus has occurred. Incidentally, the necessity for arising immediately after intercourse is a serious objection to the douche as a contraceptive method. As we shall see later, it is desirable that a certain period of rest and relaxation should follow the sexual relation, and this rest is disturbed if the woman has to douche immediately after contact."

"*What is the best way of taking a douche?*"

"It can be taken either in the lying or sitting posture, but the latter is just as effective and more convenient. The bag should hang so that its top is about on a level with the top of the head when standing. This supplies sufficient pressure for the purpose. The nozzle should be inserted for about three inches, but that would vary with the depth of the vagina. While the water is flowing in, the woman should contract the internal muscles of the vaginal outlet, or else close the latter with her hand, relaxing the muscles and opening the canal at intervals to permit the water to flow out. In this manner the canal is well distended and a thorough flushing is obtained."

"*I have noticed lately in drug stores quite an array of different kinds of devices for douching purposes; is there an advantage in any particular type?*"

"There are two kinds of douching appliances, the usual rubber bag and the hand-bulb syringe. The nozzles range in type from the thin hard rubber kind to complicated mechanical devices which are supposed to occlude and dilate the vaginal canal during douching. In my opinion the ordinary bag and nozzle is just as satisfactory as any of the more complicated types, and certainly less apt to produce injury."

"*Is the use of a douche alone sufficient to prevent conception?*"

"No, I should say that the douche alone is not at all a reliable measure. You will remember that it is possible for the spermatozoa to enter the uterus during or immediately after the ejaculation. It is even maintained by some that at the end of the sexual act the female uterus exerts an actual suction, so that a certain amount of the seminal fluid is drawn into it directly, but this has not been definitely proven. At any rate, the douche can remove only the fluid which is in the vagina, but will not affect the sperm cells that have already entered the uterus. Furthermore, you will recall that the vaginal walls are not smooth but thrown into numerous small folds. Unless the vagina is thoroughly distended and cleansed during douching there is some possibility that a little of the seminal fluid may remain in these folds and not be affected by the solution employed. While some women use the douche satisfactorily for long periods of time, the percentage of failures with this method is nevertheless very high, and it should not be relied upon as the sole measure of protection. It is, however, often useful as an accessory measure.

CHEMICAL CONTRACEPTIVES

"Another means of preventing the male cells from entering the uterus is by the use of chemical contraceptives. The chemical ingredients are generally incorporated into certain bases, and made up in the form of suppositories, tablets, powders or jellies. These are inserted into the vagina by the woman prior to the sexual relation. In the vaginal canal these preparations are supposed to dissolve or spread along the vaginal walls and uterine opening forming a mechanical barrier to the passage of the sperms, while the liberated chemical ingredients presumably mix with the seminal fluid, immobilize the sperms and render them incapable of entering the uterus and fertilizing the egg."

"I remember having read an advertisement in one of the magazines about a certain kind of suppository which was claimed to be a particularly perfect method for 'feminine hygiene.'"

SUPPOSITORIES

"'Feminine hygiene' is an advertising euphemism for contraception, and all kinds of products are extravagantly recommended for that purpose. It is unfortunate, indeed, that many of the commercial concerns are so unscrupulous in their exploitation of these products. Some of them make statements and claims which I know cannot be substantiated. In the matter of suppositories, for instance, the fact is, and I judge from the reports of many thousands of women, that they are not altogether reliable as contraceptives, and failures with them occur rather frequently."

"*Why are they not effective?*"

"For several reasons. Suppositories are made by incorporating one or more chemical ingredients in a cocoa-butter, gelatine or some other base which is solid under normal temperatures but melts at body heat. When introduced into the vagina, the suppository is supposed to dissolve and liberate its chemical contents. It is assumed that the base, after melting, will form an oily or gelatinous layer over the mouth of the uterus, producing a mechanical barrier to the entrance of the spermatozoa, while the chemicals will serve to immobilize the cells. To be effective, therefore, the suppository must melt readily, but this is often enough not the case. In studying this question I have frequently inserted suppositories into the vaginal canals of women and have sometimes found them unmelted there even half an hour later. Then, again, and this is the most important reason why these preparations are often ineffective, even if the suppository does melt, it may not cover the uterine opening, and since it appears to be possible for the sperms to be injected directly into the uterus during coitus, it is obvious that the suppositories will have no effect under such circumstances. There is always, therefore, a strong element of chance in relying on suppositories for protection. I might also mention that many people object to them because of the excessive oiliness which is produced by the melting of the usual cocoa-butter base.

TABLETS AND POWDERS

"The same drawbacks, as far as reliability is concerned, apply to the chemical contraceptives which are put up in the form of tablets or powders. The tablets, for instance, on dissolving are supposed to liberate a gas which, in turn, forms a foamy mass in the vagina, and acts both as a chemical and mechanical contraceptive. In order for the tablet to dissolve, however, a certain amount of moisture is required, and sometimes the moisture naturally present in the vagina is insufficient. I have seen tablets remain in the vagina for half an hour without dissolving. And, on the other hand, when they do dissolve, the foam in some instances disappears so quickly that it can hardly have any effect. The same applies to powders, except that, in addition, they have a drying effect upon the vaginal walls which is sometimes rather uncomfortable."

"In many of the drug store windows I have lately seen displays of various kinds of jellies which are obviously intended to be used for the prevention of conception. How are these employed?"

"Jellies are another type of chemical contraceptive. They are put up in collapsible tubes to which a special nozzle can be attached. The nozzle is inserted into the vagina, and by compressing the tube or turning a special key at the bottom of it, a certain amount of the jelly is expressed into the vaginal canal. A number of different devices have been developed with the object of making the introduction of the jelly more simple and effective. The principle, however, is the same—to introduce a sufficient quantity into the vagina and particularly around the neck of the womb. This has to be done, of course, prior to the sexual relation, either immediately, or within a quarter of an hour or so before the act."

JELLIES

"How do the jellies compare with the other chemical methods?"

"Of the several chemical contraceptives available, the jellies, I believe, are the most adequate. They do not have to melt or dissolve in order to be effective because they are already in a semi-solid or gelatinous state, and on account of their consistency they can be distributed much more readily along the vaginal canal and across the uterine opening. Nevertheless, I would say that even the jellies are not entirely reliable, except in specially selected cases. Like the other methods, jellies should not be depended upon without a previous physical examination, in spite of the exaggerated claims of manufacturers. The suitability of the method would depend upon the anatomical condition of the genital organs of the individual woman. I know of a great many failures which have resulted from too ready a reliance upon jellies.

"Recently another chemical contraceptive has been developed—known as the 'foam powder' method—which consists of a foam-producing powder used in conjunction with a small sponge. The powder contains a non-soapy, lathering agent which, in the presence of moisture and friction, produces a foamy mass. The sponge is moistened

FOAM POWDER

and a little of the powder sprinkled on it; then it is kneaded between the fingers until a foam is produced and inserted into the vagina. The foam is supposed to act as a chemical and mechanical barrier to the progress of the spermatozoa. The chief advantage of this method is that it does not require individual medical instruction and is therefore applicable on a wide scale. It is, however, still in the experimental stage and there is some doubt as to whether it is entirely harmless to the tissues and sufficiently reliable."

"*Is there any danger that chemical contraceptives might be injurious in some way?*"

"Generally speaking, I should say that the usual chemical contraceptives are not apt to be injurious. Should the ingredients of a particular product be too strong or too concentrated, or should a woman happen to be particularly sensitive to any of the chemicals employed, there is a possibility of some irritation to the tissues. In an examination of a very large number of women, however, I have seen but very few instances of local irritation that could be ascribed to the use of chemical contraceptives. Nevertheless, I feel that it is important that the ingredients employed in contraceptives, whether in suppositories or jellies, should be mild and harmless, and that strong solutions should be avoided for douching purposes.

MECHANICAL CONTRACEPTIVES

"The chemical methods, as I have said, are intended primarily to prevent the entry of active sperms into the uterus. The same result can be obtained, and much more effectively, by the use of certain mechanical devices which cover up the entrance to the womb. These are placed either directly over the cervix, that is the neck of the uterus, or else diagonally across the vaginal canal, and form a mechanical barrier to the passage of the sperms upward from the vagina. They are made of several kinds of material and come in a large variety of shapes and sizes. Those intended to cover the cervix, called cervical caps, are made either of soft rubber or of a firm material; they are cupshaped and vary from one to two inches in diameter. The caps designed for vaginal use called diaphragms or pessaries, are made of soft rubber with a flexible metal spring around the circumference; they are hemispherical in shape, and range from two to four inches in diameter."

CAPS AND DIAPHRAGMS

"How are these mechanical devices employed?"

"Like the chemical methods, these are also employed by the woman. To be effective, however, they must be anatomically suitable for the individual woman. As we have already seen, considerable variations exist in the pelvic organs, and consequently each woman must be examined individually so that the exact type or size of cap or pessary can be selected for her. There are, for instance, over twenty different sizes of diaphragms, and it is not possible to tell the size that a woman requires without a gynecological examination. Some women, in fact, are not at all suitable for this type of contraceptive and cannot rely upon it. After the choice has been made by the physician, the woman is then taught the technique of its use. Generally, the diaphragm is inserted before retiring and removed the following morning. Before insertion, however, it is well to smear the pessary with a small quantity of a contraceptive jelly which serves both as a lubricant and as an additional safeguard."

"When a pessary is used can sexual relations take place without the need of any other precaution?"

"Yes. The guard acts as a veil over the opening of the womb and prevents the seminal fluid from entering it, so that no other precautions are necessary. There is, in the main, direct contact between the male organ and the vaginal wall, and the seminal fluid is discharged into the vagina in a normal manner. This, in fact, constitutes one of the chief advantages of this particular measure, for sensation is not affected, and the normal sequence of the sexual act is not disturbed."

"When a pessary is in place does the woman feel its presence at all?"

"Not as a rule. If the pessary is of the correct size for the particular woman, and properly inserted, she should not feel its presence. Nor should the man be conscious of it to any degree during the sexual relation."

"How long must the pessary remain in place after intercourse?"

"That depends entirely upon the convenience of the woman. If she wishes, she may remove it immediately, or else she may leave it in until the next morning, or even for twenty-four hours. If she prefers to remove the guard soon after the act, however, she should first douche in order to wash out the seminal fluid from the canal."

"*But didn't you say before, doctor, that the douche is unreliable because it does not always prevent the sperms from entering the womb?*"

"Yes, but that applies only where the douche is the sole measure of protection. With the pessary in place, the sperms cannot go up into the uterus during intercourse, and the fluid remaining in the canal can be washed out quite thoroughly with an ordinary douche."

"*Is a douche necessary if the pessary is left in place until the next morning?*"

"In a number of examinations I have found that with the pessary in place there were no active sperms in the vagina six hours after sexual contact, and it is quite likely that they lose their vitality long before that. Hence, if the pessary is permitted to remain in place that length of time, or preferably twelve hours, it may be removed without a preliminary douche. Even then, however, a douche is generally advisable before and after removal of the pessary, as a hygienic measure, if it is convenient."

"*Is it necessary to add any antiseptic to the douche?*"

"No. Plain, warm water or water rendered slightly soapy with an ordinary mild soap is sufficient and as effective as any of the antiseptic solutions."

"*I once heard a woman speak of some kind of metal device made of silver or gold which she was given by a physician. Is that different from a pessary?*"

FIRM CERVICAL CAPS

"Well, there are several types of such appliances. Some are made in the form of small caps which fit snugly over the mouth of the womb. They are made of some metal such as aluminum, chrome, silver, or of other firm substances like hard rubber, resin, or celluloid. Caps of this type are rather widely used in Europe, and in some of the clinics which I visited in Germany, Austria and Russia they were being prescribed quite extensively. Their advantage is that they may be left in place for several days, and even for a month at a time, but they require frequent medical examinations and replacement and we are as yet not certain of their practicability for general use."

"From what I understood, the woman mentioned some appliance that the doctor had placed in her womb and it was to remain there for several months."

INTRA-UTERINE APPLIANCES

"Yes, there are other types of appliances, called 'buttons' or 'stems,' which are placed directly into the cavity of the neck of the uterus and are allowed to remain there for varying periods of time. However, many serious complications have been reported from the use of such devices, and the general medical opinion today is that such methods are harmful and unhygienic. Such appliances are not prescribed in any of the birth control centers in this country.

THE SILVER RING

"A few years ago, Graefenberg developed a small, flexible, spiral ring to be inserted into the cavity of the womb. The supposed advantage of this method was that it was less apt to give rise to complications than the 'button' type, and could be left in place for a year at a time. The results, however, have not proved to be entirely satisfactory or reliable, and various harmful effects have been reported. American gynecologists in general disapprove of it."

"Before we leave this subject I should like to ask one more question. In a newspaper article I read that it is now possible to make a woman sterile for a certain length of time by giving her certain injections. Is there any basis for this report?"

IMMUNIZATION AGAINST CONCEPTION

"Yes, I had intended to discuss that with you, and I am glad that you mentioned it now. Some thirty-five years ago it was first shown by Metchnikoff and Landsteiner, and later by Guyer, McCartney, Jarcho and others that the injection of male sperms into the tissues of a female produces in the latter a temporary immunity to spermatozoa and a consequent sterility. The same, it seems, can be accomplished by the use of certain glandular hormones. Experimental work along these lines has been conducted on animals for many years, and it has been proven quite conclusively that animals can be rendered infertile for varying periods of time by the use of such injections."

SPERMATOXINS

"Has this method ever been tried on human beings?"

"Within comparatively recent years attempts have been made to immunize human females by means of sperm injections. Work in this field has been carried on notably in Russia. Several hundred women were given injections, and apparently a temporary sterility lasting from several months to a year had actually been induced in a large percentage of the immunized women. Either human sperms, preferably the sperms of the husband, or the sperms of animals were used for the injections. Similar work has been carried out in this country, too, with apparently satisfactory results."

"*Can the woman have children later on, if she receives these injections?*"

"Yes, the immunity is only temporary. As it wears off, the fertility returns. Many cases have been reported of women who had given birth after the period of sterility had passed.

"This field of biological immunization must still of necessity be considered to be in the experimental stage, and observation must be continued over a long period of time before conclusions concerning its value can be reached. Not only must the effectiveness and reliability of the method be determined, but also whether there is any likelihood of some later ill effect upon the woman or her future offspring. It is not at all impossible, however, that in the future a simple injection, or perhaps even a few tablets of some glandular hormone, may serve to render a woman infertile for a definite period of time."

"*Which of the methods you were discussing do you consider to be the most satisfactory?*"

THE IDEAL CONTRACEPTIVE

"The ideal contraceptive still remains to be developed. It should be not only harmless and entirely reliable, but also simple, practical, universally applicable and esthetically satisfactory to both husband and wife. None of the methods in use today meets all the necessary requirements. Generally speaking, I would say that the vaginal diaphragm in conjunction with a contraceptive jelly is probably the most adequate and satisfactory method available at present. This method cannot, however, ordinarily be prescribed while the hymen is still intact, and at the beginning of marriage it is the man who has to employ preventive measures, if a conception is to be avoided. The vaginal diaphragm, furthermore, is not suitable for every woman, and as I have already emphasized can be prescribed only after a gynecological examination. We have not as yet a universally applicable contraceptive which could safely be employed without an individual consultation."

"*One would think that a subject of such universal need and importance would have been thoroughly studied and perfected long ago.*"

"One would think so, but such has not been the case. Please realize that until recently very little scientific work has been done in the field of contraception. The first birth control center in America, the present Birth Control Clinical Research Bureau established by Margaret Sanger, was opened only a little over a decade ago. The whole subject was until recently considered tabu even by scientific investigators. It is only within the last few years that extensive research in this field of medical science has been undertaken, and I would say that a considerable amount of progress has already been made. At the present time investigations in contraception are being carried on in a number of laboratories and clinics in many parts of the world, and we may confidently expect many new developments as time goes on.

"The action of the American Medical Association at its 1937 convention is an important step in that direction. After many years of comparative apathy the American Medical Association has now officially recognized the importance of contraception as an essential health measure. It has adopted a resolution to promote instruction in medical schools concerning the clinical considerations and therapeutic applications of contraceptive methods, and also to undertake an investigation of the methods generally recommended or employed with a view to determining their physiological, chemical and biological properties and effects. This change in attitude should in itself serve to further materially the progress of contraceptive knowledge and research.

"Some twenty-five years ago Tushnov, a Russian biologist, in a report about the possibility of human sterilization with sperm cells, ended by saying—I have his report right here—'And thus at his own will man will be able to control the great fertility of nature . . . the human mind conquers. It is not the first time that man has come to grips with nature and been crowned with laurels to celebrate his victory.' We are still, perhaps, far from celebrating the victory, but we are ever going onward. In the birth control work of tomorrow, we may safely look for two developments—a sane and intelligent social outlook and simple, effective and satisfactory contraceptive methods.

"I presume you would like me to recommend several books on birth control. I shall mention a few, though they deal chiefly with the theoretical and social aspects of the subject. The books on contraceptive methods available in this country are mostly technical in nature and are designed primarily for the medical reader."

SANGER, MARGARET. "My Fight for Birth Control." Farrar & Rinehart (1931).

A vivid and vital autobiography. Margaret Sanger's personal story of birth control in America.

SANGER, MARGARET. "Motherhood in Bondage." Brentano's (1928).

Poignant letters from American women to Margaret Sanger. A revealing picture of the intimate problems of the American family.

KNOPF, S. ADOLPHUS, M.D. "Various Aspects of Birth Control—Medical, Social, Economic, Legal, Moral and Religious." American Birth Control League (1928).

A discussion of the subject by a pioneer medical advocate of birth control.

FIELDING, MICHAEL, M.D. "Parenthood." The Vanguard Press (1935).

An able, clear and practical volume, written by an English physician.

ROBINSON, WILLIAM J., M.D. "Birth Control or Limitation of Offspring." Eugenics Publishing Company (1928).

The arguments for and against birth control succinctly and keenly analyzed by a pioneer of the movement.

HAIRE, NORMAN, M.D. (Editor). "Some More Medical Views on Birth Control." E. P. Dutton & Co. (1928)

A symposium of essays by a number of leading physicians.

BLACKER, C. P., M.D. "Birth Control and the State." E. P. Dutton & Company (1926).

A lucid and persuasive discussion of birth control by the General Secretary of the British Eugenics Society.

BROMLEY, DOROTHY, D. "Birth Control—Its Use and Misuse." Harper and Brothers (1934).

A factual discussion of birth control and its problems.

HIMES, NORMAN E. "A Medical History of Contraception." Williams & Wilkins Co. (1936).

A scholarly and comprehensive history of the medical aspects of birth control.

HIMES, NORMAN E. and STONE, ABRAHAM, M.D. "Practical Birth Control Methods." Modern Age Books, Inc. (1938).

Thoroughly practical and well illustrated. Designed for the professional and lay reader.

GUCHTENEERE, RAOUL DE, M.D. "Judgment on Birth Control." The Macmillan Co. (1931).

An able critique of birth control by a Catholic physician.

LATZ, LEO J., M.D. "The Rhythm of Fertility and Sterility in Women." Latz Foundation (1932).

A non-technical booklet on the safe period. (Published with ecclesiastical approbation.)

COUCKE, VALÈRE J. and WALSH, JAMES J., M.D. "The Sterile Period in Family Life." Joseph F. Wagner, Inc. (1932). (Published under the imprimatur of Cardinal Hayes.)

A clear and temperate presentation of the safe period by a Professor of Moral Theology and an eminent physician.

CHAPTER VI

PROBLEMS OF REPRODUCTION

"We shall continue with the story of procreation today. First I should like to go a little more fully into the problems of human fertility. This is a subject of practical importance and concern to every married couple, and might well be included in our discussion."

"*I am not quite certain that I understand what you mean by the term fertility.*"

FERTILITY

"By fertility I mean the ability to beget offspring. Not all couples, obviously, possess this capacity to the same degree. Some marriages are very fruitful, and the progeny very numerous; other unions are much less prolific, and even when no attempts are made to limit the number of offspring, the woman bears but few children; some couples, again, remain childless altogether. These variations in fertility are often a matter of vital concern in marriage."

"*What are such differences due to?*"

FACTORS INFLUENCING FERTILITY

"There are a great many factors which seem to be capable of influencing the fertility of an individual or a couple. In many instances fertility is determined by inherent racial or individual variations, the nature of which is as yet not clearly understood. In other cases, environmental factors, such as climate, diet, nutrition, and general bodily conditions, play an important part. Darwin showed long ago, for instance, that domestic animals breed faster than wild animals of the same species, and he ascribed this to the effects of a more ample and more regular food supply. On the other hand, wild animals in captivity frequently do not breed at all, and remain sterile in spite of continued sexual relations. It has also been shown that in animals, at least, the absence of certain vitamins from the food may cause a diminution or complete loss of fertility. In humans, too, diet and general bodily health appear to have a very definite effect upon reproductive capacity. Then, of course, age is a very significant factor, and influences to a considerable degree the capacity to beget offspring."

"*At what age can a girl or a woman first become pregnant?*"

"In the human female the maturing of the ova, or eggs, and their release from the ovaries begin at puberty, and it is at this time that conception can first occur. This coincides more or less with the appearance of the menstrual flow, and, as a rule, therefore, a girl first becomes fertile when her menses have been established. The age at which this occurs is not the same in all cases but is subject to many individual variations. Rare instances of pregnancies in girls of ten, nine and even eight years have been recorded, but generally speaking, a woman becomes capable of bearing a child between the ages of twelve and fifteen."

"*How long does a woman's childbearing period last? When is she no longer capable of conceiving?*"

THE CHILD-BEARING PERIOD OF A WOMAN

"The reproductive life of a woman extends from puberty until the 'change of life,' or menopause. When her menses cease, her fertility also comes to an end. As the age at which the menopause occurs is subject to great differences, the duration of a woman's fertility varies correspondingly. Exceptional cases of childbirth at very advanced ages are recorded now and again. Only recently someone sent me a newspaper clipping of a story about a Mexican woman who was reported to have given birth to twins at the ripe age of seventy years. While one may doubt the authenticity of this particular story, the woman who sent me the clipping and, who, incidentally, is still menstruating at the age of 54, was nevertheless somewhat alarmed, and expressed the quaint hope that she would not be running in competition with this

Mexican woman's extended fertility. According to Kisch, pregnancies at a comparatively advanced age are by no means unusual in Northern Europe, and he states that from 3-4% of women in Denmark, Sweden and Ireland give birth after the age of fifty. Such late pregnancies, however, are much more rare in the United States. In general, the reproductive life of a woman is considered to extend from the age of 15 to 49, or perhaps more usually from 15 to 45."

"*To what extent does the age of a woman affect her chances of a pregnancy? Is it more difficult for her to conceive later in life?*"

AGE AND FEMALE FERTILITY

"Matthews Duncan, who published a classic study on fertility and sterility in 1866, maintained that the fertility of a woman increases gradually from the beginning of her reproductive life until about the age of thirty, and then it slowly declines. More recent statistical studies in America have also shown that over 90% of children are born to women between the ages of 20-39, and only 10% of births are by mothers under 20 or over 39. It is generally accepted that the fertility of a woman starting at puberty gradually rises to its height somewhere between the ages of 25 and 30, and then diminishes again, at first slowly and then more rapidly. With the onset of the menopause in the forties, fertility decreases at a faster rate, and the chances of a conception are correspondingly reduced."

"*Is there any basis for the statement I once heard that a woman may conceive more readily during the 'change of life' than during the years prior to it?*"

"Perhaps you recall the story of Sarah who, according to the Bible, conceived for the first time at the full age of ninety, long after 'it had ceased to be with her after the manner of women.' This story might be quite plausible if the biblical year were half of our own, for occasionally a pregnancy does occur towards the end of the menopause. In some cases this is due to a premature abandonment of contraceptive care, but in rare instances there seems to be an actual reawakening of reproductive capacity at this time. Several years ago, a woman came to consult me about the general hygiene of the menopause. She was 43 years old, her menses had ceased for two months, and she was certain that she had now reached her 'change of life.' To her great amazement and even greater joy, an examination revealed that she was pregnant. She had been married for fifteen years, had never conceived before, and had given up all hope of ever bearing a child. The reasons for such sudden returns of fertility are still obscure.

"Generally, the menopause comes on rather gradually, and it takes several years before the process is completed. The menses do not cease at once but become more and more irregular, with a gradual increase in the interval between successive periods. While it is possible for a woman to conceive during these years of 'change,' a pregnancy is not very likely to occur. Nevertheless this is a time of great anxiety for many women, for with the menstrual irregularities they are often puzzled to know whether the cessation of the menses is the result of menopausal changes, or of a possible impregnation. To avoid the recurrent uncertainties of this period, it is advisable to continue the use of contraceptive measures until the menses have ceased completely."

"*But if the menstrual flow becomes so irregular during these years, when does a woman know that her periods have ceased entirely and that she can no longer be impregnated?*"

"It is indeed sometimes difficult for a woman to know whether her fertile period has passed or not. There is no exact way of determining whether ova are still maturing. It is possible, in fact, for a woman to ovulate even without menstruating, or, for that matter, to menstruate without ovulating. Perhaps a good rule to follow is for a woman not to regard herself as having completed her reproductive life until a year has gone by without a menstrual flow."

"*Is the fertility of a man also influenced by his age?*"

AGE AND MALE FERTILITY

"A man also first becomes fertile when he reaches puberty, that is, between the ages of 12–15. It is at this time that the sperm cells begin to be formed in the testes, and that he becomes capable of a seminal emission which can cause impregnation. His fertility, however, lasts much later in life than that of the woman. Cases of men who become fathers at sixty and even seventy are not infrequent. I myself have seen on several occasions numerous active sperms in the seminal discharges of men over sixty, although one could not tell whether these sperms were capable of fertilizing an ovum, for motility in itself is not a definite indication of fertilizing capacity. It is accepted, however, that men, too, become less fertile as they pass beyond their middle age in life."

"*You spoke before about some marriages being childless. What is the frequency of childlessness at present?*"

STERILITY

"A number of studies have shown that about ten per cent of all marriages remain sterile or childless, although it is difficult to obtain exact statistics on this point. There are of course different degrees or grades of sterility. Some unions are sterile from the very start, and no conception occurs in spite of a normal marital life over many years. In others, sterility ensues after one or more children have already been born so that the marriage is not entirely childless."

"*A schoolmate of mine who has been married for nearly three years has been very unhappy over the fact that she has not become pregnant yet. Both she and her husband are very anxious to have a child.*"

"Sterility is a serious marital problem whenever it occurs. The begetting of children is the ultimate aim of practically every marriage, and when this cannot be attained, the entire marital relationship is apt to be deeply affected. A woman who cannot conceive will generally take every possible measure, even subjecting herself to serious operations, in order to overcome her sterility. It is the natural desire of almost every normal, healthy, married couple to have offspring, and nearly every woman who applies for birth control advice wants first of all to be assured that the use of contraceptive measures will not prevent her from having children later on."

"*When is a marriage regarded as sterile? I mean how long a period must elapse without a pregnancy before a marriage is considered barren?*"

"While a conception may follow a single sexual contact, the first pregnancy, even when no preventive measures are used, may not occur for several months after sexual relations have been established, and sometimes not for a year or even two or three years after marriage. One cannot, therefore, tell with certainty when a marriage is to be considered infertile. Kisch says that a marriage should not be regarded as sterile until three years of involuntary childlessness have elapsed, and this is the view which is quite generally accepted. Nevertheless, it is not advisable to wait that long before seeking medical aid. Meaker rightly maintains that a thorough investigation should be made if one year passes by without a conception, and it might even be better, I feel, to make a preliminary study at the end of six months."

"*What is usually the cause of childlessness in marriage?*"

THE CAUSES OF STERILITY

"Let us understand once more that for a fruitful conception to occur it is essential that a healthy sperm cell should meet and fuse with a healthy egg cell, and that the fertilized egg should then imbed itself in the womb. There are many conditions either of the wife or the husband or of both which may interfere with or disturb the proper functioning of this mechanism, and thus lead to sterility. One of the most significant recent advances in the understanding of sterility has been the realization that the fruitfulness of a marriage depends upon the degree of fertility of both mates, and that the responsibility for childlessness must be shared by both husband and wife. Formerly it was the woman who was nearly always considered responsible for a sterile mating, and even today we are most apt to regard her as being at fault when a union proves to be childless. Barrenness has always been looked upon not only as an unfortunate circumstance, but also as a source of reproach to the woman. In many countries sterility is a cause for divorce, and the childless woman is regarded with contempt and scorn. It is only within comparatively recent years that the male factor in the causation of sterile marriages has come to be appreciated more fully. Today it is considered, in fact, that a very high percentage of sterile unions, variously estimated as from 30-50 per cent, is due to a lack of fertility on the part of the male. It should be emphasized, however, that the fruitfulness of any particular marriage does not always depend entirely upon the condition of either the husband or the wife, but rather upon the degrees of fertility of both of them."

"*Is it possible that a man and a woman may not be able to have children with each other and yet beget offspring with other mates?*"

"Yes, that may happen. Instances of this sort are due in the man to the fact that fertility is not an absolute quality, and that a man or a woman need not necessarily be either completely fertile or completely sterile. There are many varying degrees of reproductive capacity. If both mates happen to have a low fertility, they may be unable to have children with each other, yet if each one should remarry a mate with a high grade of fertility, the subsequent unions may prove to be normally fruitful."

"*In what way may the husband be the cause of a childless marriage?*"

STERILITY OF THE MALE

"The function of the male in reproduction is to deposit active and healthy spermatozoa at the entrance to the womb. If the spermatozoa are defective in quantity or quality, or if the seminal fluid cannot be deposited into the genital tract of the female, the union will be sterile. In some cases of male sterility the seminal fluid contains no spermatozoa at all, a condition known as 'azoöspermia.' This may be due to a failure of sperm-formation on account of some local or general disturbance, such as glandular dysfunctions, inflammation of the testes, congenital abnormalities, or long standing ailments; or else, the azoöspermia may be caused by a blockage of the seminal ducts leading from the testes, which prevents the spermatozoa from reaching the seminal discharge. Of three cases of sterility due to an azoöspermia which came to my attention within the last year, in one the failure of sperm production was due to undescended testes; in another to a severe attack of mumps in youth, which had been complicated by an inflammation and subsequent atrophy of the sex glands; while the third had had a gonorrheal infection which had involved the ducts leading from both testes, causing a complete blockage to the passage of the sperms.

"More frequently, however, in cases of male sterility, the spermatozoa are produced and transmitted through the several channels, but they prove to be so few in quantity or so poor in quality that fertilization is not possible. This deficiency in number or vitality may be caused by long continued debilitating diseases, glandular disturbances, chronic infections and inflammations in any part of the body, inadequate diet and a number of other factors. Abnormalities of the structure or quality of the sperms are now considered to be a comparatively frequent cause of sterile matings.

"In some cases, the sterility of the male is due to his inability to transmit the seminal fluid into the female genital tract. Sexual impotence, for instance, may prevent the deposition of the seminal fluid into the vagina. The fluid may be entirely normal, but if no sexual union can take place, sterility will obviously result. We shall, however, return to the question of impotence at some other time."

"*Is there any way of determining the quality of the sperm cells?*"

"Yes, methods of diagnosis have recently been made available by Moench, Cary and others whereby both the quantity and quality of the spermatozoa in the seminal fluid can be determined with a fair degree of accuracy. In addition to the observation of their motility and vitality, it is now possible to estimate the approximate number of sperms in the ejaculation, as well as to study the form and structure of the individual cells. A healthy sperm cell is known to possess a specific shape and form. If the percentage of abnormal forms is high, the fluid is considered defective in quality and fertilizing power."

"*What is usually responsible for childlessness on the part of the woman?*"

STERILITY OF THE FEMALE

"In the main, sterility of the woman may be due either to deficiencies in egg formation, or to conditions which prevent the meeting and fusion of the sperms and the egg, or prevent the implantation of the fertilized egg in the womb. It is now generally assumed that the same types of bodily disturbances which may affect sperm production in the male, may be responsible for deficiencies in egg formation in the female. Glandular disorders, particularly of the thyroid and the pituitary, ovarian disease, malnutrition, chronic infections, and many other conditions may adversely influence the ripening and the release of the egg cells, or lower their vitality to such a degree that fertilization and implantation are not possible.

"Most frequently the cause of the sterility is due to some condition which prevents the spermatozoa from entering the uterus or the tubes and meeting the ovum. Abnormal positions or inflammations of the uterus, particularly of its neck, infections of the fallopian tubes, growths and malformations of the genital organs frequently block the passage of the sperms, so that they cannot come in contact with the egg cell. Then, again, even though fertilization does occur, some uterine abnormality may make it impossible for the egg to implant itself, and the pregnancy does not continue.

"In some instances a sexual maladjustment which prevents normal sexual relations may be the underlying cause of sterility. Not so long ago, for instance, I had occasion to examine a woman for sterility who, although she had taken no contraceptive precautions, had not conceived after eighteen months of marriage. An examination disclosed the fact that because of a local irritation around the external genitals, actual penetration had never occurred, and her hymen was still intact. After the inflammatory condition was cleared up, and normal sexual relations were established, a pregnancy soon resulted."

"*Is it possible to determine the quality of the egg cells in the woman?*"

"No, we have no definite means of ascertaining the quality or vitality of a woman's egg cells as we do in the case of the spermatozoa. The ova are, of course, not accessible to direct examination, and their condition has to be determined indirectly from a general study of the woman and of her reproductive system."

"*Would an examination reveal whether the tubes leading from the womb are open or closed?*"

TESTS OF THE FALLOPIAN TUBES

"Yes, a comparatively simple and accurate method is now available by which it can be determined whether the tubes are open or not. This test was developed by Dr. I. C. Rubin of New York some fifteen years ago, and it has proved to be of very great value in the study and treatment of sterility. The test consists of the introduction of a gas, either carbon dioxide, oxygen or air, into the uterus under a certain degree of pressure. As the cavity of the womb becomes filled, the gas soon forces its way into the tubes, and, if one or both of them are open, passes through them into the abdomen. If they are closed, the gas cannot pass beyond the point of obstruction. The degree of pressure required to force the gas through, the bubbling sounds which can be heard by listening over the abdomen, the sensations of the patient, and, if necessary, a subsequent x-ray determine very accurately the condition of the tubes. In a similar manner it is also possible to introduce an opaque liquid into the uterus and tubes and then x-ray these organs. By this method the condition of the tubes can be studied even more thoroughly."

"*What are the chances of curing a sterility?*"

THE CURE OF STERILITY

"With modern means of diagnosis and treatment it is possible to obtain satisfactory results in a high percentage of sterility cases. It has been variously stated that in from twenty to forty per cent of sterile marriages, a pregnancy eventually results after appropriate treatment. Out of one hundred consecutive cases of sterility which I had occasion to observe during the last few years, twenty-nine have already borne children and four are pregnant now. In some instances, the cause is relatively minor in character and may be corrected quite easily; in others prolonged and extensive investigations and treatment may be required before conception results, while many cases are, unfortunately, still incurable. Our increasing knowledge of the physiology of sex and reproduction, however, is constantly making the treatment of sterility more effective and successful."

"*Not long ago there was some discussion in the newspapers about 'test tube' babies. Is it really possible to produce babies artificially?*"

ARTIFICIAL INSEMINATIONS

"The phrase 'test tube babies' is merely a journalistic expression, for we have by no means approached the stage where babies or, for that matter, any form of life, can be produced artificially. The newspaper discussions referred to the subject of 'artificial insemination' which implies merely the artificial or mechanical introduction of male seminal fluid into the female genital tract for the purpose of inducing impregnation. You can readily see that the only artificial element in this procedure is that the sperms are mechanically introduced into the vagina and uterus of the female. The spermatozoa, however, are still the natural spermatozoa of the male, and the egg must, of course, be the natural egg of the woman, and conception will occur only when the two meet in the woman's fallopian tube, and not in a laboratory test tube."

"*Is this a recent development in medicine?*"

"No, not at all. Artificial insemination has been practiced for a long time, but at first only on animals. The first recorded experiment of an artificial impregnation was made by the Italian scientist, Spallanzani, in 1784. In his *Dissertations,* he tells how he confined a female dog in a room, and later when she showed evidence of being 'in heat,' he obtained a small amount of seminal fluid from a male dog of the same breed and injected it through a syringe into the vagina and uterus of this female. Sixty-two days later she brought forth three young ones, which resembled in color and shape both the mother and the absentee father. After describing the original experiment, Spallanzani very quaintly adds—here is his statement—'Thus did I succeed in fecundating this quadruped; and I can truly say that I never received greater pleasure upon any occasion, since I first cultivated experimental philosophy.'

"Since then this type of 'experimental philosophy' has been cultivated extensively on a variety of animals. Mice, guinea-pigs, dogs, cows and horses have been successfully inseminated artificially on numerous occasions."

"*What is the object of artificial insemination? Is it being performed only for experimental purposes?*"

"No, not necessarily. In animals artificial inseminations are frequently performed for the purpose of eugenic breeding. With this method a large number of females can be impregnated with the sperms of a single selected male. With proper care, the collected seminal fluid of the male can even be sent to far distances, so that the procedure is well adapted for animal breeding. In Russia the method is being widely employed at the present time for the raising of select horses and cattle. Artificial insemination is also employed in cases of animal sterility where because of some anatomical difficulty copulation and direct insemination by the male is not possible."

"*What about the human female, have artificial inseminations been used successfully in women, too?*"

ARTIFICIAL INSEMINATION IN HUMANS

"Yes, indeed. The first artificial human insemination was performed, it seems, nearly one hundred and fifty years ago by the famous English surgeon, John Hunter. It was not, however, until seventy years later that it came into more general use. At the present time artificial impregnations of women are resorted to quite frequently for the purpose of overcoming certain types of sterility. We have already seen that some conditions make it impossible for the spermatozoa to enter the uterus, and under such circumstances it is sometimes helpful to introduce a few drops of the seminal fluid directly into the uterine cavity by means of a special syringe. The entire procedure must, of course, be carried out under strictly aseptic conditions."

"*But if the husband is suffering from a deficient production of sperm cells, would this procedure be of any value?*"

"No, an artificial insemination with the husband's seminal fluid can be successful only when his spermatozoa are normal in quantity and quality. In cases of azoöspermia, for instance, such a procedure would be of no value. When a man is found to be incurably sterile, the question of inseminating his wife with the sperms of another male sometimes comes into consideration."

"*Are artificial impregnations with the fluid of a man other than the husband actually done?*"

"Yes, every now and then an artificial insemination of this type is performed. Where a marriage is childless on account of the husband's sterility and where the desire of the couple for an offspring is very strong, they may feel that an artificial impregnation of this type may give them a child that would inherit the qualities of at least one of them, rather than adopt a child which would possess the characteristics of neither. Let me tell you of one such instance. This woman was married for eight years, and, in spite of many examinations and treatments by various doctors, she was unsuccessful in becoming pregnant. It was later found that the sterility was due to an incurable azoöspermia of the husband, and that there was consequently no chance of a conception occurring in a natural manner. The woman and her husband were both extremely anxious to have a child, and the fact of their barrenness weighed heavily upon them and was the cause of a great deal of unhappiness. In spite of their deep mutual affection and attachment they were seriously contemplating a divorce. It was at this time that they heard of the possibility of an artificial insemination, and after due deliberation, they decided upon this step as the only means which could solve their problem. An artificial insemination with a qualified donor's seminal fluid was eventually performed, and in due time she gave birth to a normal child."

"*What was the attitude of the husband towards the child, doctor?*"

"The husband, even during the period of pregnancy, had begun to look upon the coming child as his own, and both he and his wife have found an immense joy and peace of mind in the baby. However, I would emphasize the fact that an artificial insemination of this type should be undertaken only after careful deliberation on the part of the couple and the physician. It should be done only with the full consent of both husband and wife, and preferably without their knowing the identity of the donor, or the donor knowing the identity of the recipient. It is essential, of course, that the donor should be medically and eugenically thoroughly qualified for this purpose. Incidentally, artificial inseminations are often unsuccessful, and at times many attempts have to be made before the desired conception results."

"*But if the wife is the one who is incurably sterile, is there any artificial measure of this kind that could be employed?*"

"No, obviously not. It is not possible to isolate the ovum of the woman, or to substitute another instead. However, apropos of your question, a rather unusual suggestion came to my attention last year. A woman, 35 years of age, and very happily married for ten years, found that she was permanently sterile. She had even submitted herself to an operation in the hope that her condition could be corrected, but during the operation it was found that she had a congenital abnormality which made impregnation and childbearing impossible. The woman felt very keenly that it would be unfair to deprive her husband of an offspring because of her disability, and after months of deliberation and discussion with him, she made a rather unusual proposal,—but let me quote her words: 'Would it be possible to get in contact with some woman who would be willing to bear a child by my husband for us. The procedure, I believe, could be carried out in a purely scientific and impersonal manner, by hospitalization and artificial impregnation. I feel that there are women of desirable types who would be glad to provide such service for a reasonable fee.' In other words, this woman was looking not for a substitute father, but for a substitute mother—for a woman who would be willing to be artificially impregnated with the seminal fluid of her husband, bear a child, and then surrender the child to them.

"In this connection I might tell you of a very interesting experiment which was performed only recently by two biologists at Harvard. They removed ten egg cells from a female rabbit and fertilized them in the laboratory with rabbit sperms. They then transplanted the fertilized cells into the fallopian tube of another female rabbit. These eggs proceeded to develop within the body of this third rabbit, and after thirty-three days, seven young rabbits, bearing the coloring and characteristics of their real parents, were born to this 'artificial mother.'"

"*Are there any forms of life in which it is possible to bring the eggs and sperms together artificially and produce offspring outside of the body?*"

ARTIFICIAL FERTILIZATION

"Yes, but only in those species where fertilization normally takes place outside of the female body, as in fish, frogs and other types of aquatic organisms. Here, as we have already seen, the female discharges her eggs to the outside, while the male emits his sperms in the immediate vicinity, and the union of the two sex elements occurs in the surrounding medium. Under such circumstances it is comparatively simple to obtain the female eggs and the male sperms and bring them together in the laboratory or breeding tank. As a matter of fact, I believe that this is being done on a rather large scale in the breeding of certain fish for commercial purposes.

"However, biologists have gone even a step further, and have shown that in certain species of animals, it is actually possible to cause the development of the egg by artificial means without any sperm cells at all."

"*Can an egg which has not been fertilized by a sperm develop into a mature form?*"

PARTHENOGENESIS (VIRGIN-BIRTH)

"Yes. As a matter of fact, it has long been recognized that the eggs of certain species of animals are normally capable of developing without fertilization. The queen bee, for instance, lays two types of eggs, fertilized and unfertilized. Both develop into mature bees, except that the unfertilized eggs grow up into males or drones, while those that are fertilized produce workers or queens. The development of eggs without fertilization is known by the rather long name of parthenogenesis, or 'virgin birth,' and occurs in several species of animals under certain circumstances. Now, what several scientists succeeded in doing was to cause eggs which normally require sperm fertilization to develop into new individuals without the intervention of spermatozoa. They accomplished this by substituting certain physico-chemical stimulants for the fertilizing action of the sperm cells. Thus, Jacques Loeb, the American biologist, for instance, found that by adding in a definite sequence various kinds of chemicals to sea water containing the eggs of sea-urchins, he could induce the complete development of these eggs into the adult form. Among the substances which were employed as substitutes for male sperms were such prosaic chemicals as salt, alcohol, ether, chloroform and even potassium cyanide. Later it was found that the eggs of frogs could be induced to develop by merely puncturing them with a needle. Loeb treated frogs' eggs in this manner and actually succeeded in raising about half a dozen frogs to the adult stage. These were really parthenogenetic, or virgin-born frogs, produced from eggs without the aid of any male element, and they could in no way be distinguished from frogs which develop in the normal manner through fertilization with spermatozoa. Strangely enough, however, the virgin-born frogs all proved to be males.

ARTIFICIAL PARTHENOGENESIS

"The fact that an ovum can develop without fertilization would indicate that, at least in the lower forms of life, the potentialities for developing new organisms is inherent in the egg itself. The ovum, as Chambers says, is like a wound-up piece of mechanism, ready to start unfolding under the proper stimulus, and this stimulus may be supplied either by a sperm cell, or by other physico-chemical means."

"*These are rather ambitious experiments. I wonder what the future methods of reproduction will be. I recall having read in one of Shaw's plays, I believe it was 'Back to Methuselah,' the phantasy of a human child being incubated in an egg outside of its mother's body, and coming out of the egg fully matured.*"

"Yes, but the British scientist, Haldane, went even further. In his imaginative booklet on the future of science, *Daedalus,* he suggested a time when the majority of human children will be born in the laboratory, or ectogenetically, as he termed it. The ovary of a woman will be removed at puberty and kept in a suitable medium, and, as the eggs mature each month, they will be artificially fertilized with spermatozoa, the resulting embryo incubated in the laboratory for nine months, and then brought out into the world. Naturally, only the sex cells of the most eugenically suitable men and women will be selected for breeding purposes. However, these are but scientific fancies, and for the present we must still content ourselves with the old-fashioned mode of having children.

STERILIZATION

"To return to the more immediate problems of reproduction, however, I should like to discuss with you briefly another subject which is closely related to fertility and sterility—that of sterilization. Sterilization implies an artificial production of sterility, the individual being made incapable of procreation by surgical or other means. Within recent years the subject of sterilization has received considerable attention, and it may well become an important social issue in the near future."

"*On what grounds are sterilizations generally performed?*"

"Well, first of all, there are the compulsory sterilizations which are carried out by the State as a social measure. Enforced sterilizations of this kind have been performed either as a punishment for certain crimes, or else as a eugenic measure to prevent the transmission of certain hereditary defects to future generations. In addition, however, many individuals voluntarily seek to be sterilized. Men or women who feel that for medical, eugenic or even social reasons they should not bear offspring frequently wish to be sterilized in order to avoid the possibility of an unwanted conception."

"*What methods are used for sterilization at present?*"

"The usual procedure is to produce an artificial obstruction to the passage of the sperm cells from the testes in the case of the male, or of the egg cells from the ovaries in the case of the female.

"In the male it is the vas deferens which is blocked for this purpose. You will recall that in order to reach the outside, the sperms have to pass through the seminal duct, or vas, which runs from the testes through the groin and then backwards into the urinary channel. If these ducts are cut or tied in a special manner, the sperms will be unable to reach the exterior. This operation is called a vasectomy. As the bulk of the seminal fluid comes from the seminal vesicles and from the prostate which are not affected by the vasectomy, the ejaculations will continue in a fairly normal manner, but the seminal fluid will not contain any spermatozoa, and the individual will be rendered sterile. The operation is comparatively simple because in the scrotum and groin the vas lies close to the surface; it can be performed under a local anesthetic and requires but a few days of rest."

STERILIZATION OF THE MALE (VASECTOMY)

"*What becomes of the sperms, then, if they are prevented from coming to the outside?*"

"Vasectomy sterilizations are now usually performed in such a manner that the sperms are diverted into the scrotum, and from there they are gradually absorbed into the system. With this type of operation, the formation of the sperms is not interfered with, but they do not appear in the seminal discharge."

"*I have been under the impression that sterilization involves the removal of the sex glands, and that a sterilized individual loses all sexual feelings and undergoes other physical and mental changes.*"

"No, at the present time a sterilization does not involve the removal of the testes or of the ovaries. With the modern methods, the sex glands are not affected at all. The operation merely renders the individual incapable of reproduction, but it does not diminish sexual desire or capacity, nor does it produce any other adverse physical or psychic changes."

"*What method of sterilization is employed in the case of the woman?*"

"In the woman the fallopian tubes are closed off. When these are cut or tied, the eggs from the ovaries cannot reach the uterus, nor can the sperms gain access to the egg. An operation of this kind, however, requires an abdominal incision and hospitalization for about two weeks, and is therefore a much more involved undertaking than a male sterilization.

"Sterilizations both of men and women may also be accomplished by the application of x-rays to the sex glands. This method, however, must be employed cautiously, for its effects are still rather uncertain, and it may lead to an undesirable premature onset of the menopause. Its use, therefore, is definitely limited for the present to individuals near the menopausal age.

STERILIZATION OF THE FEMALE (SALPINGECTOMY)

"A simplified method of closing the tubes which does not require an abdominal incision was recently perfected. An instrument is introduced through the vagina into the uterus, the tip of the instrument is brought in contact first with one and then with the other opening into the fallopian tubes, and by means of an electric current these openings are closed or sealed. This method was first suggested by Dr. Dickinson many years ago, but now it is being improved for practical use and may eventually offer a simple and effective means for female sterilization."

"*But suppose a man or a woman wants to have children later on, is it possible to open the passages again?*"

"Several methods have been suggested from time to time whereby the closed ducts or tubes could be reopened at a later date, but, as far as I know, none of these procedures have proven to be practical or successful. When the seminal ducts or fallopian tubes are cut, the individual must be considered permanently sterile. This, incidentally, is the reason why sterilization cannot be used for the temporary prevention of conception, and is indicated only where a permanent sterility is desired."

"*From time to time we have read accounts of the recent compulsory sterilizations in Germany. It has seemed to us that to force anyone to be sterilized is an arbitrary assumption of power by the State over the rights and life of the individual.*"

COMPULSORY STERILIZATIONS

"I quite agree with you that the resort to enforced sterilizations is altogether too severe and oppressive a measure. Compulsory sterilizations have been urged both as a punishment for criminal acts, and as a eugenic measure to prevent the reproduction of the unfit. In either case, however, they constitute, I believe, a dangerous social policy. As a punishment sterilization has long been held to be too unjust and too severe. In several American States, in fact, punitive sterilization laws have been declared by the courts to be unconstitutional on the ground that sterilization is an 'unusual and cruel' punishment for any criminal offense.

"As a compulsory eugenic measure, too, sterilization is a hazardous program because it harbors too many possibilities of grave abuse. The chief object of eugenic sterilization is to prevent the reproduction of individuals who bear defective hereditary qualities, but we have already seen that there is still a great divergence of opinion as to which traits or characters are inherited and which are acquired as a result of environmental influences. There is grave danger, therefore, in adopting too drastic and arbitrary laws. Landman, for instance, tells that in the state legislature of Missouri, a 'eugenic' sterilization bill was introduced in 1929, which provided among other things for the presumably eugenic sterilization of those 'convicted of murder (not in the heat of passion), rape, highway robbery, chicken-stealing, bombing, or theft of automobiles,' the inference apparently being that all these tendencies, including chicken-stealing, are hereditary in nature and transmissible to one's offspring. Of course this bill, which incidentally was not adopted, was probably designed as a punitive measure, but even so, it is an indication of the possible dangers of the misuse of compulsory sterilization. A special Committee on Sterilization of the English Board of Health, after completing a thorough survey of the subject, stated, in a report published in 1934, that they were convinced 'that the harm done by compulsion would far outweigh any possible advantage resulting from it.'"

"*Are many sterilizations being performed in this country?*"

STERILIZATIONS IN THE UNITED STATES

"Since 1907, when the first eugenic sterilization law was passed in this country—in Indiana, thirty States have enacted statutes which permit or order the sterilization of certain types of mentally defective or diseased individuals. From two to three thousand eugenic sterilizations are now being performed annually in the United States, and a total of 11,700 men and 16,300 women have thus far been officially sterilized. Nearly 50% of these operations were performed in psychiatric institutions of the State of California, where a eugenic sterilization law was first adopted in 1909. In spite of the fact that in most States sterilization is compulsory, the general procedure has been first to obtain the consent of the patient, or, if the individual was incapable of judgment, the permission of the nearest relative or legal guardian. This, at least, has been the rule in California, where in 90% of the cases the written consent of the patient or relatives was obtained prior to the operation. A detailed study of the experiences in that State was published by Gosney and Popenoe in a book on *Sterilization for Human Betterment.*

"In addition, however, to the official State sterilizations, many similar operations are being performed privately by physicians all through the country. It is my impression that in the last few years there has been an increased interest in the question of voluntary sterilizations."

"*For what reasons do people seek to subject themselves to sterilization?*"

VOLUNTARY STERILIZATIONS

"There are many reasons why a man or a woman may wish to be sterilized. Some seek sterilizations on purely medical grounds. A woman, for instance, who has had one or more cesarean operations may well want to be sterilized in order to avoid the possibility of another conception. Many men consider the advisability of a sterilization for themselves because their wives are suffering from ailments which would make a pregnancy extremely dangerous. Not long ago a man consulted me about this very subject. He had been married for twelve years and had three children. His wife, since the last childbirth, has had several abdominal operations, and she was warned that any further childbearing might prove most serious for her. The husband thought that a sterilization of himself would be the most satisfactory means of preventing the possibility of another conception.

"Then, again, many wish to be sterilized for eugenic reasons. A person suffering from a hereditary disease, for instance, might be anxious to avoid any possibility of transmitting the disease to a future generation. The individual might consider himself or herself fit for marriage and yet unfit for reproduction. Here, for example, is a letter from a woman inquiring about the possibility of a sterilization, which illustrates well this type of case. Let me read a part of it: 'I am contemplating marriage and I want to be sterilized. . . . I want sterilization because several members of our family during the last few generations have been afflicted with epilepsy. My sister is an epileptic, and during the last few years I have had many attacks myself. I do not feel that I have any right to bring forth children. My fiancé understands the situation and he agrees with me.'

"There are also some people who want to be sterilized because they feel that they already have a sufficiently large family and they do not want to rely upon or cannot employ the usual contraceptive methods. Havelock Ellis, for instance, has recently advocated the use of sterilization for cases where there are already a sufficient number of children in the family, where the wife's failing health renders it undesirable to have more children, or where it is undesirable ever to have any children at all, a classification which would include medical and eugenic, as well as social indications."

"*What is your opinion of such voluntary sterilizations, doctor?*"

"Personally I feel that when there are valid indications, an individual who wishes to be sterilized should have the privilege of having this operation performed. In many instances, indeed, it is a useful therapeutic measure, and should become a recognized medical procedure. When there is definite evidence of hereditary feeble-mindedness, insanity, epilepsy and similar disorders, the transmission of these defects to future generations should certainly be avoided, and such people might well be urged to submit themselves to a voluntary sterilization. Sterilization should not be regarded as a punishment or stigma but as a valuable medical measure.

"It is not at all advisable, though, in my opinion, for an individual to seek a sterilization merely as a means for the prevention of conception. Sterilization is an irreversible step, and there are so many unpredictable possibilities in life, that one should exercise great caution and deliberation before submitting to this operation for contraceptive purposes.

MISCARRIAGES AND ABORTIONS

"I see that we still have some time left, and so perhaps we can discuss today one other important problem of reproduction—the subject of miscarriages and abortions. This refers to pregnancies which are either voluntarily or involuntarily ended prematurely. It has been estimated that from 20-40% of all pregnancies terminate in this manner, and it therefore constitutes a very serious medical as well as social problem."

"*What is the difference between a miscarriage and an abortion?*"

"Both imply a premature termination or interruption of a pregnancy. Technically there is a distinction between the two words according to whether the pregnancy ends in the early or later months. If it terminates before the fifth month, it is called an abortion; between the fifth and seventh months—a miscarriage. In ordinary usage, however, the term miscarriage is applied to a spontaneous and involuntary ending of a pregnancy before its full time, while abortion is used to indicate an artificial and deliberate interruption of a pregnancy."

"*What causes a miscarriage to occur?*"

THE CAUSES OF MISCARRIAGES

"It would lead us into too technical a discussion to mention all the many factors which might cause a woman to miscarry. Generally speaking, a miscarriage may result either because the fertilized egg cannot go on to complete development and dies prematurely, or else because the uterus sets up untimely contractions and expels the fetus. Glandular disturbances, inflammations of the generative organs, displacements of the uterus, infectious diseases of the mother, physical injuries and severe emotional shocks—any of these might lead to a miscarriage. It is interesting to note, however, that in some instances the underlying cause can be traced to the husband. If his sperms are subnormal in quality, the resulting embryo may have a low vitality and die prematurely."

"*A neighbor of ours who was three months pregnant recently fell down several steps and had a miscarriage a few days later. Are accidents of this kind apt to produce a miscarriage?*"

"There is a rather widespread, though much exaggerated, fear that some slight accident during pregnancy might result in a miscarriage. Some women, it is true, are very sensitive to shocks or injuries and are apt to miscarry as a result of a comparatively trivial fall, overexertion, or even an emotional disturbance. As a rule, however, even severe shocks or violent exercise do not influence the progress of a pregnancy."

"*Are miscarriages avoidable?*"

"By proper care and supervision during pregnancy it is often possible to prevent an untimely termination. The onset of a miscarriage, furthermore, is usually preceded by such forewarning symptoms as a vaginal discharge of a blood-stained fluid and bearing-down pains in the back and lower abdomen, and at this time it may still be possible to prevent the interruption of the pregnancy by complete rest and appropriate medical treatment. Any genital bleeding during pregnancy should be regarded as abnormal, and the cause should be investigated."

"*As for abortions, doctor—for what reasons are pregnancies interrupted artificially?*"

ABORTIONS

"Well, in some instances a pregnancy has to be terminated prematurely in order to save the life of the mother. Occasionally complications arise during the course of a pregnancy, particularly where there is a preëxisting heart, kidney, lung or other grave disease, which actually endanger the life of the woman and necessitate an interruption of the pregnancy. Abortions on such grounds are designated as 'therapeutic,' and according to present legal statutes may be performed as a necessary medical measure.

"The majority of abortions, however, are undertaken for much less threatening reasons. Minor medical indications, eugenic, social or economic factors frequently prompt a woman to seek a termination of a pregnancy. An unmarried girl, for instance, who becomes pregnant may feel that its continuance will prove socially disastrous to herself and the child; a woman who has already given birth to a large family may be afraid or unwilling to go through another pregnancy; economic distress, unemployment, marital difficulties, separation, and any number of other family problems may drive a woman to terminate a pregnancy. Legally, however, a pregnancy may not be interrupted on any but valid medical indications, and abortions performed on other grounds are therefore referred to as 'illegal' or 'criminal.'"

"*What is the nature of a therapeutic abortion?*"

"An abortion is a surgical operation which involves the removal of the embryo from the uterus. As a rule, the neck of the womb is first dilated, and then the fertilized ovum with its surrounding tissues removed by curetting. It is a rather painful surgical procedure and frequently requires an anesthetic."

"I understand that many women take various kinds of drugs to stop a pregnancy. Are there medicines that can be used for that purpose?"

"I do not know of any drugs available at present which can be safely used for the purpose of interrupting a pregnancy. Drugs are frequently taken or prescribed for a delayed menstrual period, but a delay does not necessarily denote a pregnancy. Any number of physical or psychic conditions, such as exposure to sudden changes of temperature, bodily ailments, debility, an unbalanced diet, disturbances of the glandular functions, emotional strain and worry, may cause a postponement of the menstrual flow for days or even weeks. Certain drugs and glandular extracts are frequently prescribed to correct the underlying condition and to restore the normal menstrual function in such cases. When the cessation of the menstruation is due to a conception, however, medication is of little value."

"Are abortions dangerous or injurious?"

DANGERS OF ABORTIONS

"It is estimated that about 2% of the abortions performed in the United States end fatally. In addition there are a large number of women who remain chronically ill as a result of these operations. This high percentage of mortality and sickness is no doubt due largely to the fact that because of legal restrictions the majority of abortions are carried out secretly, often under very unsanitary conditions and by untrained and incompetent individuals. Under such circumstances injuries and infections are very apt to occur. When performed by trained surgeons under strictly aseptic conditions, the dangers are greatly reduced, but it is well to bear in mind that the interruption of a pregnancy is never a slight matter, and that it is usually accompanied by some sort of physical and psychic shock to the woman."

"How widespread are abortions at the present time?"

"The number of abortions performed annually in the United States has been variously estimated as between 800,000 and two million. Because of the illegality of the procedure, the actual number cannot be determined. In a recent book, Dr. Taussig stated that in urban communities the rate is one abortion or miscarriage to two pregnancies that go to full term, and in the rural districts the rate is one to five. In a study of the reproductive histories of 2000 women which I made not long ago, I found that approximately one out of every four pregnancies terminated prematurely. When one considers the possible injury to the woman and the enormous biological and economic waste which this practice involves, it becomes evident that the subject of abortions presents a grave social and medical problem. To solve it we shall have to approach the question from a more rational and realistic viewpoint than we have heretofore.

EXTENT OF ABORTIONS

"It is true, of course, that the practice of abortion cannot be considered as a purely modern problem. Even primitive peoples resorted to abortions, and often indeed to infanticide, as a means of limiting their population. All through history one finds records of these practices in one form or another. In modern times, however, and especially within the last few decades, the rapid changes in social and economic conditions, together with changing attitudes towards religious and moral codes, have caused a very marked increase in the resort to artificial interruptions of pregnancy."

"*What is the status of abortion in Russia, doctor? I understand that at one time they had made abortions legal but that lately these laws have been changed.*"

"That is quite true. In 1920, not long after the Soviet regime came into power, abortions were legalized in Soviet Russia. This step was taken, it was claimed then, primarily as a public health measure—to safeguard the health of women who, because of the very difficult social and economic conditions of the time, were already resorting in large numbers to the interruption of pregnancies. Abortions had been widely practiced in Russia long before the revolution, but because these operations were being performed secretly, under unsanitary conditions and by untrained individuals, the mortality rate and the resulting complications were very high. For the protection of the health of the women, the Soviet authorities decided to bring this 'underground' practice into the open so that it could be adequately supervised and controlled. Special government hospitals were set aside where a woman in need

THE STATUS OF ABORTION IN SOVIET RUSSIA

of an abortion could have the operation performed by trained physicians and under strictly sanitary conditions, and she was required to remain in the hospital for three days following the operation. A pregnancy, however, was not to be interrupted if it had advanced beyond the tenth week, and when a woman was pregnant for the first time, an abortion was not to be performed unless there were urgent social indications or serious danger to her health.

"This law did apparently serve to decrease to a considerable degree the number of deaths and other complications following abortions. Nevertheless, it became evident after a time that even under the best hospital conditions abortions were not always without danger or subsequent harm to the health of the women, and that the large-scale resort to the interruption of pregnancies led to many physical disabilities among women. As a result, a widespread educational campaign was instituted by the public health authorities to acquaint the people with the nature and the dangers of abortion and with the advisability of preventing conceptions rather than resorting to the interruption of pregnancy. Finally, in June, 1936, the Soviet government completely rescinded the legalization of abortion, partly because of the medical reasons, and partly no doubt because of the changing social and political conditions at the time. At present an abortion is permitted only in those instances where the continuation of a pregnancy constitutes a danger to the life or threatens serious harm to the health of the woman."

"*What is your opinion, doctor, about the abortion problem in this country? Are there any steps being taken here to control this practice?*"

SOCIAL AND MEDICAL ASPECTS OF ABORTIONS

"The question of abortions is not purely a medical one; it is intimately bound up with our social, moral, ethical and religious views, and the problem cannot be solved without a considerable social and ethical reorientation. It seems obvious, however, that our present restrictive measures have failed in their purpose and that other means will have to be adopted. From a biological and a medical point of view, it would seem that even now two valuable steps could well be taken which would materially aid in the solution of this grave problem. First, we should extend the scope of the legal medical indications for abortions. At the present time it is legally permissible to interrupt a pregnancy if it places the life of the mother in danger. There are, however, many medical, eugenic and even social conditions which, though they do not exactly endanger the life of the woman, definitely contra-indicate a pregnancy on physical or psychic grounds, and such conditions might well be included among the therapeutic indications for abortions. Dr. Rongy discusses these in some detail in his book on *Abortions, Legal or Illegal,* and he even goes to the extent of suggesting that the State should authorize abortions in cases of acute economic distress. Let me read to you also a few pertinent sentences from an article on this subject by Dr. Taussig:

> A further gain in reducing abortion deaths would result from broadening the indications for therapeutic abortions. At present such interference is limited to conditions that are directly threatening the life of the mother. Is it not also justified when the continuance of a pregnancy would make her a semi-invalid, unable properly to care for the children she already has? Especially where poverty is added to ill-health should we not prevent the further break-down of the family by relieving her of this added burden? . . . Such measures to include the social economic indications for abortion would certainly reduce the number who now in desperation seek the aid of a mid-wife or themselves employ dangerous measures.

"A second measure for the control of abortion, and one which I believe to be of paramount importance in this respect would be the wide dissemination of contraceptive information. If every woman were supplied with adequate and reliable contraceptive knowledge, the incidence of abortion would be greatly decreased. Indeed, the wide dissemination of birth control information is the most effective way of combating abortions and must be included among the first steps of any program for the control of this practice. The prevention of abortions can best be achieved by the prevention of conception.

"Now, as for books on the subjects we have been discussing today, you will find a very fine chapter on Fertility and Sterility in Guttmacher's *Life in the Making* and Marshall's *Physiology of Reproduction.* And here are several other pertinent volumes."

LAUGHLIN, H. H. "Eugenical Sterilization." American Eugenics Society (1926).

An authoritative book by a pioneer in this field.

LANDMAN, J. H. "Human Sterilization." The Macmillan Co. (1932).

An able critique of sterilization and a discussion of its present status.

GROSNEY, E. S. and POPENOE, P. "Sterilization for Human Betterment." The Macmillan Co. (1929).

A detailed analysis of the California experiences with sterilization.

WHITNEY, LEON F. "The Case for Sterilization." Frederick A. Stokes Co. (1934).

A plea for the extension of voluntary sterilization.

RONGY, A. J., M.D. "Abortion: Legal or Illegal?" The Vanguard Press (1933).

A recent study of the problems of abortion.

ROBINSON, WILLIAM J., M.D. "The Law Against Abortion." Eugenics Publishing Co. (1933).

A clear, non-technical analysis of the present attitude towards abortion.

CHAPTER VII

THE ART OF MARRIAGE

"Until now we have concerned ourselves mainly with the biological aspects of marriage and reproduction. Today I should like to consider with you briefly the sex side of marriage—the physical, psychological and emotional factors involved in the sex union. Within recent years it has become more generally recognized that sex plays a dominant role in marriage, and that a satisfactory sex relationship is essential for a happy union. What is perhaps less frequently appreciated is the fact that a harmonious and dynamic sex adjustment does not necessarily develop spontaneously, but that a satisfactory sex life in marriage requires an understanding of the nature and the mechanism of the sex union as well as the exercise of an art in sexual love."

"*Isn't there a tendency at present to stress the sex side of marriage too much? From some of the discussions on the subject one gets the impression at times that sex is the only purpose and the only basis of marriage.*"

SEX AND MARRIAGE

"I quite agree with you that sex alone does not make a marriage, and that no really lasting relationship can be based merely on a sexual attraction. For a truly happy marriage, there must of course be present mutual love and affection, a community of ideas, of interests, of tastes, of standards, an adequate economic arrangement and a satisfactory adjustment in many personal, family and social relationships. On the other hand, it is also true that a successful marriage can hardly be expected where sexual attraction does not exist, or where the marital sex life is unsatisfactory and inadequate. In our work we have constantly found that many domestic difficulties can be traced directly or indirectly to sexual disharmonies, and that the sex factor plays a leading role in marital satisfaction. A number of studies in recent years have also emphasized this fact. Dickinson and Beam, for instance, in a summary of their analytical survey of a thousand marriages state as follows: 'If the data in this study reinforce any one concept it is that satisfactory sexual relations are necessary to fully adjusted and successful unions.'"

"*Does not, though, the constant emphasis on sex tend to place the marital relation on a mere physical level and destroy some of the ideals of marriage?*"

THE ETHICS OF SEX

"Unfortunately, not all of our present marriage ideals lead to an ideal marriage. The very disposition, which is still widespread, to regard the sexual embrace as essentially sinful, impure and degrading is a serious deterrent to a satisfactory marital life. In a wise discussion of marriage and the ethics of sex, John Haynes Holmes once said,—but let me quote to you his words—

> How many men and women there are—not as many today as there were yesterday, but millions of them still—who believe that there is something wrong about the sex life! How many husbands and wives there are who have entered upon their relationship together with the secret conviction that what they are doing is something to be ashamed of and hidden away. How many wives there are who cherish the suspicion, never to be reached by any argument or logic, that their practice of sex is an ignoble yielding to the flesh, and who have never surrendered to their husbands except with feelings of protest and humiliation! I know of nothing so disastrous to happiness in marriage as this feeling of shame which is so often attached to what possesses us with so insistent a drive upon our energies.

"It would be well, indeed, it seems to me, if we were to cease to look upon the sex urge as one of our 'baser' instincts and as an unworthy motive in matrimony. If anything, the development of a harmonious sex life should constitute one of the aims and ideals of the marital union.

"It is quite likely, of course, that in the transition from the prudishness and false modesties of the former generation, some have leaned a little too far in the opposite direction. We must remember, however, that we are only now emerging from the puritanical era with its tabus and inhibitions, and that any undue emphasis on sex and sexual technique at the present time may be but a reaction to the suppressions and repressions of the previous age."

"*What has really been responsible for the present day change in attitude towards sex values generally?*"

"Many social and cultural factors have undoubtedly combined to bring about a newer attitude toward sex. The growing emancipation and independence of woman have enabled her to exercise greater freedom and initiative in the choice of a mate and in the expression of her sexual needs. The spread of birth control knowledge has made possible the separation of sex from reproduction and the realization of a more dynamic sex expression in marriage. The rise of Freudian psychology with its emphasis upon the libido, and the wider dissemination of books on sex questions—the books of Havelock Ellis, Margaret Sanger, of Marie Stopes, Van de Velde and others, have brought about an increased awareness of the significance of the sexual impulse, and have centered greater attention upon the importance of the sex side of marriage. At the same time, the widespread and rapid industrial, economic, and political changes of our age, by giving rise to new social problems, have forced a revaluation and reappraisal of our former sex ethics and standards.

"As for the problems of sexual technique, the recognition of the fact that some preparation is necessary for sexual love is not at all a novel idea of modern times. Among primitive peoples guidance in sexual matters is regularly given to young people by their elders, often constituting a part of the initiation ceremonies at puberty. Malinowski, for instance, relates that the boys and girls of the Trobriand Islands regularly receive instruction in erotic matters from their companions. Among the Samoans, too, according to Margaret Mead, definite information concerning the details of sex life is generally imparted to young people and 'the need of a technique to deal with sex as an art' is fully recognized among them. As far as civilized peoples are concerned, books on the art of sex have been written long before our present era. The manner of wooing and the art of sex were dealt with in an Egyptian papyrus which dates back some three thousand years; they were described in great detail in the Hindu *Kama Sutra*, written about 1600 years ago; in the poems of Ovid who lived during the first century, and who, in fact, originated the term 'art of love'; in the *Perfumed Gardens* of Arabia, written in the 16th century, and in many other ancient books. It is only in the last few centuries that the art of sex has been largely neglected and even suppressed. Now we are once again realizing the importance of an understanding approach in sexual love, and are placing greater emphasis upon an adequate technique in the marital sex relation."

"*Why should there be a need, though, for so much discussion about the details of the art of love, doctor? Are not the natural human instincts and impulses a sufficient guide to a satisfactory sex life?*"

THE SEX INSTINCT

"No, I do not think that either in our social sex conduct or in our individual sex relations can we rely entirely upon our instincts. Generally speaking, an instinct is an innate tendency to behave in a specific manner when confronted by a certain stimulus. In civilized human life, however, we long ago ceased to respond in an instinctive manner to sexual stimuli. From early infancy our sex impulses are subjected to restrictions, suppressions and tabus which effectually modify our normal sex instincts and condition us against a natural sex expression. These inhibitions are not easily thrown off even after wedlock, and the development of an adequate sex life in marriage cannot, therefore, be 'left to nature' altogether. It requires a conscious and intelligent effort for its realization.

"Furthermore, it is a significant biological fact that the sexual urge of men and women is in itself not sufficient to guide them to a satisfactory physical union. An instinct implies the ability to act in a certain manner without previous education in the performance. In the human species, however, the actual technique of sex is not an instinctive attribute. Without some previous knowledge and understanding of the mechanism of coitus, difficulties in the sexual union are very apt to occur. Let me quote to you an interesting passage on this topic from a recent article by Parshley:

> In most mammals . . . copulatory behavior is instinctive, being not at all dependent upon imitation, learning or experience. Experiments show that individuals reared to maturity in isolation can at once perform the act, if the mate is presented when in

> proper physiological condition. . . . In contrast complete copulatory behavior among the primates (that is among monkeys, apes and men) is reached only after a long period of experimentation and experience. It is not an instinctive behavior pattern, but rather a complex adjustment between two individuals, made possible through early training and facilitated by more or less prolonged association.

"In other words, adequate copulatory behavior does not come instinctively to men and women. The technique of the sexual relation has to be understood and learned in order to develop a satisfactory sex life."

"*What specifically do you mean by 'sexual technique'? What particular knowledge does it require?*"

SEX TECHNIQUE

"Well, by the technique of sex I have reference to the effective performance of the sexual act. This requires, first of all, an understanding of the mechanism involved, of the anatomical and physiological processes of sexual union; and secondly, an appreciation of the art of sexual love, that is of the means by which the sex relationship may be rendered most satisfying to both mates.

"From a physical viewpoint, the sex act involves the union or coaptation of the male and female genitals. It is well that both the man and the woman should have some understanding of the nature and location of the sex organs, their respective relations to each other, the changes which occur during sexual stimulation and excitation, the position to be taken in order to bring the organs into satisfactory apposition—in other words, of the actual mechanism of the sexual union. It may not be necessary to follow Balzac's rhetorical suggestion that a man should not marry 'before he has studied anatomy and has dissected at least one woman,' but it is certainly true nevertheless that some knowledge of sexual anatomy is of considerable help to the satisfactory consummation of the sex act.

"On the psychological and emotional side, it is desirable that the couple should know something about the nature of the sexual impulse, the stimuli which lead to sexual excitation, the differences in the sexual responses and reactions between the male and the female, and the value and importance of a delicacy, finesse and skill in the sexual approach."

"You spoke of the changes that occur during sexual stimulation. Could you describe them briefly?"

THE NATURE OF THE SEX ACT

"Generally speaking nearly every part of the body is brought into activity during sexual stimulation and sexual union. The nervous mechanism, the glandular system, the muscular apparatus—all of them play an important part in sexual activity. The special senses, too, particularly the senses of touch, of sight, of odor, contribute greatly to an adequate sexual expression. The physical changes which take place during the sexual relation are, therefore, widespread and really involve the entire organism.

"The physical sex act itself consists of the intromission of the male organ into the vaginal passage of the female, and of the reciprocal copulatory movements which lead to the climax or orgasm. Under ordinary conditions the penis is soft and flaccid, but during sexual excitement it becomes firm, erect and sufficiently rigid to penetrate into the vagina. The female genitals, too, undergo certain changes when the woman is sexually aroused. The walls of the vagina become congested, the vaginal orifice widens and even pouts to some extent, while the clitoris and the smaller labia become tense and slightly erect. At the same time the glands of the vulva secrete a slippery fluid which moistens the surfaces of the external genitals and facilitates the entry of the male. Accompanying the local changes there are general physical and emotional manifestations of sexual stimulation—the stronger and quicker pulse, the faster breathing, the dilated pupils, the flushed face, the increased muscular activity and nervous excitation. The coital movements increasingly heighten the erotic sensation and general tension until the release is reached in the climax or orgasm."

"Do the first sex experiences really have an important bearing upon the future happiness in marriage? Sometime ago I read that sexual troubles at the beginning of marriage may affect the marital life for a long time later."

"The importance of the experiences on the so-called 'bridal night,' as far as future marital happiness is concerned, has been rather exaggerated, I should say. It is quite true that awkwardness, clumsiness and much discomfort at the beginning may make the future adjustment more difficult. The woman, particularly, may feel keenly disillusioned and upset by such an experience, and she may resent further sexual contacts for a time. It is not, however, the first relation only that counts but rather the attitude and approach towards the sex union throughout the following months and years of marriage. I think it is well to bear in mind that at the beginning some difficulty and perhaps even discomfort are very likely to be encountered, and that the first sex relations may not be entirely satisfactory. Such an occurrence is not at all unusual, nor is it serious, and it should not be particularly disappointing or distressing. Gradually, with greater understanding and increasing experience, a mutually satisfactory sex life can generally be established."

THE FIRST SEX ACT

"*Is the first sex act actually very painful for the woman?*"

"Not necessarily. The first or first few sexual contacts differ from the subsequent relations in that the hymen is penetrated at this time. Any pain experienced is due to the actual stretching or breaking of the hymen, and the degree of the discomfort depends largely upon the texture and condition of this membrane. If it is thin and elastic it will dilate or give way with but little discomfort; if it is firm and tense, it may prove to be quite resistant and its breaking will then cause considerable pain. Even this, however, can be greatly lessened, if not entirely avoided, by an understanding and patient approach on the part of the husband, as well as by the coöperation and willing yielding on the part of the wife."

THE DEFLORATION

"*Is the hymen always broken during the first sex act?*"

"It is, if complete penetration takes place at this time. The hymen surrounds the vaginal entrance, partially closing it in, and the male organ must pass through it in order to enter the vaginal canal. The diameter of the erect penis is about an inch and a half, while that of the opening through the hymen is generally less than an inch. The pressure of the male organ first causes the hymen to stretch or dilate, and if this is not sufficient to permit entry, the continued pressure results in the breaking or splitting of the membrane at one or more points. This constitutes the defloration."

"*How much bleeding usually occurs when the hymen is broken? Does it require any particular treatment at the time?*"

"As a rule the bleeding is slight and is rarely serious enough to require any special treatment. It usually stops in a short time, though there may be a slight recurrence during the first few subsequent relations."

"If the first experiences prove uncomfortable, is it advisable to postpone sex relations for a time?"

"In the *Kama Sutra*, a Hindu classic on marital conduct, Vatsyayana gives the advice that a husband should take ten days in gradually gaining the confidence of his wife before even attempting to consummate the marital union. I doubt whether this counsel is either suitable or necessary for the modern couple who most likely have already had a long period of intimacy beforehand. It is usually best for the sexual union to be consummated during the first few days after marriage, if feasible. If the defloration should prove to be very painful, or if there is much apprehension and fear on the part of the wife, complete penetration need not take place during the first sex act. A gradual and gentle dilatation carried out during the several successive relationships will considerably ease the discomfort and lessen the anxiety for the woman.

"In general, however, even if the first experiences prove uncomfortable, it is not advisable to put off the consummation of the sex union for any length of time. The longer the first relations are postponed the greater will be the feeling of anxiety on the part of the wife and of frustration on the part of the husband. When the completion of the sex union is avoided from day to day under one pretext or another, it is usually a sign of the existence of some sexual difficulty, and it is not advisable to permit such a situation to continue too long.

"At the beginning of marriage, many women find it difficult to yield to the sexual union, and, either because of their inherent feminine modesty, or because of their early training and upbringing, or because of an exaggerated fear of the possible discomforts, they may actually physically resist the sex act. Ordinarily the intimacies during the premarital courtship tend to develop a feeling of confidence and trust on the part of the woman and to lessen her resistance in this respect. At times, however, it may persist for some period after marriage. Such a reaction may occur irrespective of the wife's affections for her husband, or of her desire to respond to the sexual embrace. As a matter of fact, she may feel a very deep attraction for her mate and possess a strong sexual urge, and yet be unable to prevent the instinctive resistance to the relationship. This may make the first sex experiences more difficult to consummate, and cause considerable anxiety during the early weeks of marriage. It is well, therefore, for both the man and the woman to recognize this situation, should it arise, and to treat it with the necessary understanding and patience. The woman, in particular, should realize that complete relaxation on her part and an active coöperation are necessary for the consummation of the sexual union."

"I once read that among certain primitive peoples the hymen is artificially removed or broken before marriage."

PRIMITIVE ARTIFICIAL DEFLORATION

"Yes, it seems that this was and still is a rather widespread practice among primitive races in various parts of the world. Books on anthropology abound with examples of this custom. Among many peoples the membrane is artificially destroyed either at puberty or just before marriage as a tribal ritual. In their classic book, *Das Weib*, Ploss and Bartels state that in certain countries the hymen is even removed early in infancy. This is so, for instance, in some parts of China, where the membrane is unintentionally destroyed by the mother or nurse as a result of the too energetic cleansing of the infant's genitals, and many Chinese physicians are said not even to know of the existence of the hymen. The social, emotional and sentimental significance attached to virginity is a comparatively recent development in the evolution of human society."

"Is it advisable to have the hymen surgically dilated before marriage? I know many young women who have had this done."

SURGICAL DEFLORATION

"Yes, a premarital surgical defloration is often of value as a hygienic measure and as an aid to early marital adjustment. It is indicated particularly, however, when the hymen is found to be unusually thick and resistant, so that much difficulty might be expected from a natural defloration. A surgical dilatation of the hymen is a comparatively simple procedure and can be made practically painless with the use of a local anesthetic. Such a surgical stretching requires no cutting, causes very little bleeding and does not incapacitate the woman in any way. This step, however, should be taken only with the express consent of the fiancé, for many people still have strong traditional, sentimental or other objections to such a procedure.

"I should emphasize once more, though, that with a mutually sympathetic attitude and an understanding coöperation on the part of both the husband and the wife, the first sex relation need not be accompanied by any considerable physical discomfort, and certainly not by any emotional strain."

"*After the first sexual relations have been consummated, what would aid in bringing about a satisfactory sexual adjustment?*"

"It is well to bear in mind that the sexual union is both a physical and emotional experience; it combines sensuality and sentiment. To render the sexual embrace most satisfying in marriage, the husband and the wife should make every effort to understand and appreciate each other's reactions and responses, to harmonize their sexual needs, and to cultivate what has been called an 'art of sex' in their relationship."

"*But what exactly constitutes an art of sex, doctor?*"

THE ART OF SEX

"The art of sex, I would say, is the harmonious blending of the physical, emotional and esthetic qualities of the sexual relationship. The sexual embrace should become neither a duty nor a routine of marriage, but rather the expression of mutual desire and passion, while the response and reaction during sexual union should be shared and experienced by both mates. In his quaint little *Ritual for Married Lovers,* Guyot, a French physician, says: 'The joy of sex union is peculiar in this, that it is far greater for the man when he feels it in the woman, and for the woman when she feels it in the man.' In other words, the joy of sex is increased for both when it is mutual, and an art in sexual love must aim at achieving this harmony."

"*Isn't it usual though for sexual desire and response to be mutual?*"

"Not necessarily. Too often either the husband or the wife will fail to consider the physical and emotional needs of the other. The husband may not appreciate the fact that a woman's sexual desires and responses differ from those of the man and require a more sensitive and delicate approach for their satisfactory expression; while the wife may not understand the sexual reactions of the husband and may fail to share and coöperate in the sexual embrace."

"*It is rather generally assumed, though, that most men have some sexual experiences before marriage. Wouldn't that give them the necessary knowledge and understanding of the art of sex?*"

"First of all, a large number of young men abstain from premarital sexual experiences and remain continent until marriage—many more, perhaps, than is generally assumed. Then, again, in most instances sexual contacts before marriage, especially when they are confined to casual relationships, do not necessarily provide a suitable preparation for the later association with one's wife. Let me read to you an interesting passage by Havelock Ellis on this very point:

> The training and experience which a man receives from a prostitute, even under fairly favorable conditions, scarcely form the right preparation for approaching a woman of his own class who has no intimate erotic experiences. The frequent result is that he is liable to waver between two opposite courses of action, both of them mistaken. On the one hand, he may treat his wife as . . . a novice to be speedily moulded into the sexual shape he is most accustomed to. . . . On the other hand . . . he may go to the opposite extreme of treating her with an exaggerated respect, and so fail either to arouse or to gratify her erotic needs.*

"To this I might add another significant difference. In a casual relation a man need not and does not take into consideration the woman's sexual feelings or responses. He seeks merely to obtain relief for himself and the satisfaction of his own sexual urge, and he does not even expect to arouse or to gratify the woman. Such contacts do not, therefore, necessarily supply him with an understanding of the differences in sexual needs between men and women, or with an appreciation of a proper sexual approach to his wife, a relationship which has so many emotional and esthetic implications."

"*Are there great differences in the degree or intensity of sexual desire between men and women?*"

"The degree of woman's erotic sensibility has long been a matter of considerable dispute. For a time it was seriously maintained that sex desire was primarily or entirely a masculine attribute and that woman was devoid of sexual feelings. Acton, a well-known English physician who was considered an authority on sex matters some fifty years ago, wrote that 'the majority of women, happily for society, are not much troubled with sexual feelings,' and that the supposition that women possessed any erotic desires was a 'vile aspersion.' Other writers of that period maintained a similar point of view. Today, with our fuller knowledge of the nature of the sexual impulse, such assumptions are, of course, regarded as entirely baseless. It may be quite true that lack of sexual desire, or frigidity, is met with more frequently in women than in men, but that does not necessarily indicate an inherent absence of the erotic urge. After a rather exhaustive survey of this subject, Havelock Ellis comes to the conclusion that the sexual impulse is fairly well balanced between the two sexes. It is rather generally assumed at present that the woman's erotic desires are just as strong as those of the male, although the manifestations of the sexual urge may vary considerably in the two sexes."

THE SEX IMPULSE IN THE MALE AND THE FEMALE

"*In what way do the sexual reactions of men and women differ?*"

"Well, in practically all species the male is sexually the more aggressive and active, while the female is the more receptive and passive. These differences are expressed even in the very character of the respective sex cells. The sperm is active, restless, constantly in motion, while the egg is quiescent, immobile, waiting, so to speak, for the coming of the sperm. Perhaps in this striking difference in the character of the reproductive cells one sees a counterpart of the profound psychic and emotional differences between the two sexes. At any rate, it is well recognized that the sexual impulse of man shows greater activity and is more easily aroused, while his erotic desires are as a rule directed more specifically toward sexual consummation. The woman, on the other hand, is sexually more passive, her desires are aroused more slowly, and they express themselves at first in a rather diffuse urge for general bodily contact and sexual play. Only after a certain degree of erotic excitation is the woman prepared for the consummation of the sexual act. In general, sentiment and emotion seem to play a much more significant role in the sexual reactions and responses of the woman than those of the man.

"Another important difference in the sex reactions of the man and the woman is the time element involved in reaching a climax or orgasm during intercourse. In the man the entire sexual cycle is much shorter; he is more easily aroused and, unless he specifically restrains himself, he is capable of reaching the climax in a comparatively short period. The woman, again, takes a longer time to become erotically stimulated and also a longer period to reach the orgasm. Her sexual reactions are generally more diffuse and more variable than those of the male."

"*In what way can the difference in the time element be adjusted if it takes the woman so much longer to be aroused?*"

THE PRELUDE TO THE SEX ACT

"With an understanding attitude, mutual sympathy, a conscious effort and deliberate restraint, an adequate adjustment can usually be established. To make the sex relation a mutually satisfying experience it is necessary that the woman's erotic impulses should first be aroused to a degree where she desires the consummation of the union. The woman usually requires a period of courtship, of wooing, of caressing, of love play, of bodily contact and erotic manipulation before she is physically ready for the sex act. The husband, as Ambroise Paré, a renowned French surgeon of the 16th century wrote, 'when lying with his companion and wife must fondle, caress, pleasurably excite and arouse her emotions if he finds her unready in response.' This does not imply, or should not imply, merely a physical stimulation but rather an attitude, an approach, a prelude which would place the wife in a receptive mood for sex union.

"As a matter of fact, there seems to exist a biological need for this preliminary courtship and fore-play. A certain amount of wooing and play prior to sex union has been observed among many forms of animal life. Among animals intercourse is not possible unless the female willingly receives the mate, and the male, as a rule, has to pursue and win the female before she will accept him sexually. It is only in the human species that sexual relations may occur even when the female has no desire for the act at all. It must be obvious, though, that for a fully adjusted and satisfactory sex life in human marriage, the sex act should be made mutually desirable, and that it should be entered into only at a time when the husband is acceptable to the wife. Balzac once wrote that 'a man must never permit himself the pleasure with his wife which he has not the skill to make her desire.' In other words, the sexual union should be preceded by a suitable type of wooing and love play which adequately arouse the wife to desire the sexual union.'

"*What should the prelude to the sexual act include?*"

THE SEXUAL RELATION

"In the sexual relationship the emotional and physical factors are intimately bound together, and in the prelude to sexual union it is necessary to take both of these aspects into consideration. On the emotional side, the actual manner of wooing will depend upon the cultural background, the individual sensibility, the temperament of the mates, as well as upon the mood and general circumstances of the moment, and is obviously subject to numberless variations. An approach which may prove highly stimulating to one person at one time may be quite repellent to another individual, or at another time. Sometimes a word, a gesture, an allusion, an odor is more effective than prolonged erotic play. It is neither possible nor desirable to prescribe any routine form of behavior or any set rules to be followed. In this intimate sphere of human relationship, dependence must be placed largely upon individual spontaneity and skill, as well as upon a mutual understanding and adaptation.

"A sensitive emotional approach may be sufficient to arouse a high degree of sexual desire, yet in most instances it is also well to employ direct physical stimulation prior to the actual union. This consists largely of the touch, the caress, the kiss. Unlike the male, in whom the sexually excitable areas are more or less localized, the erogenous zones of the woman are extensive and diffuse. Under favorable psychic circumstances, contact with any part of the body may, in fact, be productive of sexual excitation. Mantegazza once described sexual love as a higher form of tactile sensation. The lips, the neck, the lobes of the ears, the breasts, particularly the nipples, are especially sensitive, and the caress or kiss of these parts will often give rise to strong erotic desires. In the early period of marriage, in fact, the woman may be more responsive to general bodily stimulation than to direct genital contact. It is only after the natural shyness and reserve have gradually been thrown off that direct contact with the genital region is sexually stimulating. The entire vulvar area is erotically sensitive, and the gentle stroking of the labia minora, of the orifice of the vagina, and especially of the clitoris, is highly stimulating to the responsive woman. These organs, as well as the nipples, are supplied with erectile tissue and they therefore become more firm and erect under sexual excitation. Special care must be taken, however, that these contacts be gentle and delicate, for undue pressure and rough manipulation may give rise to painful sensations and unpleasant reactions. Gentle stimulation, on the other hand, may quickly result in a responsiveness of the entire organism and a readiness for sexual union."

"*Is it necessary that all of these preliminaries precede every act of intercourse?*"

"That would depend entirely upon individual inclinations, desires and reactions at the time. I would say that any of these measures might be employed whenever it becomes advisable to increase the erotic excitability and pleasure of the woman and to bring her to a state of tumescence or sexual readiness. The character, degree and duration of the preliminary play will depend upon the reactions and responsiveness of the woman, upon the length of time that the husband is able to maintain an erection before ejaculation, and upon any number of other factors. It is largely a question of individual insight and divination.

"In some of the books I shall mention you will find detailed descriptions of the art of erotic love. You will read of the odors which are intended to arouse sexual desire, of the various types of contact and stimulation suitable for the purpose, of the erotic kiss, and the love kiss, of the love bite and the genital kiss, of any number of bodily manipulations which may be employed to increase sexual desire and pleasure. The chief value of these descriptions, in my opinion, is that they help to remove many inhibitions and fears from the sphere of sexual behavior and to show that there is nothing abnormal in any type of love play. Variations in the sexual approach appear, in fact, to be a part of the biological pattern of the species to which man belongs, and I believe that no form of sex play is wrong in itself, unless it gives rise to physical injury or to an undesirable emotional or esthetic shock. It is doubtful, however, whether it is necessary to become book-conscious in this respect or to follow any particular routine in the art of sex. One should preferably develop one's own ingenuity and skill in this field, and make sex life a mutual adventure, rather than be guided in every detail by the instructions of a Baedeker in the art of love."

"*I should think that to follow any set erotic practices would remove the spontaneity from the sexual relation.*"

"Quite so, and this is what sometimes actually happens when people try to follow too literally the specific instructions to be found in some books on erotic love. Time and again women have told me that after having read certain passages on the art of sex, their husbands would endeavor to carry out in detail the given directions, with the result that the marital relation would become altogether too conscious, artificial and strained a procedure. It is much better to give fuller expression to one's own imagination and inclinations in the pursuit of a satisfactory sexual adjustment.

"In this connection I should also like to emphasize that during the intimate contacts of sex life, the wife need not and should not be entirely passive. It may be quite true that a woman frequently prefers to be forced to do the thing that she may very much desire herself, yet it is a serious error for her to remain entirely inactive and inert during sex play. Nothing will dampen the desires of even an ardent husband more completely than actual or feigned sexual indifference on the part of the wife. This is a frequent source of marital disharmony which I intend to discuss with you more fully again. At the beginning of sex life most women are naturally diffident and timid in their sex behavior, and the husband must assume all the initiative at this time, but after complete intimacy has been established it is well that she, too, take an active part in the love play, and at times even initiate the sex relation. It is neither abnormal nor degrading for the woman to make use of all the erotic plays that a man does. For just as the husband's attempts to stimulate his wife sexually serve at the same time to arouse his desires and increase his own tumescence, so does active participation on the part of the woman excite her own erotic desires and prepare her more fully for the sexual union and response."

"*What are the signs that a woman has been sufficiently aroused and that she is ready for the consummation of the sex act?*"

"The husband can usually learn quickly enough to recognize the emotional and physical signs which indicate that the wife is ready for union. There are any number of ways, indeed, in which the wife may express her desire or readiness, and where there is complete mutual confidence and an absence of inhibitions, it will not be difficult for the husband and wife to appreciate each other's reactions. On the physical side, the wife's sexual excitation and readiness for intercourse are evidenced by the appearance of a mucoid secretion around the vulva which comes from the glands of Bartholin, and it is well, when possible, to wait until the external genitals become bathed with this moisture before actual entry takes place. The secretion renders the vulvar region and the opening to the vagina moist and lubricated, and this serves to make penetration easier and also to heighten the sexual sensations. In the early days or even weeks of marriage physical and mental anxieties and restraints may inhibit the functioning of these glands and the moisture may not appear, and it may be desirable to employ an artificial lubricant, in the form of some greaseless jelly, at this time in order to render entry less painful, and to increase the possibility of a mutually satisfactory climax or orgasm."

"*What actually constitutes the orgasm?*"

THE ORGASM OF THE MALE

"The term orgasm applies to the spasmodic contractions of the muscles surrounding the genitals at the climax of the sex act. It occurs in both sexes at the time when the sexual sensation reaches its highest intensity. In the male it is accompanied by the ejaculation of the seminal fluid. The vas, seminal vesicles and prostate contract forcibly and expel their contents into the urethral canal where the several secretions mix to form the seminal fluid. During the orgasm this fluid is ejaculated through the penis in a number of jets by the rhythmic contractions of the surrounding musculature. The number of contractions experienced by the male varies in different individuals and also in the same person at different times, but generally they average from ten to twenty, while the total quantity of the ejaculated seminal fluid amounts to about one teaspoonful."

"*Does the woman experience the same kind of a reaction as the male at the time of the orgasm?*"

"In the woman, too, the orgasm signifies the acme of the erotic sensations and is manifested locally by involuntary and rhythmic throbbings of the sexual parts. The sensations are more or less localized to the region of the vulva, particularly around the vagina and clitoris.

THE ORGASM OF THE FEMALE

Sometimes the contractions extend to other muscles of the body, too, and there may even be a few general convulsive-like movements at the time of the orgasm. As a rule the local throbbings are fairly strong and distinct and the woman is usually definitely aware of their occurrence. Sometimes, however, the contractions are rather feeble and transient, so that the woman is barely conscious of them. The duration of the orgasm of the female is generally more prolonged than that of the male, and the climax subsides more slowly and more gradually.

"The emotional and erotic sensations accompanying the orgasm are subject to considerable variation both in the man and the woman depending upon individual sensitivity and general intensity of emotional response. In some, the sexual pleasure may be comparatively slight, while in others it may reach the height of mental and physical exaltation. Between these two extremes there is a wide range of gradations of sensuous response and reaction."

"*Is there a fluid discharged by the woman at the time of her climax?*"

"In the male, the ejaculation represents the discharge of his spermatozoa into the genital tract of the woman and is therefore an essential part of the physiological process of reproduction. The woman, however, does not discharge her sex cells during intercourse, and there is, therefore, no emission on her part corresponding to the ejaculation of the male. The moisture of which she may be conscious during sexual excitement is due, as I have said, to the secretions of the glands around the vulva and is not a part of the orgasm. Some maintain that a small amount of the mucoid secretion is expelled from the mouth of the womb into the vagina during the climax, but even if this is so, this discharge cannot be compared to the ejaculation of the male, nor would the woman or the man be conscious of its occurrence."

"*Can either of the mates tell when the other has reached the climax?*"

"The actual contractions of the sexual parts are not always felt by the other partner, especially if the orgasm is simultaneous. This is particularly true of the female contractions which often cannot be felt at all by the male. However, the other manifestations which accompany the climax, the sudden release of the increasing tension and the relaxation and sense of completion can frequently be observed or recognized by both."

"*If it takes the woman much longer to reach a climax can a mutually satisfactory relationship always be attained?*"

"There are great variations in the degree of sexual response in women and particularly in their ability to attain a satisfactory climax during intercourse. At the beginning of marriage, especially, a woman's sexual desires may still be dormant as yet, and there may, therefore, be but little erotic response to the sexual act. With a sympathetic understanding and patience on the part of the husband, a harmonious adjustment may soon be achieved, and if the woman is at all capable of reaching a climax, there should be but little difficulty, even if her 'reaction time' is slow. Delicacy in the sexual approach and stimulation, variety in the positions assumed during intercourse, and a general sensitivity and skill in the art of sexual love will generally arouse the woman to a degree where she will be able to reach an orgasm together with her husband. There are, unfortunately, a certain percentage of women who cannot obtain complete sexual release even after a prolonged period of sexual stimulation, but this is a problem which we shall discuss a little more fully later on."

"*How long should sexual intercourse normally take?*"

DURATION OF THE SEX ACT

"That would depend upon what we consider the term to include. Van de Velde, for instance, in his *Ideal Marriage*, a book which deals in some detail with the art of love, considers sexual intercourse to consist of the fore-play, the sexual union and also the after-play, that is, the period of rest and relaxation which normally follows intercourse. With such a definition, the sex cycle would obviously be subject to any number of variations. Even, however, if we consider coitus to extend only from intromission until the completion of the orgasm, there is normally a marked individual variation in the duration of the act. The length of time that the man is able to retain an erection without an ejaculation, the ease or difficulty with which the woman is capable of reaching an orgasm, the degree of sexual tension at the time of intercourse, the frequency of the sexual relations and many other factors determine the duration of the act at any particular time. While some men are able to continue active coitus for fifteen or twenty minutes and even longer before ejaculation, others can hardly prolong it for a minute or so. The average duration of the sex act is probably from three to five minutes. Stekel states that few men are able to continue the sex act for more than five minutes. In Dickinson's study of 362 cases, 40% of the men are said to have reached an orgasm in less than five minutes after intromission, 34% in from five to ten minutes, and the remaining 26% in from fifteen minutes up to an hour or longer. 'The median man,' says Dickinson, 'holds an erection from five to ten minutes.'

"From inquiries among a large number of couples it is my impression that these figures are rather high. There is a difference, of course, between simply 'holding an erection,' even in intromission, and between maintaining it during active copulation. When both partners are passive, a man may learn to retain an erection for a comparatively long time, but with active coital movements the orgasm occurs, in most instances, in less than three minutes. It is difficult to obtain exact data concerning this question, but I should rather be inclined to say that the average duration of active coitus is from one to two minutes."

"*You spoke before of a variety in the positions that may be assumed for intercourse. Does it make any difference just what particular posture is employed?*"

COITAL POSITIONS

"I am glad that you brought up the question of coital positions, for I had had in mind to discuss this with you today. Ignorance concerning the postures suitable for the sex act is no doubt one of the frequent causes of awkwardness and difficulties in sexual adjustment, and it is well that we should give this subject some consideration in connection with the question of the art of marriage. We need not, of course, discuss all the possible varieties of coital positions. The erotic literature of the East and the Orient contains detailed descriptions of nearly a hundred different modes of intercourse, but the majority of these are but minor modifications of the usual postures, and many are altogether fantastic. I shall consider only the positions which are most generally employed and which appear to be most adequate and satisfactory both from a physical and psychological standpoint.

"FACE TO FACE" POSITION

"The usual position for coitus and the one which is probably the most easily assumed is the anterior, front, or 'face to face' posture. Here the woman lies on her back with her thighs separated and her knees bent or drawn up toward her, while the man inclines over her, with the upper part of his body lightly in contact with hers. By supporting himself on his knees and on one or both hands or elbows, he avoids putting his weight upon the woman, and the position is comfortable to both. With this mode of coitus, entrance can be accomplished with ease, and there is good approximation or coaptation of the male and female organs. It is important to bear in mind, however, that in this position the knees of the woman have to be bent and her thighs drawn up towards her body."

"*How far should the knees be drawn up?*"

"Well, the knees may be flexed but slightly with the feet resting on the bed, or they may be drawn up so that the legs of the wife will encircle the husband's body. Some bending of the knees, however, is necessary. I know a large number of couples who were having difficulties in consummating the sexual union merely because they had failed to take this factor into consideration. They were attempting to have intercourse with the wife lying straight on her back with her limbs outstretched or extended, a position which makes penetration very difficult, if not impossible. When the thighs and legs are straight, the inclination of the pelvis is such that the opening of the vagina is further back and points more or less downward, and as the male organ is elevated at an acute angle during erection, approximation is not easy. When the woman flexes her knees and separates her thighs, however, the vaginal orifice is tilted upward, and at the same time it is slightly opened so that penetration can be accomplished with greater ease. In some instances it is even advisable to place a pillow underneath the wife's hips in order to increase further the tilt of the pelvis and bring the orifice of the vagina forward. This permits deeper penetration and closer contact, and serves to heighten the sexual sensation and to facilitate the attainment of a climax.

"After entry has been made, the wife may slowly straighten her knees, and bring her thighs together. Although full penetration is not possible in this position, it affords closer approximation between the male organ and the external genitals of the woman, which is especially desirable when there is some difficulty with the potency of the man or the sexual response of the woman.

"A simple modification of the 'face to face' posture is the 'side' position. Here instead of lying on her back the woman lies on her side, with her knees drawn up and her thighs separated, while her husband lies facing her, resting between her limbs. If she lies on the right side, her right thigh is underneath him and her left is over his body. This posture is simple to adopt, and is comfortable because both the husband and the wife rest on the bed and there is very little weight placed upon either.

"SIDE" POSITION

"There is another form of the side position in which the couple lie facing each other sideways as before. If the husband lies on his left side he draws up his left thigh, and the wife rests upon it. She then places her left leg over his body. This position sounds somewhat complicated, but it can be readily assumed, and many find it very comfortable. Ovid long ago advised the Roman ladies that 'the simplest and the least fatiguing is to lie on your right side.' "

"*Is it possible to have intercourse with the woman lying above the man?*"

"Yes. The woman may assume the 'superior' or upper position, and either sit astride or lie over her husband. The man lies flat on his back, with his thighs together, while the woman kneels or squats across him, and intromission is accomplished in this position. If the husband raises his knees slightly to support the wife's hips, she can bend her body forward over his, so that closer contact of the upper part of their bodies is possible. In some instances a small pillow placed under the lower part of the husband's back makes this method more satisfactory and comfortable. In general, this position gives the woman greater freedom of motion, and permits deep and complete penetration and close sexual contact.

"REVERSE" OR "WOMAN SUPERIOR" POSITION

"SITTING" POSITION

"The 'sitting posture' in which the man sits on a chair and the woman sits or rather is suspended across his separated thighs, facing him, is also used occasionally. This is not particularly practical or convenient, but in some instances it is found to be a stimulating variation."

"*In the positions you have mentioned the man and the woman always face each other during intercourse.*"

"Yes, this is the characteristically human attitude during the sexual act, although it may not always have been so. Among quadrupeds, generally, coitus is effected in the posterior or 'back' position, that is with the male behind the female. This may also have been the original human method, but today it is resorted to but infrequently, except among certain primitive peoples who use this posture regularly. It may be accomplished either with the woman lying on her side and the man lying behind her, or else with the woman in the so-called 'knee-chest' position, that is kneeling face downward, with her elbows and chest resting on the bed, while the man kneels behind her. However, aside from presenting an element of variety, and in some cases of permitting closer compression of the clitoridal and urethral area, there does not seem to be any particular advantage to this posture. It does not allow complete penetration, it is not very comfortable, it often places a physical strain upon both the man and the woman, and, above all, it does not permit the face to face contact and caress, which is so important an accompaniment of sexual intercourse among civilized peoples.

"BACK" POSITION

"I have mentioned the several positions which are probably the most suitable and convenient. There are a great many others indeed. Ovid, perhaps with true poetic license, said that 'love has a thousand postures.' To detail too large a number of them at this time, however, might only prove confusing and more of a hindrance than a help. In fact, as in other fields of sexual play, it is best, it seems to me, to allow for a certain degree of spontaneity and ingenuity on the part of the individual couple. After a while, they will learn to adopt the postures which will prove most comfortable and most satisfactory to them."

"*But are not some of the positions you have mentioned unnatural and abnormal?*"

"I do not think that we can consider any particular method of sexual union as the normal one and the others as abnormal. The use of one or another mode of intercourse is largely a matter of social, cultural and esthetic traditions and attitudes. What is considered as natural in one place may be regarded as quite the opposite in another. Ploss and Bartels, for instance, state that the inhabitants of Kamchatka use the side position for intercourse, supposedly because this is the mode of contact among fish which constitute their chief food supply, and they regard anyone who practices coitus in any other fashion as committing a grave sin. Similarly, the peoples of Trobriand who employ a rather difficult squatting posture for coitus, consider the European positions not only impractical but also improper. Obviously, then, it is largely a question of environment, training and conventions as to whether a particular form of sex contact is considered normal or abnormal. One might say, indeed, that no position which appears suitable need be regarded as tabu or indecent, and that a variety in the sexual approach is much to be desired for a mutually satisfactory sex experience."

"*Sometime ago I saw a quotation to the effect that 'all animals feel sad after intercourse'; is there any truth in this saying?*"

THE EPILOGUE TO THE SEX ACT

"This statement, which was supposedly made by the Greek physician, Galen, many centuries ago, is still frequently quoted, yet I doubt whether there is really any psychological or physiological basis for it. The intense physical and mental excitement which usually precedes and accompanies the sex act may be followed by a period of some languor and at times even of fatigue or exhaustion, but this does not imply sadness or mental depression. On the contrary, a satisfactory sexual experience is more apt to leave the individual with a sense of well-being and agreeable repose.

"As a rule the sexual embrace should be followed by a feeling of gratification and relaxation. Van de Velde considers this period, which he calls the 'epilogue' or 'after-glow,' as a part of the sex union, and he has wisely emphasized its importance to the completion of the act. When a couple are physically, emotionally and sexually well attuned and adjusted, the sexual embrace should be succeeded by a sense of restfulness and close intimacy.

"We have spoken at some length today about the technique of the sexual relation, and there are many other related problems which we shall probably discuss next time. I should like, however, to stress again at this point, that the art of sex is but one phase, although an important one, of the art of marriage. Marriage is a complex relationship and to be satisfactory requires any number of mutual adjustments and adaptations. Happiness in marriage does not come spontaneously. It is a goal which must be attained. It is, as Dr. Holmes has so well said, 'not a gift which is bestowed but a result which is achieved,' and that is perhaps why we should aim to make an art of marriage.

"I should like to mention a few of the more recent books which deal with the subjects we have discussed today. You will no doubt find much instructive information in many of them.

ELLIS, HAVELOCK, M.D. "The Psychology of Sex." Long & Smith (1933).
A one volume summary of Havelock Ellis' classic and authoritative studies in the psychology of sex.

VAN DE VELDE, TH. H., M.D. "Ideal Marriage." Covici, Friede (1931).
An instructive and detailed presentation of the physiology and technique of the sexual relation.

SANGER, MARGARET. "Happiness in Marriage." Brentano (1926).
A non-technical, practical volume on premarital and marital problems.

EXNER, M. J., M.D. "The Sexual Side of Marriage." W. W. Norton & Co. (1932).
The problems of sexual adjustment presented in an able and enlightening manner.

STOPES, MARIE C. "Married Love." G. P. Putnam (1918).
A frank discussion of the factors involved in marital adjustment.

WRIGHT, HELENA, M.D. "The Sex Factor in Marriage." Vanguard Press (1931).
A brief and clear presentation of sexual technique.

HUTTON, ISABEL E., M.D. "The Sex Technique in Marriage." Emerson Books, Inc. (1933).
A well written, concise exposition of the sex factor in marriage.

EVERETT, M. S. "The Hygiene of Marriage." Vanguard Press (1932).
The physical and psychological aspects of marriage ably and comprehensively discussed.

ROBIE, W. F., M.D. "The Art of Love." Eugenics Company.
Sexual behavior and technique treated with considerable frankness and insight.

BUTTERFIELD, OLIVER M. "Marriage." Oliver M. Butterfield (1929), LaVerne, Calif. (private).
A concise and lucid booklet on the marital relation.

*ELLIS, HAVELOCK. "Studies in the Psychology of Sex," Vol. VI, page 523. F. A. Davis Co., Phila.
Quoted with the permission of the publisher.

CHAPTER VIII

SEXUAL DISHARMONIES

"We are to consider today several other topics in relation to the art of marriage. Last time we spoke of the nature and technique of the sexual union and of the importance of attaining a mutually satisfactory sexual relationship; this time I should like to discuss with you certain types of sexual disharmonies which sometimes arise, and which, when they do occur, are apt to affect seriously an otherwise successful union."

"As a matter of fact, doctor, we had intended to speak to you about the question of sexual incompatibilities, and we are glad that you are bringing the subject up now."

"Frankly, I should not like to dwell upon the potential incompatibilities and maladjustments of marriage, nor do I want to give you the impression that marriage is necessarily beset with pitfalls and disharmonies. Yet I feel that young people about to enter the marital relationship should be aware of the possible difficulties and not find themselves totally bewildered, perplexed and distressed should some unexpected problem arise. It is well indeed for them to know something of what Balzac calls the 'sandbanks, the reefs, the rocks, the breakers, and the currents' on the sea of matrimony, so that they may be able to steer their barques clear of the dangerous areas. I am quite convinced that much unhappiness in marriage can be obviated by a more realistic understanding of the problems which may arise in the sexual relationship.

"You will understand, of course, that, as I have already emphasized on several occasions, I do not consider the sex relationship to be the only important factor in marriage; personal, social, economic, family, and any number of other problems play their part in the success and happiness of a union. If I shall discuss with you primarily the subject of sexual harmony and disharmony, it is because just now we are chiefly concerned with this aspect of the marital relation."

"*Is it likely for sexual difficulties to occur at the very beginning of marriage?*"

DIFFICULTIES IN THE CONSUMMATION OF THE SEXUAL UNION

"Yes, sexual disharmonies of a minor or major character may develop from the start, and they are apt, in fact, to render the first weeks or months of marriage very trying. I might mention, for instance, the difficulties which are sometimes encountered in connection with the consummation of the sexual union. I frequently come across newly married couples who have been unsuccessful in completing their marital relation, and who are very much astonished and disconcerted by such an unexpected complication. Sometimes these difficulties persist for a long time, and the wife remains a post-marital virgin, so-to-speak, for weeks, months and even years after marriage. I am not speaking, of course, of instances where, for one reason or another, sexual contact is deliberately avoided, but of those couples where the failure to consummate the sex act is entirely involuntary, and is due to the existence of physical or psychic conditions which make the completion of the union difficult or impossible. Such a situation might be much less disturbing if the husband and wife were aware of its possible occurrence, and were prepared to meet it intelligently."

"*But why should a couple be unable to consummate their sexual relation?*"

"A number of causes may account for the failure to complete sexual union. Ignorance of the mechanism of coitus and consequent awkwardness in technique; an involuntary contraction of the genital muscles of the female which makes penetration impossible; persistent pain to the woman during attempts at intercourse; lack of sufficient potency on the part of the husband, and many other physical or emotional disturbances may lead to failure in the consummation of the marital union.

IGNORANCE OF SEX TECHNIQUE

"Let me give you a somewhat typical story of one such case. A young couple, married for seven months, had somehow not been able to have satisfactory relations. Repeated attempts at coitus were unsuccessful, and defloration had not yet occurred. They were both deeply in love and were happy together in every respect, except for the fact that they could not adjust themselves sexually. Upon examination both the wife and the husband were found to be physically normal. The sex relation, however, had not been consummated and the hymen was still intact. The difficulty in this case proved to be the fact that neither of them had any clear understanding of the elementary facts of intercourse. They had but a vague idea, for instance, of the actual mechanism of copulation, or of the position to be taken during the act. The wife had kept her body rigid and tense without any attempt to relax and to flex the knees, so that complete intromission was hardly possible. An explanation of the cause of their difficulties, and some brief instruction in sexual hygiene served to solve their problem in a short time."

"*I can well understand the wife's lack of knowledge, but it is rather surprising that the husband should have been equally ignorant.*"

"In this particular instance the husband had had no sexual experiences prior to marriage, and had learned very little about the sexual relation beforehand. Often, however, even if a man has had sexual relations before marriage, it does not necessarily mean that he acquires sufficient sexual knowledge. His premarital experiences may have been limited to cohabitation with women who had taken the initiative and guided him in the relation. After marriage, however, it is the man who has to play the role of initiator, and he may then find himself quite unequipped for the purpose."

"*Is it only a question then of lack of understanding?*"

"No, not all of the early difficulties are due to ignorance or lack of skill in the art of love. Sometimes it is the woman's reactions which make intercourse difficult. I mentioned last time that many women have a natural tendency to resist sex relations at first. Ordinarily such resistance disappears in a short time so that normal relations are soon established. In some cases, however, it persists for a long time, for weeks and months, and constitutes a serious obstacle to a satisfactory sexual adjustment. Let me cite an instance of such a case. At the time this couple came for a consultation they had been married ten months. Their story was that in spite of numerous attempts they had found it impossible to have a normal sex union, and their marriage had not as yet been consummated. The husband stated that he had normal sexual desires, and that there was no difficulty whatsoever with his potency, yet penetration seemed impossible. At every attempt his wife would resist him, would express a fear that he was injuring her, and would draw back in a defensive attitude. Both had been looking forward with much anticipation to a perfectly happy union, and they were greatly bewildered by the unexpected difficulties they were encountering. They were certain that there was some serious incompatibility, or that the wife had some anatomical abnormality, and they felt that they were evidently sexually mismated. In this case, too, it was found upon examination that the young woman was entirely normal, but that defloration had not yet occurred and the hymen was still intact. The difficulty proved to be due to the fact that whenever coitus was attempted, the woman would bring her thighs together and forcibly contract the muscles around the entrance to the vagina, making intromission impossible. Such a muscular spasm, a form of the condition known as vaginismus, is not infrequently the cause of early marital difficulties."

VAGINISMUS AND GENITAL SPASM

"*In such instances, doctor, does the woman consciously resist because she objects to the relation?*"

"No, the resistance is in the nature of a reflex action which is beyond her voluntary control. The woman may be entirely normal in every other respect, she may even have strong sexual desires and be both willing and anxious to submit to the sexual embrace, yet every time intercourse is attempted, a reflex spasm of the genital muscles occurs, which definitely prevents penetration. I have called this condition 'genital spasm.'"

"*What causes this spasm? Is it due to nervousness?*"

"Well, an involuntary contraction of the vaginal muscles may be due either to physical or to psychic factors. Any abnormality of the woman's sex organs, for instance, which would render intercourse painful to her is apt to result in a spasm of the muscles around the vagina. On the other hand, the genital spasm may represent a purely subconscious defense reaction against sexual relations. Fears and anxieties of one kind or another, strong sexual inhibitions and tabus inculcated in early life, an unfortunate sexual experience in the past, or some other conditioning factor may be responsible for the development of this type of muscular spasm at marriage."

"*In what way can early experiences or impressions cause this resistance to develop later on?*"

"Ordinarily, you see, the female child is taught from infancy to regard her genitals as distinct from any other part of her body. She is continually warned against touching them, and the danger of harming them is strongly impressed upon her. In the child's mind the sexual organs soon become associated with a sense of shame and tabu, and with the feeling that she must ever be on guard against any injury to them. Even though in later life the young woman may become emancipated from the sex tabus, she may still retain many of the inhibitions and protective instincts of her youth, and these may seriously interfere with her reactions and responses during sexual contact. She may involuntarily shrink from intercourse and set up a protective mechanism in the form of this genital spasm. The outer resistance is but an expression of an unconscious inner resistance to sexual union."

"*Are such inhibitions really carried over into marriage? I should think that in the intimate daily life of two people fears and feelings of this kind would soon disappear naturally.*"

"It is quite true that in the majority of instances the early apprehensions and resistances soon give way to a normal sexual expression. In some, however, they tend to persist for a long time, particularly where such a reaction on the part of the wife is complicated by an unskilled and awkward approach of the husband. The fears and inhibitions accumulated by a woman during a lifetime cannot after all be thrown off by her on the very day she is united in wedlock, and the husband must understand her behavior. If he is impatient and unsympathetic, it may only serve to aggravate her anxieties and to increase her resistance."

"*How can inhibitions or fears of this kind best be removed?*"

"The best way, of course, is to prevent their occurrence. This implies an intelligent sex education in youth and a more adequate preparation both of the man and the woman for the sexual relation in marriage. The husband, especially, should learn to realize that he has to exercise judgment and restraint at the beginning, and that he must make every effort to win the complete confidence and trust of his wife. Let me read to you some advice on this subject from Vatsyayana's *Kama Sutra;*

> Women, being of a tender nature, want tender beginnings, and when they are forcibly approached by men with whom they are but slightly acquainted, they sometimes suddenly become haters of sexual connection, and sometimes even haters of the male sex. The man should therefore approach his bride according to her liking, and should make use of those devices by which he may be able to establish himself more and more into her confidence.

"This was written some 1600 years ago, but is still applicable today, and may very well serve as excellent advice for the prevention of many sexual disharmonies.

"When a genital spasm does develop, however, it is essential first of all to understand its character and its significance. Once the husband and the wife recognize the nature and reason of the difficulty, it will render the possibility of correction so much easier. Instruction or reinstruction in the physiology and psychology of the sexual relation and in the art of sexual love, an adequate individual discussion of the underlying factors, and, when necessary, an artificial defloration and dilatation of the hymen, are usually sufficient to remedy the condition."

"*You mentioned before that pain during intercourse may be a cause of sexual difficulties. Were you referring to the pain caused by the breaking of the hymen?*"

PAINFUL COITUS

"No, not necessarily. The pain caused by defloration is only temporary, and by the end of the first week coitus should not be accompanied by any discomfort. The painful disturbance I had reference to is due to other factors. Anatomical abnormalities, inflammations of the external or internal sex organs, irritations due to clumsy and awkward attempts at coitus—these, and other conditions may be responsible for pain during sexual union. If the discomfort is severe enough, it may render sexual contact so unpleasant for the wife, that she may even try to avoid sexual relations altogether.

"Painful intercourse is not at all infrequent, and if it should occur, it is important not to let it continue for too long without medical attention. It may become a source of serious marital dissatisfaction and unhappiness, yet simple medical care and advice may often serve to relieve this difficulty. Several months ago, for example, a woman came to see me because of painful coitus. This woman began to be troubled with pain during intercourse soon after marriage. The pain had persisted long after the defloration and became more acute as time went on. After a while it reached a stage where sex relations had become so unpleasant to her and so unsatisfactory to her husband that for many months they practically avoided all sexual contact. They were ascribing their difficulties to some anatomical disproportion of their sex organs, and each secretly regarded the marriage as a failure. A medical examination of the wife at this time disclosed the presence of an inflammation of the vulva and vagina, which responded readily to local treatment. The relief of the condition soon led to the disappearance of the pain during intercourse, and eventually entirely normal and satisfactory sex relations were established. I am citing this case because the history is rather characteristic of this type of sexual disturbance."

"*May I ask you whether this inflammation was due to a venereal disease?*"

"No, it was not. As a matter of fact, in this particular case, the condition was due to an infection with an organism technically called trichomonas, which is not considered a venereal disease. This infection is not infrequent in women and occurs occasionally in men, and it may even affect those who have never had any sexual relations. When severe in form, it may render intercourse quite painful to the woman."

"*You mentioned before the question of sexual weakness on the part of the man. Is this a frequent factor in marital difficulties?*"

"Well, deficiencies in male potency are not at all uncommon, and when sufficiently marked to interfere with normal sexual activity, serious marital disharmonies may indeed result. Sometimes it happens that the man is sexually inadequate from the very beginning of marriage. I am not speaking of temporary difficulties or hesitancies which may occur during the first few days, but rather of those which are more or less lasting.

SEXUAL IMPOTENCE OF THE MALE

"The potency of a man depends upon several factors: the strength of his libido or sexual desire, his ability to have a satisfactory erection, and his capacity to maintain the erection for a certain length of time. If his sexual urge is very low, if he is incapable of attaining a sufficiently strong erection, or if his coital cycle is very brief, that is if he reaches the orgasm very quickly, the man is more or less sexually inadequate. Under any of these conditions, normal and satisfactory sex relations are not possible.

"If sexual inadequacy happens to exist from the beginning of marriage, defloration may not be accomplished, and the sexual union will not be consummated. Here, for instance, is another history of a couple who had been married for over two years without having had complete sexual relations. During the first few months the husband had made some attempts at intercourse but these were apparently unsuccessful, and thereafter there had been very rare sexual contacts of any kind. The woman had been brought up in a strictly puritanical fashion and knew very little about the nature of the sexual relation, so that her husband's failure to consummate the marital act and his apparent lack of sexual desire were not regarded by her as anything unusual. She had even looked upon it at first as an evidence of his self restraint and of his great consideration for her. After a time, however, she became aware that there was something abnormal in their relations and sought medical advice. It developed that the husband was totally impotent and had not approached her because of his disability. It later became evident that his condition was more or less permanent, and eventually an annulment of the marriage was obtained."

"*But why should a man who is not capable of having sexual relations marry?*"

"In the majority of instances, I would say, the man marries without being fully aware of the extent of his inadequacy. It may also happen that the impotence manifests itself only after marriage. A man may have had fairly normal sexual experiences before marriage and yet, for various psychological or emotional reasons, find himself sexually inadequate with his wife. Occasionally, of course, a man marries in spite of the knowledge that he is not altogether sexually competent, believing that the deficiency will be cured by marriage. This, in my opinion, as I mentioned once, is a serious mistake. It is far better to have the condition remedied beforehand if possible. At any rate, the marriage should not be entered into unless the future wife is fully cognizant of the man's disability, and is willing to accept him in spite of his condition and of the possible later disharmonies. There are some men and women, particularly those of somewhat advanced age, who come to look upon marriage merely as a means of establishing a friendship, companionship and a home, and they are willing to disregard the sexual factor—but this is a matter for individual understanding and adjustment. They should certainly both have a clear idea of the situation, and should be well aware of the potential difficulties which they may encounter in their relations."

IMPOTENCE AND MARRIAGE

"*If a man reaches his orgasm very quickly is it a sign of sexual weakness?*"

"The duration of the act of coitus, as we have already discussed, is subject to wide variations, and men differ greatly in their so-called 'staying-power.' Ordinarily the erection should be maintained for many minutes, and the ejaculation should not come for about one or two minutes after intromission, at least not until after shall we say ten, twenty or more coital movements. Some men, however, cannot maintain an erection for even that length of time, and reach their orgasm very rapidly. This condition is technically known as 'premature ejaculation,' and can be considered as one form of sexual inadequacy. In men suffering from this disturbance, the seminal discharge and the orgasm come on very quickly, often immediately upon intromission. In the more severe cases the ejaculation may even occur as soon as the male organ comes in contact with the external genitals of the female, before actual entry has taken place, so that penetration and normal cohabitation is not possible. Disturbances in the sexual function of the male involving rapid ejaculations in one form or another are not uncommon, and they constitute a rather frequent source of sexual maladjustment and marital disharmonies."

PREMATURE EJACULATION

"*What causes sexual weaknesses of this type?*"

"For its complete fulfillment the sexual act requires an adequate coördination of the psychic, nervous, glandular and muscular functions of the body, and a disturbance of any one of these or of their proper coördination may lead to a diminution of potency. Perhaps the repressions and the inhibitions, the conflicts and the strains occasioned by our present moral standards and social life have been responsible to a large degree for the development of these disturbances of the male sexual functions. Among the more primitive groups, where the sexual morals and the social conduct are more simply organized, there seem to exist but few of the sexual inadequacies that we so often encounter among the more civilized peoples.

CAUSES OF SEXUAL IMPOTENCE

"Generally speaking, disturbances of the male sex function, in the form of premature ejaculations or of complete impotence, may be caused by either physical or psychic factors. General constitutional diseases, local disorders of the reproductive organs, disturbances of glandular functions, severe sexual abuses or strains, or even an inadequate sexual technique, may be the underlying cause of the difficulties. Or else, the lack of potency may be entirely psychic in origin and develop as a result of marked inhibitions, mental conflicts, fear complexes, anxiety neuroses, abnormal sex tendencies and other psychopathological influences. The psychologists, in fact, ascribe all instances of disturbed sexual capacity to some underlying mental factors. 'Sexual incompetence,' says Havelock Ellis, 'is, to a large extent, a special manifestation of incomplete social adaptation,' and Stekel maintains that 'behind most cases of premature ejaculation lies a fear.' However, in the disturbances of the sexual function it is not always possible to distinguish clearly between the physical and psychic causes. In sexual life the physique and the psyche are so closely interrelated that of necessity one constantly reacts upon the other."

"*Can anything be done to correct or cure sexual weakness?*"

"Yes, indeed. Generally, of course, it is advisable to obtain competent medical care, for the treatment will vary according to the nature and cause of the disturbance in the particular instance. Attention to constitutional disorders, the administration of certain hormones, local treatment of the genital tract, electrotherapeutic measures and other forms of medical care are often effective. In many cases, however, such medical measures are of little value, and main dependence must be placed upon psychiatric analysis and guidance.

"In the milder forms of rapid ejaculations, it is often possible for the man to remedy the condition by persistent self-training and control. The coital act should not be carried to its climax immediately after intromission; the man should attempt to remain quiescent and passive after entry, without resorting to any coital movements. As the possibility of an imminent ejaculation passes off, motion may be commenced and then stopped again before the ejaculation. Deep breathing and a conscious relaxation of the genital muscles when an ejaculation is about to occur are helpful. With such intervals of rest it may be possible gradually to maintain the erection for a longer period and to strengthen the power of sexual control. It is essential, however, that during these preliminary attempts, the wife should fully coöperate with her husband, and by a sympathetic attitude and either passive or active assistance give him the necessary encouragement and help."

"*You spoke before of the strength of the sexual desire as one of the factors in the potency of the man. Is there a great difference in the degree of the sexual impulse between one individual and another?*"

SEXUAL FRIGIDITY

"Yes, indeed. Aside from the profound differences in the sexual impulse between the two sexes, there are wide variations in the intensity of the sexual urge in members of the same sex. It may vary from a strong sexual drive to a total lack of any erotic desire. Some men and some women are 'highly sexed,' others only moderately so, and there are those who seem to have few or no sexual demands. Such a diminution of the sexual impulse is generally spoken of as frigidity or coldness.

SEXUAL FRIGIDITY IN MEN

"A low degree of sexual desire is not an uncommon condition in the male and constitutes one of the problems which are encountered every now and then in marriage. Not infrequently, perhaps more often than is generally realized, a woman will complain of her husband's sexual apathy, and of his apparent lack of erotic desire. She may accuse him of lack of affection, or even suspect him of infidelity. While in some instances the sexual coldness may indeed be the result of an absence of physical attraction between the mates, it is much more often the expression of a relatively low degree of sexual endowment of the man, or of the existence of some physical condition or mental conflicts and anxieties which inhibit and repress his libido, irrespective of the particular mate he may have."

"*But isn't sexual coolness more frequent in women than in men? That at least seems to be the general impression.*"

SEXUAL FRIGIDITY IN WOMEN

"Yes, it is quite true that frigidity is encountered much more often in women than in men. In women, the sexual impulse is subject to greater variations, and frigidity may manifest itself in a number of different ways. Some frigid women seem to lack all sexual desire and have no sexual 'appetite,' so to speak; others, even though desire is present, experience no pleasure from the sexual act and are sexually anesthetic; and there are women who even have a positive distaste or aversion to intercourse, and regard the sexual relation merely as an unpleasant marital duty."

"*When a woman is frigid does it mean that she has no sexual desires or feelings at all, or merely that she does not respond to a particular mate or under certain conditions?*"

"This is exactly the point which has to be determined in each instance. A woman may be totally frigid, and she will then presumably have no sexual desire under any circumstances; or her sexual coolness may be only temporary and relative in degree, the result of a number of personal, social and marital factors. The general consensus of opinion, I would say, is that absolute and permanent frigidity is rare. 'Frigidity,' says Dickinson, 'is not a fixed state which comes on whole and is borne to the grave,' and Stekel, who has written on the subject from a psychoanalytical point of view, maintains that 'no woman is absolutely anesthetic,' and that the woman who has no sexual feeling is merely one who has not as yet discovered the form of erotic gratification which would be adequate in her case. In my own experiences, I have found that in the case of most women who claim even complete sexual indifference, a history of some degree of sexual desire at one time or another and of sexual gratification from masturbation or some other form of sex play, can usually be obtained. In these cases, then, it is not a question of the total absence of any sexual impulse, but rather of the suppression and inhibition of erotic feelings, or of a failure to respond to a particular form of sexual approach or stimulation.

"Total frigidity, as I have said, is probably very rare. Robie claimed that not one-sixth of one per cent of women are really cold and unresponsive, and Hamilton in his study of one hundred cases found only one instance of actual frigidity. On the other hand, a relative degree of sexual coolness and lack of sensuous response appears to exist among a fairly high percentage of women. In reply to a questionnaire sent to 1000 married women by Katherine Davis, only 62% of the wives stated that sex relations were definitely pleasurable to them; 16% claimed that they were 'neutral' towards sexual union; 10% that the act was definitely distasteful to them, while the remaining 12% were doubtful concerning their reactions. In other words, at least 26% of the women could be considered as obviously sexually frigid. A similar incidence of deficiency in sexual response was found among the patients of the New York Birth Control Clinical Research Bureau. At the Bureau, we have been recording the patient's attitude towards sexual relations as a part of the clinical history, and in an analysis of some 9000 of these records, Kopp found that 76% of the women reported what may be considered as a normal sexual attitude; 20% stated that they were indifferent to the sexual act; and 4% claimed a definite aversion to intercourse. Here, too, then, we find that about one out of every four women is sexually unresponsive."

"*But what accounts for this lack or loss of sexual desire? Is it due to any physical abnormality or disturbance?*"

THE CAUSES OF FRIGIDITY

"The normal development and expression of the sexual impulse is dependent upon both physiological and psychological factors, and consequently any organic, psychic or emotional disturbances may affect the extent or intensity of the libido. Physiologically, there is considerable evidence to show that sexual activity is controlled to a large degree by various hormones. In the female of lower animals, for instance, the periods of increased sexual desire are closely associated with the processes of ovulation and with the increased hormone production which occurs at this time.

It has also been shown that the administration of the female sex hormone actually stimulates sexual activity. It is very likely, therefore, that the sexual drive is to some degree, at least, dependent upon the adequate production of the essential hormones, and that a lack of sexual desire may be due to some disturbance in the function of the internal glands.

"However, the available data indicate that the sexual impulse in humans, at least, is not controlled entirely by the secretion of the glands. Social, cultural and emotional factors play a definite part in the development of the sexual impulse, and a woman may have a diminished libido not because of any inherent physical or physiological deficiency but because of extrinsic or environmental influences."

"*Do you refer to general environmental influences or to maladjustments in the particular marriage?*"

"Well, in a large percentage of cases the lack of response is undoubtedly due to influences which had existed long before the marriage. 'I am inclined to think,' says Rachelle Yarros in an able analysis of woman and sex, 'that the cause of the high proportion of apparent frigidity among women is due to lack of sex education and inability to throw off the control they have built up.' I have already mentioned some of the factors which might generally disturb or misdirect the sexual impulse in women, and these same conditions may, under certain circumstances, completely inhibit the sexual appetite. A repressive attitude toward sex on the part of the parents, the association of sex with sin and immorality, the belief that any sexual expression is base and degrading, unfortunate sexual experiences at some time in early life, fears and anxieties concerning the sexual relation, fears of pain, fears over former acts of self-gratification, fears of childbearing and so on—all of these may so condition the woman that the sexual impulse will fail to develop normally or naturally.

"Let me read to you, as an illustration, a paragraph from a letter which bears upon this point. This letter came to me from a young woman, a college graduate, happily married, physically normal, but with a certain degree of sexual anesthesia. In telling of her early life, she writes:

> 'I always considered sexual intercourse a sign of extreme weakness, sinful, and not to be condoned. Up to about 16 years of age

I had the notion that a woman was destined to have a certain number of children, and that only one sexual congress of the parents was necessary. That was the only way I could explain why my parents, who were extremely poor, should keep on having babies. Because of the extreme poverty in our home and the frequent additions to the family, I worked up a strong dread of marriage and of the sexual act. . . . My dread of intercourse and what I considered the misery of married life even increased as I grew older.'

"Here we find a number of factors—the total lack of any intelligent sex education, the association of intercourse with weakness and sin, the dread of childbearing—all of which had obviously combined to inhibit any normal sexual expression on the part of this young woman. As a matter of fact, it took some time before she was finally able to overcome these early impressions and conditionings.

"On the other hand, the lack of response may be due to factors which exist in the particular mating. It is well to bear in mind that in cases of frigidity the husband's sexual capacity and behavior, as well as that of the wife, must be taken into consideration, and that in many cases the frigidity is not a quality inherent in the woman but rather a problem of the particular marriage. 'It takes two persons to make one frigid woman,' says Dickinson. If the husband is awkward and clumsy in his approach, if he is inconsiderate and tactless in his sexual relations, if he lacks any art or skill in sexual love, if he makes no attempt to arouse and stimulate his wife before coitus, she may never be fully awakened and may remain quite unresponsive to sexual contact. Then, again, if the husband's sexual capacity is inadequate, if he has a low degree of sexual desire, if his ejaculations come on rapidly or prematurely, or if he frequently resorts to coitus interruptus and withdraws before the wife is sufficiently aroused, the wife may develop an antipathy and even a definite aversion to sexual union. She either does not become stimulated at all, or else the repeated frustrations gradually lead to a loss of any pleasurable sensation and eventually to a loss of desire for sexual intimacy."

"*Suppose a man finds after marriage that his wife is unresponsive, what measures can be taken to correct the condition?*"

"First of all one has to take into consideration the fact that the sexual impulse of the woman may normally remain dormant for a long period. Her sexual instinct may not, in fact, develop to its full capacity until she is well beyond her twenties, or even later. Moll once divided the sexual urge into two elements: the impulse toward general bodily contact, 'to approach, touch and kiss another person of the opposite sex,' and the impulse toward actual sex union, toward the relief of sexual tension. In the woman the desire for bodily contact is at first, at least, much more strongly developed than the desire for genital contact, and the caress, the embrace and the kiss may be more gratifying to her than actual sex union. Many women are indeed passionate from the very beginning of marriage, but in many other cases it takes months or even years before the sexual emotions of the wife are awakened to a degree where she consciously and actively desires full sexual contact and takes pleasure in the sex act. The lack of complete sexual response at first may therefore be only due to the fact that the latent sexual capacities of the wife have as yet not been fully developed.

THE TREATMENT OF FRIGIDITY

"If the frigidity persists, however, the measures which may have to be taken to overcome or correct the condition will depend upon the nature and the cause in the individual instance. Adequate sexual education, or, more usually, re-education of the wife and of the husband, instruction in the technique and art of sexual love, the removal of baseless apprehensions and fears, the provision of satisfactory and reliable methods for the prevention of conception, these and other medical and psychiatric measures are often of great value. It is especially important that the husband should acquire the knowledge and understanding, the delicacy and the skill, the ability and the art of arousing the sexual impulses of his wife and of finding the means of gratification which are most satisfactory in her individual case.

"As far as the wife is concerned, she must make every effort to obtain an insight into the nature of her disability, to recognize her deficiency, and to appreciate the importance of correcting it. Every now and then a woman will tell me with a considerable show of satisfaction and pride that she is indifferent to sexual contact and that she derives no pleasure from sex union. She looks upon her sexual anesthesia as an indication of her moral virtue and spiritual superiority. 'Oh,' she will say, 'I am not that kind, sex doesn't mean anything to me. I wouldn't care if he never touched me.' Obviously such an attitude is in itself a contributing cause of her sexual failure. The woman should be made to understand that a mutual sexual response is of paramount importance to marital harmony, and that her frigidity is not a matter for pride and satisfaction but a sign of a physical or emotional inadequacy. She must realize that her husband cannot long retain his sexual ardor if she herself is totally unresponsive, and that for her own welfare, as well as for the happiness of the marriage, she should endeavor to develop a sexual interest and response.

"As a matter of fact, I should go a step farther and suggest that even if her sexual desire is not very strong, a wife need not constantly emphasize the fact of her indifference to her husband, or always inform him of her lack of response. At times it may even be well for her to simulate an interest in the sex act and to indicate a greater reaction to sexual stimulation. This in itself might help to create a greater marital harmony, and aid in gradually correcting her sexual indifference."

"*Last time you mentioned that some women have difficulty in reaching a satisfactory climax during intercourse. Is this condition a form of frigidity?*"

ORGASM INCAPACITY

"The inability to attain an orgasm is really quite distinct from frigidity. In frigidity, the woman either experiences no sexual desire at all or else the sex act gives rise to no pleasurable sensations; in orgasm incapacity, the desire may be quite normal and the sensations during the act even intense, but the final climax is not reached.

"This failure to reach an orgasm is, in fact, another frequent source of sexual disharmony. Ordinarily the completion of the sex act is characterized by a rather distinct emotional and physical reaction, by keen erotic sensations and by the local muscular contractions which constitute the orgasm. Many women, however, rarely or even never reach this culminating reaction, and this inadequacy sometimes leads to marital unhappiness and discord."

"*Are there many women who have difficulty in reaching an orgasm?*"

"Yes, I would say that orgasm incapacity is more frequent than is commonly recognized. It is perhaps the most frequent sexual complaint of women who are otherwise entirely normal. It should be made clear, however, that the capacity to reach a climax cannot be classified either as definitely positive or definitely negative. The orgasm may vary in degree and intensity from a very transient sensation to a very profound physical and emotional reaction, and it may also vary in the frequency of its occurrence. Some women reach a satisfactory climax during every sexual relation; others only at certain intervals, as once in every three, four or more cohabitations; to some women it comes as a very rare experience, only when some special combination of physiological and emotional circumstances makes a complete sexual release possible, while not a few never reach this culmination of the sex act.

"As far as the frequency of these variations is concerned, the figures of several studies on this subject may be illuminating. In his detailed analysis of 100 couples, Hamilton found that 46 of the 100 wives had what he terms 'a very inferior or wholly lacking orgasm capacity.' Dickinson, in a study of 310 cases, found that, generally speaking, out of every five women two reached an orgasm fairly frequently, one attained it 'sometimes,' and two did not reach any climax. In the series from the Birth Control Clinical Research Bureau, out of over 8500 women, 34% reported that they had experienced an orgasm 'usually,' 46% experienced it occasionally or 'rarely,' and 20% stated that they had never reached an orgasm. The orgasm capacity of another group of 3000 women whose records I have recently analyzed showed somewhat similar figures. Over 41% reached an orgasm regularly, 43% experienced it only occasionally or rarely, and 16% never attained the final reaction. As the women in these several studies did not come primarily because of any sexual difficulties or maladjustment, the figures can be considered as a fair index of the average status of women as far as orgasm capacity is concerned."

"*Why is it that so many women fail to respond fully during intercourse?*"

THE CAUSES OF ORGASM INCAPACITY

"There is no general agreement as yet as to the actual cause of orgasm failure in so high a percentage of normal women. Some, indeed, maintain that the orgasm of the female is not a universal physiological phenomenon, and that female animals generally do not reach any particular climax during the sexual act. They regard the development of the orgasm reflex in women as a special human attribute, an attribute which is still not deeply rooted in her organism and therefore subject to frequent and wide variations and anomalies.

"It seems to me, however, that the failure of response must be looked for in some more specific cause, either physical or psychic in character. From a physical point of view the orgasm difficulty may in part, at least, be accounted for by the relative positions of the erogenous zones of the woman's genital organs. There is one point which is of particular interest in this respect. As we have already noted, a woman's erotic sensations are centered mainly in and around the clitoris. Before sexual relations are established, erotic gratification is frequently obtained through stimulation of the external genitals and particularly of the clitoris. Repeated excitation of this area during youth and adolescence may even further concentrate the sensuous feelings to this region. It is only after the beginning of sexual experiences that the vaginal walls, too, become erotically sensitive, but even then the clitoris still remains, perhaps, the chief point of sexual feeling. In many women, indeed, these sensations are probably never transferred to the vagina, but remain confined to the clitoridal area even after sexual relations have long been established. Hence it is that so many women will attain an orgasm with comparative ease upon stimulation of the external genitals, and yet will have very little sexual gratification and will not reach a climax from the actual sex act."

"*But is not the clitoris stimulated during intercourse?*"

"Not directly and perhaps not sufficiently. This, it seems to me, is one of the anomalies in the sexual physiology of the human female. If you will look at the diagram of the female genitals you will notice that the clitoris is situated about an inch or more above the orifice of the vagina. During intercourse there is therefore comparatively little direct contact between the male organ and the clitoris. It is only when penetration is deep and complete that there is pressure upon the clitoris and the surrounding area. The difficulties in sexual response which many young women experience at the beginning of their marital relations may therefore be due to the fact that penetration is not complete at this time and proper approximation does not occur.

"It is likely that the distance between the clitoris and the opening of the vagina in the individual woman may have some bearing upon her capacity to reach an orgasm during intercourse. The higher the clitoris is located, and the further away from the vaginal entrance, the less contact there is apt to be, and the greater the difficulty in obtaining a satisfactory climax. During the last few years I have taken measurements of the span between the clitoris and the vagina in a large number of women, and I have found it to vary from one-half to two and a half inches, with an average of one and a half inches. While the results have not been conclusive, and at times rather contradictory, it has seemed to me that there was a distinct correlation in this respect, and that where the distance between the clitoris and the vaginal orifice was short, the woman was more apt to belong to the group who reach a satisfactory climax. This, however, is but one anatomical factor, and its importance in the individual case can be judged only when considered in connection with the other physical and emotional problems which enter into the sexual relationship."

"*What particular kind of emotional conditions may affect a woman's orgasm capacity?*"

"To discuss the various psychic or emotional conditions which may be responsible for orgasm difficulties in the female, I should have to repeat much of what I have already said in connection with the other forms of sexual disharmonies. The same psychological factors which may lead to genital spasm, to frigidity, to impotence, may also result in orgasm incapacity. Faulty sex instruction, subconscious inhibitions, fears and anxieties, sexual shocks of one kind or another, infantile fixations, homosexual or other forms of abnormal sexual tendencies—any of these may account for the development of orgasm difficulties in the woman. The inability to reach a climax may represent a subconscious reluctance to surrender completely to the sexual embrace."

"*Is it possible to tell from a medical examination whether a woman is or is not able to respond fully to the sex act?*"

"Generally speaking, a woman's capacity for sexual response cannot be determined from a physical examination, nor does a woman's general physique, except where there is some definite congenital abnormality or evidence of gross glandular dysfunction, indicate the degree of her sexual aptitude or orgasm capacity. Neither can the menstrual and reproductive history serve as a criterion in determining sexual response. The inability of a woman to react fully to the sexual relation is rarely related to any specific organic abnormality which could be revealed by a physical examination."

"Does the husband's sexual capacity or technique influence the wife's ability to reach a climax?"

"Yes, in many instances a wife's failure to reach a satisfactory climax may be due to her husband's sexual inadequacy. A woman's sexual reaction-time is as a rule much slower than that of the male; it usually takes her longer to become erotically aroused, and a longer period to attain an orgasm. If the husband looks upon the sexual relation merely as a means of satisfying his own biological urge, if he makes no effort to arouse his wife's desires before sexual union, or, else, if he can maintain an erection for only a brief period and reaches an orgasm quickly, the wife, although possessing a normal orgasm capacity herself, may not be stimulated to a degree where she, too, could reach a climax before the completion of the act. This is one reason, perhaps, why a woman will sometimes respond fully to one mate and yet fail to do so with another.

"Sometimes, again, it is a question of the contraceptive method employed. Not infrequently a woman will be unable to react completely when a certain form of contraceptive is used, and yet will respond normally when another method is substituted. Only recently, for instance, a woman who has been married for three years told me that during the first two years of her marriage, when her husband was resorting to coitus interruptus and the sheath, she had many difficulties in her sexual adjustment and was rarely able to reach a climax. Since she began to employ a different method of contraception, their sexual relations have been entirely harmonious, and she has been able to attain a mutual and simultaneous climax with her husband almost every time. In such instances it is evidently largely a problem of technique and of a suitable adjustment, rather than of any inherent incapacity on the part of the woman.

"I should emphasize, however, that the extent of the woman's orgasm response is not a problem only of the husband's sexual vigor or skill. I constantly come across instances where the husband's function is not at all in question, and where even an adequate sexual approach, a long period of precoital play and a considerable prolongation of the sexual act are unsuccessful in bringing about a culmination for the woman. Here, some of the other physical, psychic or emotional factors which I have mentioned may be responsible for the orgasm incapacity of the woman."

"*If a woman is frigid, doctor, or is unable to reach an orgasm, does it in any way indicate that she does not love her husband or that she is not sufficiently attracted to him physically?*"

"There are many men who believe that the failure of a woman to respond fully to the sexual embrace is a sign of her lack of affection or devotion. As a matter of fact, though, the absence of erotic gratification and the failure to attain an orgasm during intercourse does not at all indicate a lack of love or attraction. A woman may be profoundly and sincerely attached to a man and yet be unable to obtain any keen satisfaction from sexual relations with him. A large number of women, as we have already noted, obtain greater pleasure from intimate love play than they do from actual intercourse, and the failure to reach an orgasm during sexual union is therefore not at all a sign of insufficient physical attraction."

"*Is the failure to reach a satisfactory orgasm apt to affect a woman's health in any way?*"

THE EFFECTS OF ORGASM INCAPACITY

"First of all, I should like to stress the fact that if a woman responds actively to the sexual embrace and takes pleasure in the sexual union, her inability to reach an orgasm may not be of any serious import. Please understand that even if a woman does not attain an intense culmination, it does not mean that she does not derive a great deal of gratification from the sex act. Some women, indeed, are not at all aware of any orgasm problem until they learn about it from a conversation or book, and then they become greatly worried because they believe that they are not obtaining complete satisfaction from their sex experiences. As a matter of fact, some of the descriptions in the literature about the manifestations of the orgasm are often more poetic than real, and they sometimes lead men and women to expect sensations which are but rarely experienced. When D. H. Lawrence, for instance, in speaking of a woman at the completion of the sex act says that she experienced 'pure deepening whirlpools of sensation, swirling deeper and deeper through all her tissues and consciousness till she was one perfect concentric fluid of feeling, and she lay there crying in unconscious inarticulate cries,' he may give a very lyrical description of a very intense climactic reaction, but it does not represent the sensations of the average woman. Yet I have known men who, having read this or similar passages, were greatly disturbed because their own wives would not swoon and cry out during the climax, and women, who, similarly, were very much perturbed when such ecstatic reactions did not materialize. They were troubled with the thought that they were not obtaining complete gratification from sexual union, although, in reality, their response was quite satisfactory.

"If an actual orgasm deficiency exists, however, the effect of this condition upon the woman would depend largely upon the intensity of her sexual desires and the degree of her excitation at the time of the relation. If her sexual impulse is weak, or if she has been aroused but little, the absence of the orgasm will hardly have any harmful effects. On the other hand, if she has been very much stimulated, the failure to reach a climax may leave her in a state of frustration which may prove physiologically and emotionally disturbing. During erotic excitation there is a marked local congestion of the sexual organs, as well as a general physical and emotional tension. With the completion of the act, if an acme is reached, there is a gradual release, or detumescence, and this is followed by a sense of fulfillment and relaxation. In the absence of an orgasm, however, the relief is not complete, and the woman may remain for some time in an unsatisfied and restless condition. Repeated experiences of this kind may eventually lead to various nervous or sexual disturbances."

"*Would the failure to reach a climax have any bearing upon a woman's ability to conceive?*"

"There is little relation between orgasm capacity and fertility, and it is possible, indeed, that the orgasm is not a biological necessity for the female. The male climax is, of course, essential for reproduction; it is during the climax that the seminal fluid is ejaculated into the female genital tract, and without an ejaculation insemination could not take place. In the woman, however, the orgasm plays no such physiological role. The female does not discharge any specific fluid during the climax, and ovulation, or the release of the egg from the ovary, in the human species, is certainly not dependent upon the orgasm. Some maintain that the orgasm aids impregnation because during the culmination of the sex act the uterus presumably contracts and expands, producing a suction like effect which draws in the seminal fluid, but this point is still debatable and has not yet been definitely proved. At any rate, it is quite certain that women can and do become pregnant without reaching an orgasm. I have records of a large number of women who were fertile and bore many children without ever having attained an orgasm during the many years of their marriage. The failure to reach a climax, it would seem, does not materially affect the woman's capacity to conceive."

"*What can be done to overcome a woman's inability to reach a climax?*"

THE TREATMENT OF ORGASM INCAPACITY

"The means which may have to be employed to correct an orgasm incapacity will depend largely upon the nature and cause of the deficiency. If it is found to be due to the woman's mental state, to her complexes, her inhibitions, her fears,—these will have to be treated accordingly. If the husband's sexual technique or capacity is at fault, this must obviously be corrected. If it is a question of an inadequate contraceptive, a more satisfactory one will have to be provided. If it is a matter of a glandular disturbance, some suitable hormone therapy may perhaps have to be employed, although this has not as yet proven very successful. Indeed, the ingenuity of the physician will often be greatly taxed in the management of this condition.

"As far as the husband's sexual approach is concerned, I have already spoken at some length concerning the pre-coital play and of the necessity of arousing and stimulating the wife's erotic desires before actual union. The husband should delay intromission until the wife is sufficiently aroused, and he should try to prolong the act of coitus, so that she may have every opportunity to attain an orgasm, if possible.

"Sometimes a change in the coital posture is indicated. Some women, perhaps because of the anatomical relations of their genital organs, are able to reach a climax satisfactorily in some particular position, as in the 'reverse' or 'back' posture, and not in the usual anterior position, and it is certainly advisable to employ the one most adequate for the purpose. Free sexual experimentation and variation is particularly indicated when there is some orgasm difficulty on the part of the woman.

"Because of the concentration of the sensuous impulses around the area of the clitoris, many women, although unable to reach an orgasm during sex union, can do so with comparative ease if the clitoridal region is stimulated directly. In instances of orgasm incapacity it is therefore advisable for the husband to stimulate the clitoris locally either during the progress of the sex act, or, if necessary, even after he has reached his own orgasm. It is often better to bring about a culmination in this manner than to permit the feeling of physical and mental frustration which sometimes follows an unfulfilled sexual relationship."

"*But would not such a practice be a perversion rather than normal sexual behavior?*"

"Erotic sex play can be termed perverse when it serves as the sole means of sexual gratification and comes to be preferred to normal sexual union. As long, however, as it is used merely as a preliminary preparation to the sex act or as a means of bringing about its completion and fulfillment, it can hardly be regarded as abnormal. There is nothing perverse or degrading, I would say, in any sex practice which is undertaken for the purpose of promoting a more harmonious sexual adjustment in marriage. Of course, esthetic values and sensitivities vary considerably, and it is of importance that these should not be shocked, and that no sense of impropriety or guilt should follow any such conduct, otherwise the effect may be more harmful than beneficial. This, however, is largely a matter of individual judgment and mutual understanding. Two people who are in love with one another and who are mentally and emotionally compatible should not find much difficulty in adjusting the details of their sexual relationship."

"*There is one other question in relation to sexual disharmonies that I should like to ask you, doctor. Could a lack of proportion between the male and female organs become a source of sexual difficulties?*"

"Many people believe that genital disproportions are a frequent cause of sexual incompatibilities, yet in reality this is but rarely tne case. Only in exceptional instances does a lack of proportion lead to physical difficulties in intercourse or to sexual maladjustments. While it is possible, for instance, for the male organ to be so large as to actually cause pain and discomfort to the woman during coitus, particularly when the female genitals are insufficiently developed, this is a comparatively rare occurrence. Nor is the smallness of the size of the penis a serious or frequent source of sexual disharmonies. As a rule, any deficiency in size can be compensated for very well by a suitable sexual approach and technique. As for the vaginal canal, its tissues are elastic and distensible so that it will generally accommodate itself to the male organ. It does happen that when the vaginal walls are very much relaxed and distended, as, for instance, after several childbirths, there may be a lack of sufficient contact and a diminution in sexual stimulation and gratification. Even such a deficiency, however, can usually be adjusted through the adoption of a suitable posture during coitus, and variations in sexual technique. By making use of her vaginal muscles and learning to tighten and relax them from time to time during the sexual act, the woman can bring about a much closer contact of the genital organs and increase the erotic gratification."

GENITAL DISPROPORTION

"*In speaking of sexual disharmonies, you mentioned that abnormal sexual tendencies such as homosexuality may be one of the underlying causes. Do homosexuals ever wish to marry?*"

"First of all, homosexual inclinations are sometimes subconscious or latent, and they may not manifest themselves until some particular circumstances bring them to the surface. A man or a woman may marry without being fully aware of their sexual deviations. I recall one woman, for instance, who was married at eighteen, lived a fairly satisfactory married life for a number of years, gave birth to five children, and then, under peculiar circumstances, she became aware of a very strong attraction to members of her own sex, and finally became completely homosexual in her relations. Incidentally, her erotic responses in her homosexual relation proved to be rather intense, although with her husband she had been entirely anesthetic.

HOMOSEXUALITY AND MARRIAGE

"It may also happen that a man or a woman, conscious of an abnormal sexual tendency, will marry in the hope of conquering this inclination and of establishing a normal family life and home. The existing sexual aberration, however, rarely permits a satisfactory marital adjustment under such circumstances."

"*What is homosexuality due to? Is it the result of a physical abnormality?*"

"We must distinguish between homosexuality which is merely substitutive, that is where an individual resorts to homosexual practices because of a lack of opportunity for relations with members of the opposite sex, and homosexuality which is truly compulsive, where homosexual love is definitely preferred to the normal form of sex expression. True homosexuality, or inversion, as it is sometimes called, is in most instances due to some innate predisposition. All human beings possess a mixture of both feminine and masculine elements, and whether a man or a woman will become homosexual, heterosexual, or bisexual, that is, whether they will be attracted to members of their own sex, or of the opposite sex, or of both sexes, is largely, perhaps, a matter of the proportion of these elements in their make-up. Ellis refers to inversion as a 'congenital anomaly,' and he ascribes it in the main to an imperfect sexual differentiation and to a lack of hormonic balance. We have already noted that the sexuality of an individual is dependent to a large degree upon glandular secretions, and it is likely that the development of homosexual tendencies is due to some anomaly or variation in hormone production, although the psychiatrists generally prefer to ascribe sexual aberrations to psychological rather than to organic causes.

"At any rate, it is well to bear in mind that physically the homosexual may differ in no way from the normal individual. The idea that all male inverts have feminine characteristics and that female homosexuals always have a masculine appearance is quite erroneous. The majority of homosexual men and women have the appearance, characteristics, and physique of their own sex, and their peculiarity can be told only from the nature of their reactions and experiences. Whenever a definite inversion is suspected, marriage should certainly not be undertaken without careful deliberation and expert guidance."

"*We have taken a long time today, doctor, but I should like to ask you one question with reference to masturbation. You mentioned before that the fear of self-gratification may lead to certain sexual difficulties. In what specific manner can this result?"*

"I am glad you mentioned the subject of masturbation, for I had wanted to discuss it with you more fully at some time, and we may as well do so now. The fear of the consequences of masturbation, or auto-erotism, as it is sometimes called, is one of the most common sexual anxieties. As this form of self-gratification is a very widespread practice, for it has been encountered in every part of the world and it has been estimated that nearly 90% of men and a very high percentage of women resort to it at one time or another in their lives, the subject obviously constitutes an important sexual problem.

MASTURBATION AND ITS EFFECTS

"The significant fact about masturbation is that it is very generally looked upon as wicked, sinful, and abnormal, and as fraught with serious dangers both to body and mind. Although this attitude has apparently not decreased the extent of the practice to any degree, it has served to generate in the minds of those who resort to it feelings of guilt, of shame, of remorse and self-reproach, as well as actual fears and anxieties concerning the possible physical and mental consequences. As a result, most young people who seek release in self-gratification are constantly beset with mental conflicts and anxieties which may seriously affect their social as well as their sexual adjustments.

"Let me read to you, as an illustration, a paragraph from a letter which I received not so long ago from a young man:

> I am convinced that masturbation is an evil which has created havoc in my life. It has sapped my general vitality, it has distorted my sense of intellectual values, and the consciousness of it is a perpetual embarrassment in social contacts. It has now culminated in so complete a destruction of strength, of physical health, of all incentive and zest for living that suicide, hermitage or some such refuge often seems inevitable.

"This came from a young man of twenty-two who had been masturbating rather moderately for a number of years. A fairly thorough physical examination failed to disclose any evidence of organic trouble, either general or genital. In fact, the man was of fine physique and good intelligence. It soon became evident that his complaints were in no way due to any direct physical effects of his auto-erotic practices but primarily to the fear and anxiety which his preoccupation with the problem had brought about.

"Somewhat similarly, a woman who had not conceived after two years of marriage told me that she was convinced that her sterility was the direct result of masturbation during adolescence, and she was certain that she would remain permanently childless on account of it. There is, of course, absolutely no relation between sterility and masturbation, and, as a matter of fact, this woman conceived readily after a displacement of her uterus was corrected, yet for years the sense of guilt and fear had weighed heavily upon her and had affected both her social behavior and sexual reactions. 'You can hardly realize, doctor,' she told me later on, 'what a burden had been lifted off me when I learned that I was not a doomed person because of my youthful acts.' "

"*Could self-abuse, though, produce any actual disturbances of the sexual or reproductive functions?*"

"As far as the actual effects of masturbation are concerned, you are aware, perhaps, that the medical opinion on the subject has changed considerably during the last few decades. There was a time when practically every ailment of the body and mind, from acne to insanity, was attributed to indulgence in self-gratification. Today we realize that the dangers of this practice have been grossly exaggerated, and that there is little scientific basis for ascribing any dire results to auto-erotism. There is certainly no evidence that the moderate practice of masturbation, and by this I mean a frequency of about once or twice a week, in itself leads to any physical injury or bodily harm. In a recent able analysis of the question, Havelock Ellis comes to the conclusion that 'in the case of moderate masturbation in healthy, well-born individuals, no serious pernicious results necessarily follow.'

"It is true, however, that the continued practice of masturbation may result, as I have already mentioned, in various neurotic symptoms and manifestations. This is due, first, to the fact that the odium which is attached to auto-erotism makes the one who practices it feel depraved, vicious and fearful, so that inner struggles are set up which have a disturbing effect upon character and personality. Secondly, masturbation is at best but a very inadequate substitute for normal sex relations; it does not produce the complete physical and emotional release which follows sexual intercourse, and it often leaves one with a sense of frustration and dissatisfaction, of weakness and inferiority. The mental conflicts which thus arise are apt to be unfavorably reflected in the social and sexual behavior of the individual.

"I might also mention that when carried out at frequent intervals and over a long period of time, and masturbation readily lends itself to excesses, there is a possibility that local irritations and congestions of the genital organs may develop. A gradual weakening of sexual power, premature ejaculations, and even a loss of desire for normal sexual relations may eventually result. Such consequences, however, are rather rare and represent pathological instances. They do not apply to the average individual who resorts to the moderate practice of masturbation during youth and adolescence.

"We have been discussing all kinds of potential sexual disharmonies, but let me reassure you now that I do not anticipate any difficulties in your own case. From your histories and from the physical findings, I can see no reason at all why you should not make an entirely satisfactory and harmonious adjustment. I have spoken about incompatibilities at such length because I am convinced that ignorance and evasion lie at the base of many marital troubles, and that a frank attitude and adequate knowledge are the best preventive measures.

"Our discussion next time will probably be the last one, and I should like to devote it chiefly to certain aspects of the hygiene of marriage. However, I would suggest that before you come, you discuss between yourselves the subjects we have already considered and make a note of any particular point that may not be quite clear to you.

"As for books, the few I shall mention are in the main technical in character, but you may wish to have the names for future reference."

DICKINSON, R. L., M.D., and BEAM, LURA. "A Thousand Marriages." Williams & Wilkins Co. (1931).

A comprehensive and authoritative medical study of the sex problems of marriage.

DAVIS, KATHERINE B. "Factors in the Sex Life of 2200 Women." Harper & Brothers (1929).

A statistical analysis of a questionnaire on sex experiences submitted to a group of American women.

HAMILTON, G. V., M.D. "A Research in Marriage." Albert & Chas. Boni (1929).

A psychiatrist's revealing, analytical study of the social and sexual factors of 100 couples.

KOPP, MARIE E. "Birth Control in Practice." Robert M. McBride & Co. (1934).

An analysis of 10,000 case histories from the Birth Control Clinical Research Bureau.

STEKEL, WILHELM, M.D. "Impotence in the Male." Liveright Pub. Corp. (1927) (in two volumes).

A psychiatric study of sexual inadequacies of the male.

STEKEL, WILHELM, M.D. "Frigidity in Woman." Horace Liveright (1929) (in two volumes).

A psychoanalytical study of female frigidity.

ROBINSON, WM. J., M.D. "Sexual Impotence." Eugenics Publishing Co. (1933).

A practical outline of many sexual disorders in men and women.

HIRSCH, E. W., M.D. "The Power to Love." Alfred A. Knopf (1934).

A frank discussion of the physical and psychological aspects of the sexual function and its disturbances.

YARROS, RACHELLE S., M.D. "Modern Woman and Sex." The Vanguard Press (1933).

A keen, tolerant, and enlightened discussion of woman and marriage.

CHAPTER IX

HEALTH IN MARRIAGE

"This is to be our final session, and, as I mentioned last time, I should like to devote it in the main to a consideration of several specific problems of sex and reproduction which are directly related to health in marriage. We have, of course, already dealt with many aspects of marital health as we went along, but there are several pertinent matters which we have yet to consider, and which may well serve as a closing chapter to our discussions."

"*You suggested, doctor, that we should make a note of any particular points which we should like you to take up today. We have jotted down several questions concerning the planning of a family and sexual adjustments which seem to us to be of immediate importance at the outset of marriage. Perhaps you would like to hear them?*"

"Very well. Suppose we take up your questions, then, and proceed in our usual manner. It is quite likely, for that matter, that your notes may coincide with the topics which I myself had intended to discuss with you."

"*First about children—how soon after marriage would you advise a woman to plan her first pregnancy?*"

PLANNING THE FIRST PREGNANCY

"One can hardly be dogmatic on this subject. Circumstances and conditions of the individual couple—their ages, their physical status, their social and economic situation, their preferences and predilections—would naturally have to be taken into account. As a general rule, however, I should advise a couple to wait at least one year, and preferably two years, after marriage before planning a pregnancy. Upon marriage, a man and a woman, often enough with totally different backgrounds, personalities and habits, are somewhat suddenly brought together into intimate daily contact. They need time to adjust themselves to each other's temperaments and reactions, to build up their companionship and mutual interests, to strengthen and cement their attachment and affection; they need time to establish their home and their social life; they need time, above all, to prepare themselves economically and emotionally for the task of parenthood. Unless there are some special reasons to the contrary, it is preferable that the first year or two of marital life should be free from the many problems which accompany childbearing and child-rearing.

"Furthermore, even in normal and healthy women pregnancy may give rise to various physical and emotional indispositions—to nausea, vomiting, nervous irritability, undue sensitivity and so on. If these occur too soon after marriage, before the husband and the wife have had an opportunity to adjust themselves to each other and to their new mode of life, it may place too great a strain on their new relationship and may seriously mar their happiness and affection. Ordinarily it is not desirable that a conception should follow immediately after marriage, and it is best to avoid what Margaret Sanger calls 'premature parenthood.' The first pregnancy might well be postponed until the second or third year of marriage."

"*At approximately what age, doctor, is it best for a woman to have her first baby?*"

"In a very general way, I would say that a woman should preferably not have her first child before she is twenty or twenty-one years of age, and not much beyond her thirtieth year. While a girl becomes capable of conceiving any time after she begins to menstruate, the mere onset of menstruation is not a sign of biological readiness for reproduction. It generally takes several years for the processes of puberty to be completed, and child-bearing and child-rearing are certainly not advisable until a woman has reached her full physical and psychical development. The age at which biological maturity occurs varies to some degree with race, climate, nutrition, and other environmental factors, but it is generally agreed that in temperate zones a girl is not ready for reproduction until she is at least eighteen and preferably twenty or twenty-one years of age. Duncan places the age of a woman at which she may fulfill all the duties of maternity as between twenty to twenty-five. It is true that in certain Oriental countries marriages often take place at an extremely early age, and pregnancies sometimes occur soon after the onset of puberty. Such a procedure, however, appears to be biologically unsound, and for the more northern countries, at least, it would seem that a girl should not conceive, and perhaps even not marry, before she has reached the age of eighteen.

"On the other hand, while fertility lasts until past forty, and while with modern obstetric technique it is quite safe for a woman to give birth even to her first offspring at a rather advanced age, it is nevertheless both medically and socially desirable that a first pregnancy should not be postponed much beyond the age of thirty. After the middle thirties fertility normally tends to diminish, and the problems of a first pregnancy, of childbirth and child-rearing at this time are much more involved."

"*What would you consider a desirable number of children for a couple to have?*"

THE SIZE OF THE FAMILY

"So many individual factors enter into consideration that it is hardly possible to lay down specific recommendations in this respect. The health of the parents, particularly that of the mother, their ages, their social and economic status, and many other personal and environmental factors have to be taken into account. Grothjan, who has made many studies of population problems, has advocated a three-children family as the minimum, while the United States census report for 1930 showed the average size of the American family to be 3.81. Certainly most couples will want to have at least one and preferably two children, and few American families can under present conditions plan to have more than four. It is well that the first two babies should come fairly close together, with an interval of about two to two and a half years between births. This provides greater companionship for the children, and simplifies considerably the problems of their upbringing for the parents. As for later children, it is a matter for individual planning as to whether they should come in as close succession, or at longer intervals of several years between births."

"*If no preventive measures against conception were to be taken, how soon after marriage would a woman conceive?*"

"That would depend primarily upon the reproductive capacity, or fertility, of the particular couple. If both the husband and the wife are highly fertile, conception may occur the very first month. This, however, is not always the case, and as a rule several months, and sometimes even a year or more, may elapse before the first pregnancy ensues. It would seem from certain studies which have been made that when no contraceptives are employed, the first child is born, on an average, about seventeen months after marriage, which means that in the majority of instances conception occurs about seven to eight months after wedlock. In his book on *Human Sterility*, Meaker makes the following interesting statement on this subject:

> When one hundred human couples, young and apparently healthy, marry and have regular intercourse without contraception, the results are easy to predict. In a minority of cases pregnancy will occur immediately, the wife missing her first period. The majority of the wives will become pregnant after delays ranging from a month to a year. In some few cases a pregnancy will appear a year or more after marriage. Approximately ten of the couples will remain childless.

"This, of course, is but a statistical average, and while it may be possible to give such an average for a hundred couples there is no exact way of telling beforehand how soon after marriage a pregnancy may occur in any particular case."

"*If a pregnancy is to be avoided, then, contraceptive measures have to be employed from the very beginning?*"

"Yes, indeed. If for health, social, economic or any other reasons a pregnancy has to be prevented or postponed for a time, no reliance should be placed upon the chance that perhaps the woman will not conceive immediately. The very fact that conception may follow a single sexual relation indicates the need for the use of adequate contraceptive measures from the very first.

"It is also advisable to employ contraceptive precaution in order to avoid the recurrent fear and anxiety of an unwanted pregnancy. Such fears are apt to have a very baneful influence upon the marital adjustment of a couple. They lead to restraint and tension in the sexual relation, and may prevent a normal sex expression and response on the part of both the husband and the wife."

"*I remember you mentioned the fear of pregnancy as one of the causes of sexual disharmonies.*"

THE FEAR OF CONCEPTION

"Yes. We must frankly recognize that the fear of an undesired conception is a dominant factor in marital life today. With many women this fear becomes an actual phobia which mars every phase of their marriage. Time and again women have told me that because of the possibility of an unwanted conception, they have actually discouraged any tenderness and intimacies on the part of their husbands, and have made every effort to avoid sexual contact altogether. Let me read to you a few sentences from a letter which one woman sent me: 'Ever since we were married we were in constant fear and anxiety, and all the beauty and joy of our love was lost. Our intimate life became a source of continuous worry to me, and I often dreaded it. I almost came to look with loathing upon the sexual relation.'

"Such instances of frustrated and distorted sex lives are not at all rare. It is obvious that a healthy marriage can hardly exist under such strains. Neither affection nor love can long survive the effects of constant fear and anxiety."

"*If a woman uses contraceptive measures for any length of time, however, will it affect her chances of having children later on?*"

CONTRACEPTION AND STERILITY

"The statement is sometimes made that the use of contraceptive precautions may eventually lead to sterility, yet I know of no authoritative evidence to this effect. In his study of human sterility, Meaker explicitly states that there is no reason to suppose that sterility will follow the use of approved birth control measures, and many other authorities have expressed similar opinions. During the course of my work I have had occasion to observe many thousands of women who had employed prescribed contraceptive measures for varying lengths of time, sometimes for many years, and who, when they wished to become pregnant, readily conceived upon discontinuing the contraceptive precautions. In a large number of these 'planned pregnancy' cases, I had made particular note of the time that elapsed between the abandonment of preventive measures and the onset of pregnancy, and in tabulating 250 records recently, I noted that 215 of the women conceived within six months, the majority of them, in fact, becoming pregnant during the first or second month after ceasing to employ contraceptive precautions; 28 more conceived within a year; and seven at various intervals later on. These findings would indicate that, at least as far as this group of women is concerned, contraceptive measures did not cause any diminution in reproductive capacity, for the fertility of these women was certainly as high as that of women who might never have used any measures for the prevention of conception.

"The fact, also, that many women become pregnant very readily when, either through neglect or for some other reason, they omit the use of preventive measures on but a single or a few occasions, clearly indicates that the resort to contraception does not affect adversely the fertility of a woman. Of course, as we have already seen, some ten per cent of married couples who never use contraceptives are generally found to be sterile, and there is no reason at all to assume that this percentage is in any way increased by the use of birth control methods."

"*Can the use of contraceptives lead to any injurious effect?*"

IS BIRTH CONTROL HARMFUL?

"The contraceptive methods which are currently prescribed in clinics and by physicians have been found to be entirely harmless. I have had a rather extensive experience in this field and I have seen no ill effects from the use of modern contraceptive measures. There are, of course, methods which may be harmful; the introduction of appliances into the uterus, the prolonged practice of coitus interruptus, the use of strong chemicals—these may possibly give rise to local congestions or inflammations, but this does not apply to the approved methods of contraception."

"*Now, with reference to the sex relation in marriage, doctor—how often should married people have intercourse?*"

"The question of the frequency of intercourse in marriage has long been a subject of inquiry and discussion, and, as a matter of fact, it is one of the points I had intended to consider with you today. Many attempts have been made to lay down rules and regulations concerning the frequency of marital relations. Mahomet, for instance, in the Koran, prescribed a frequency of once a week, but it seems that this applied only to the woman, and as the Mohammedan was permitted more than one wife, the man was apparently not bound by these limitations. In the Hebrew Talmud a frequency varying from once a week to once a day is advised, depending upon the general state of health and occupation of the husband. The best known advice, perhaps, is that of Luther, who is said to have stated that 'twice a week does harm neither to her nor to me,' a suggestion which coincides very well with modern medical opinion.

THE FREQUENCY OF INTERCOURSE

"Quite recently a number of statistical studies have been made with reference to the actual frequency of intercourse in marriage. Katherine Davis found that of 1000 married women, over 70% had sexual relations from once to several times a week, 20% less than once weekly, and about 10% daily or oftener. In Dickinson's study of some 500 couples, 60% had relations one to three times a week, 24% less than once weekly, and 16% daily or more often. In an analysis of 10,000 records from the Birth Control Clinical Research Bureau in New York, Kopp found that 85% of the couples had relations from one to three times a week, and only 4% daily or oftener. A survey of the histories of 3000 women which I made more recently also showed the average frequency to be between two and three times a week. It is well to remember, however, that these figures apply to couples who had been married for some time. In the early months of marriage the frequency is naturally greater, and probably approximates the higher figures of once a day or so, but gradually it diminishes to the average stated.

"It is apparent that the frequency of intercourse cannot be prescribed dogmatically, nor is it advisable to institute any routine regularity. Individual sexual capacity and desire, as well as many transitory conditions and circumstances will naturally influence the sexual relation in marriage. Some men and women are endowed with a very strong sexual drive, while others have a low degree of desire and are comparatively frigid. Between these two extremes there are many gradations and variations in the intensity of the sexual impulse and capacity.

The sexual desire is, furthermore, subject to many temporary fluctuations. Illness, insufficient diet, overwork, emotional strain, will tend to diminish the sexual urge, while rest, a rich diet, erotic stimuli and other factors may temporarily serve to heighten it considerably. All these factors will obviously affect the frequency of intercourse.

"It seems to me that the best rule to follow is to permit one's natural desire and capacity to control the frequency of the relations, but it is well not to stimulate and excite desire artificially, or to strain one's capacity to its limit. The physical reaction which follows coitus may perhaps serve as a guide in this respect. If one feels tired and exhausted after intercourse or on the following day, a diminution of sexual activity may be advisable. When the coital act, however, is succeeded by a sense of relaxation and ease without any particular feeling of fatigue, the sexual relations are probably not excessive, and their frequency should then depend entirely upon a mutually satisfactory adjustment of the couple."

"*But if the husband and wife happen to differ in the degree of their sexual desire, doctor, how should they regulate their sex life and the frequency of their relations?*"

FREQUENCY AND SEXUAL COMPATIBILITY

"You have touched upon one of the most pertinent problems in sex adjustment. Marked differences in the sexual urge of the husband and the wife may indeed become a source of sexual difficulties and disharmonies, and it may require a great deal of understanding and sympathy to make a satisfactory adaptation. There are several considerations, however, which should be taken into account in attempting to meet this particular problem. It must be remembered that in the matter of sexual activity, it is the male who is generally the initiator and who takes the more aggressive role. The female is biologically the more passive, and this passivity is constantly being reinforced in our social life by training, education and convention. Ordinarily, therefore, and certainly at the beginning of marriage, the wife can hardly be expected to take the initiative in the sexual approach, and the frequency of the relation will to a large degree be controlled by the desires of the husband. As a matter of fact, the sexual impulses of a woman often remain latent or dormant at first, and she may hardly even be aware of the extent of her sexual needs and capacities at marriage. Her erotic nature may awaken and develop only after the marital relations have been established for some time, and consequently her sexual desires cannot be taken as a guide for the frequency of intercourse at first. There is another reason, of course, why the frequency of marital relations will depend largely upon the male. While the woman is able to enter into, or rather submit to, sexual union without any desire at all, the male cannot take part in the sex act unless he has been erotically aroused and has been able to attain an erection. When he lacks desire or is sexually fatigued at the time, it may not be possible for him to have relations, so that of necessity it will be the husband's capacity which will determine the frequency of intercourse in marriage.

"At the same time, however, the sexual frequency should not be entirely a matter of the husband's choice, but should be adjusted to the responsiveness of the wife and to her acceptability of his approaches. The husband should certainly not force his wife when she has absolutely no wish for intercourse, and he should make every effort to choose a time when she is more apt to derive gratification from the union. Nor is it necessary that the husband should always be the initiator of the sexual embrace. It is conducive to much greater satisfaction in marriage if every now and then the wife, too, takes the first step in the sexual approach. A man and a woman who are compatible in other respects, who have a deep affection and sympathy for each other, and who are sexually normal, will, generally speaking, find little difficulty in adjusting the time and frequency of their relations to their mutual harmony and satisfaction."

"*Are a woman's sexual desires greater at certain times than at others?*"

THE RHYTHM OF SEXUAL DESIRE

"In nature sexual activity is usually subject to a certain periodicity. Among female animals, for instance, the sexual impulse manifests itself only periodically—once a year, every six months, every month or oftener, depending upon the particular species, and it is only at these times that copulation takes place. It has been claimed that a similar seasonal rhythm existed among the early humans, and that sexual relations took place then only at certain periods of the year—as during the Spring and Autumn festivals, but this is still an unsettled point. At the present time, certainly, no such periodic cycle of sexual desire can be observed in the human species, except, perhaps, for the general heightening and intensification of bodily activities at certain seasons of the year.

"There is, however, some evidence of the existence of a monthly rhythm in the intensity of the sexual urge of woman. The studies of Havelock Ellis, Marie Stopes, Katherine Davis and others seem to indicate that there is a periodic rising and waning of sexual desire during the menstrual month. The erotic impulses are apparently increased either a few days before the onset of the menstrual flow or, more frequently and more definitely, toward the end of the menses and during the few subsequent days, although the latter rise may partly be due to the abstinence which is usually maintained during the menstrual week. Stopes claims to have observed also a second rise of sexual desire during the middle of the menstrual month. There are apparently individual differences in this cycle of desire, and the woman can best determine for herself her own particular rhythm. It is advisable, however, to allow these periods of increased sexual interest on the part of the wife to regulate in some degree the time and the frequency of the sexual relations in marriage."

"*You spoke at one time of the fact that during certain days of the month a woman is more apt to conceive than at others. Is there any relation between this rhythm of fertility and the rhythm of sexual desire?*"

SEXUAL DESIRE AND FERTILITY

"In animal life there is a very definite relationship between these two cycles. As a matter of fact, the height of sexual desire and the height of fertility almost coincide. The greatest sexual activity of the female animal manifests itself during the period of rutting or 'heat,' and this corresponds to the period when the eggs are ripening and are being discharged, and consequently to the time when the animal is most likely to conceive. As a result, copulation among lower species occurs at a period when it is most apt to be fruitful. Among the higher animals, such as the primates, sexual union can occur at any time, but there is also a very definite period during the month when sexual desire and sexual activity are at their highest, and this period, too, corresponds to the time of ovulation and consequently of greatest fertility.

"In the human female, however, the relation between the rhythm of fertility and the rhythm of sexual desire is not so apparent. As I mentioned, the increase of the sexual desire of the woman is more apt to occur near the menstrual period, either just before or just after, but at these times the woman is presumably least fertile. The second wave of increased desire at about the middle of the menstrual month, which Marie Stopes claims to have observed, would coincide more nearly with the period of greatest fertility in the woman, but these findings have not been substantiated by other investigators. Perhaps the fact that a woman may desire to have sex relations at times when conception is not likely to result is an indication that for human beings, at least, sexual activity has a specific social and biological value in addition to its reproductive purpose. It has been suggested, in fact, that the readiness of the female to accept the male at any time is responsible to some degree for the development of mating and the family among the primates."

"*Is the male also subject to a rhythm of sexual desire?*"

"In some species of animals there is a definite periodicity of desire in the male corresponding to that of the female. In fact, during certain periods of the year the male does not produce any sperm cells at all, and his sexual activities are dormant. In the higher species, however, the male, unlike the female, produces his sex cells continually during the year, and is therefore capable of impregnating the female at any time. His sexual desires and activities are correspondingly not subject to any seasonal or periodic variations. In man no inherent sexual cycle has been demonstrated, as far as I know. He is, of course, also subject to a certain ebb and flow in his sexual drive, but this is apparently due to environmental or general bodily changes rather than to any specific physiological rhythm."

"*What about sexual relations during the menstrual period? Will intercourse at this time be harmful?*"

"There is a considerable divergence of opinion concerning the advisability of intercourse during the menstrual period. Formerly a woman was almost universally regarded as 'tabu' during her menses, and sexual relations at this time were strictly forbidden. Among many primitive tribes, the woman is even today isolated in a special hut during the days of her menstrual flow, and any article of clothing or food that she comes in contact with is considered contaminated and 'unclean.' The Bible, too, prescribed seclusion for the menstruating woman, and strictly prohibited any sexual contact with her 'as long as she is impure by her uncleanness.' Intercourse during the menstrual period has everywhere been considered as both dangerous and sinful.

SEXUAL RELATIONS DURING MENSTRUATION

"Today we realize, of course, that there is no particular 'impurity' about the woman during her menses. It is true that some investigators claim to have found certain toxic substances in the secretions of menstruating women, but whether these findings are substantiated or not, the fear of actual contagious emanations from the menstrual discharges is now generally looked upon as merely a survival of primitive superstition. In civilized communities the tabus concerning social contact with women during their menstruation have practically disappeared, and many have even come to look upon sexual relations at this time as neither harmful nor objectionable. In this respect, however, it is well to bear in mind that during the days of the menses the sexual organs of the woman are in a state of considerable congestion, and that intercourse at this time may lead to an increase of the menstrual flow and to an aggravation of the discomforts which usually accompany this period. The congestion of the organs also makes them more liable to injury and infection, for it is known that existing infections of the female genital tract are usually aggravated during the menstrual period. Furthermore, if a protective sheath is not used, intercourse during the menses is occasionally followed by a local irritation of the male genitals due perhaps to the entry of menstrual secretions into the male urethra.

"Aside, however, from these medical considerations, it would seem to me that sexual relations are esthetically undesirable during the days of the active flow. Nor is the 'unwell' woman likely to have much sexual desire at this time. Briffault, in fact, in his book on *The Mothers,* makes the interesting suggestion that the menstrual tabus were originally instituted by the women themselves, and that they correspond to the instinctive refusal of female animals to accept the male whenever they are not in a condition for copulation. There may be exceptions, of course, and some women may indeed manifest a very strong sexual desire during their menses, or there may be other circumstances which may make sexual relations advisable or necessary at this time, but this is a matter for individual consideration and decision. As a general rule, I would say, that while intercourse during the menses may not be dangerous, it is best on physiological as well as esthetic grounds to abstain from sexual contact and even from sexual stimulation during the days of active menstrual flow."

"*When a woman becomes pregnant, do the sexual relations have to cease entirely, or may they be continued for any part of this period?*"

SEXUAL RELATIONS DURING PREGNANCY

"The consensus of medical opinion is that if a pregnancy runs a normal course, intercourse may continue until about the last eight or six weeks before the expected childbirth. Towards the end of pregnancy sexual relations are contraindicated because of the possibility of bringing on labor prematurely, and because of the chance of carrying bacteria into the female genital tract which may later cause serious infections. Coitus should therefore be entirely avoided during the last six or eight weeks.

"Among mammals generally, as soon as the female conceives she will no longer accept the male, and her sexual activity ceases entirely during the periods of pregnancy and suckling. Similarly, sexual relations are tabu all through pregnancy and even during lactation among many primitive peoples. Briffault suggests that this tabu, as in the case of menstruation, was originally initiated by the woman, and that the primitive human female merely followed biological precedent in imposing a sexual prohibition upon the male during a period when her own sexual instincts were more or less quiescent. Gradually these restrictions assumed a different interpretation, and came to be regarded with superstitious awe and fear. Whatever their origin, however, these tabus have long since lost their significance and force in civilized societies, and sexual relations during pregnancy are no longer regarded as either dreadful or sinful. During the entire pregnancy, however, the relations should be moderated in frequency and in character. Because of the anatomical changes at this time, the vagina becomes shorter and shallower, and it is necessary to avoid too deep penetration so as not to cause any pressure upon the uterus. Nor should any undue weight be placed upon the woman during this period, and this can best be obviated by resorting to the side position for coitus. This posture is probably the most convenient and comfortable for the childbearing woman."

"*How soon after childbirth may relations be resumed?*"

SEXUAL RELATIONS AFTER CHILDBIRTH

"Ordinarily it is advisable that there should be no sexual contact for about six weeks following delivery. Among primitive peoples the sexual tabus of pregnancy are usually extended to the period of lactation, and sexual relations are prohibited during the entire time that the mother is nursing her baby. As this period frequently lasts for two and three years, and even longer, it is evident that there is a long span of abstinence following conception. The Biblical injunctions are much less severe in this regard. According to the Mosaic laws, a woman is considered 'unclean' for forty-one days following childbirth, if the child is a son, and for eighty days, if the offspring is a girl. Why such a distinction should have been made between the birth of a son and a daughter does not seem quite clear, at least not from any physiological standpoint, nevertheless the prescribed period of abstinence of about six weeks corresponds closely to present medical opinion on the subject. As I have already mentioned, the generative organs of a woman undergo profound changes during childbearing and delivery, and it takes from five to six weeks after childbirth before they return to their normal condition. It is usually advisable that sexual relations should not be resumed during this period in order not to hinder the natural processes of involution."

"*When a woman's menstrual periods cease entirely, I mean when she reaches her 'change of life,' does she also lose her sexual desire?*"

SEXUAL IMPULSE AFTER MENOPAUSE

"Not at all. The cessation of a woman's reproductive capacities does not involve the extinction of her sexual instincts. With advancing years the sexual urge normally tends to diminish, but a woman may continue to have a strong sexual urge for ten, fifteen and even more years after she has reached her menopause. As a matter of fact, a large number of women have spoken to me of an intensification of their erotic impulses during the years of their menopause and for a considerable time thereafter.

As a rule women can continue a moderately satisfactory sex life until well after the age of sixty."

"*How does age affect the man's sexual capacity?*"

"The man, too, gradually loses his sexual abilities with advancing age, although both his reproductive capacities and his sexual impulses may last longer than in the woman. I have already mentioned that it is not infrequent for a man of seventy to become a father, and I know of men who have continued a moderate sex life until past eighty. Of course, as a man grows older the strength of his desire and the frequency of his relations are correspondingly diminished."

"*There is one other question I should like to ask you, doctor, although it may not come directly within the field of our present discussion. Is sexual continence harmful? Is the repression of the sexual urge apt to lead to any injurious effects?*"

SEXUAL CONTINENCE

"There is no single problem in the entire field of sexual physiology about which there is greater controversy and divergence of opinion than about that of continence. Formerly, it is true, it was very generally held that even prolonged repression of the sexual instinct was altogether harmless. Some thirty years ago, for instance, The American Medical Association adopted a resolution which read that "continence is not incompatible with health." At about the same time, Ludwig Jacobsohn, a Russian physician, sent a questionnaire on the subject to the most eminent German and Russian physicians of the time, and, with but very few exceptions, they all stated that sexual abstinence would not produce any injurious effect. From the nature of the replies, however, it would seem that many of the opinions expressed were based upon what Havelock Ellis calls 'an illegitimate mingling of moral and physiological considerations,' and were influenced more by religious, moral and ethical concepts than by actual biological data. During the last two decades, particularly since the advent of Freudian psychology, the medical viewpoint on the subject of continence has changed considerably, and many physicians now believe that continued abstinence may lead to physical and mental ill-health and perhaps also to various sexual aberrations. At any rate, today one can find thoughtful and candid opinions on both sides of the question. The fact is, perhaps, that neither side is altogether convincing, for we do not possess as yet sufficiently accurate scientific knowledge upon which to base any generalizations concerning the ultimate effects of sexual abstinence.

"As to whether sexual continence might prove harmful in a particular case, that is a question for individual consideration. A number of factors would have to be taken into account. Age, for instance, is of paramount importance. Sexual continence up to the time of complete physical and emotional maturity is not only harmless, but may even be definitely beneficial. As sexual maturity is generally not reached until eighteen or twenty, continence until that age is certainly without injurious effects. Thereafter, the problem differs in each case, depending upon many physical, psychic and emotional factors, upon the strength of the sexual impulse, the type of environmental stimuli, and so on. Men and women with a strong libido, or those subjected to frequent erotic stimulation, may be considerably more affected by continence than those who possess a low degree of sexual desire or lead a more cloistered life. Freud remarks that it is a serious injustice that our standards of sexual life are the same for all persons, because while they may be easy for some, they involve most difficult psychic sacrifices for others. In my own work I have encountered a great many men and women who showed no evident injurious effects from postponing sexual activity until a comparatively late age, but I have also seen many people, who, at a much earlier age, were greatly troubled and affected by their sexual repressions. 'The practice of continued sexual abstinence,' says Ira Wile, 'may strengthen or destroy individuals,' and whether it will work one way or another in any particular instance is a matter for individual consideration.

"I might also point out in this connection that the complete suppression of the sexual instinct is in reality not very frequent. It is rarely possible to dam up entirely the flow of the sexual urge, and though abstinence, that is the avoidance of sexual intercourse, may be maintained, there are other ways in which the sexual impulse liberates itself. Involuntary nocturnal emissions, masturbations, physical intimacies which lead to a release of sexual tension—these are some of the forms of sex expression which often serve as substitutes for sexual intercourse both for the adolescent and the adult. These practices, however, offer but a temporary form of relief, and cannot be regarded as an adequate substitution for normal sexual relations."

"*What is your opinion about the advisability of remaining continent until marriage?*"

"The moderate exercise of the sexual function, once maturity has been reached, undoubtedly contributes to the physical and mental balance of a man or a woman, and from a physiological point of view, therefore, it would be desirable that sexual relations should be established soon after the completion of sexual development. In those countries where marriages take place at an early age, sexual activity commences soon after maturity. In our own social life, however, early sexual unions are usually not feasible. On the one hand, the social and economic conditions make early marriages impractical, and on the other, our moral, ethical, religious and legal standards prohibit sexual relations outside of wedlock. Thus a serious problem is created concerning one's sexual behavior during the interval between the age of maturity and the age of marriage, a problem to which no socially sanctioned solution has as yet been found. Some continue to maintain that premarital chastity is socially and morally necessary and should be preserved at all costs. Abstinence until marriage, they say, is not only desirable on religious or ethical grounds, but it is also beneficial because it strengthens will and character and contributes to personal development and achievement. Others advocate a return to early marriage and see the solution to the sexual problem in the 'companionate' or some other form of early sexual alliance. And there are not a few at present who favor the abandonment of sexual restrictions, and who hold that sex relations of adults should be their own private affair and not be subject to social or religious control.

"In this respect, however, it is well to bear in mind that the sexual relation is not a purely individual matter. It involves the rights and privileges of another person, it carries with it the possibility of a conception, the chance of acquiring and transmitting a venereal infection, and many other social implications. These are the reasons, perhaps, why a certain degree of social control over sex activity is to be found in nearly every form of human organization. Certainly as long as our present social system and moral codes prevail, complete freedom of sex expression is hardly feasible. The violation of accepted social, moral and ethical standards, particularly if it is done furtively and secretively, may prove more disturbing and disastrous to personality and emotional balance than the conscious repression of the sexual impulses. I have often come across much suffering and mental anguish among young people, especially perhaps among young women, who, while still adhering to the existing social values, were led into casual sexual experimentation and the abandonment of their own moral principles.

"We must, of course, accept the obvious fact that the standards of sexual behavior are not the same for the man and the woman. As long as our social system and moral codes remain what they are, it is the woman who will bear the greatest burden of any premarital sex experiences. Chastity and virginity are still considered essential qualifications for marriage. Among certain peoples, it is true, virginity is not valued so highly, and the girl who has already borne a child is considered a much more desirable bride than one who has never yet been pregnant, but such a refreshing biological attitude does not obtain in the more civilized communities. Virtue in a girl is still regarded by most people as a necessary prerequisite for marriage. Clearly, then, it is the woman who has most at stake socially when she decides to enter her sex life before marriage, and she should carefully consider the nature and possible consequences of the act.

"Then there is also, of course, the possibility of a conception. Through carelessness, or the inefficiency of contraceptive measures employed, a pregnancy may occur during the experimental period. It is difficult enough when a married woman conceives unwillingly or accidentally, but it is a much more serious problem when a pregnancy occurs before marriage.

"The problem for the man is much less acute. Men have generally felt rather free to experiment sexually, and this has almost become an accepted part of our moral code. Nevertheless this type of sexual freedom hardly offers an adequate solution to the insistent problem of sex expression. Transient and indiscriminate relations are neither desirable nor safe; they are fraught with many dangers, not only to the body but to personality, character and morale as well. In civilized life we can no longer regard the sexual impulse merely as a biological urge which requires satisfaction. The sexual union is not only a physical contact, it is a psychological and emotional relationship as well. Sex is not merely biology. It is the cultural aspect of sex life which brings the greatest joy and satisfaction to human relations.

"In the final analysis, the question of continence is not so much one of physiology as one of social and moral values. A satisfactory solution will be reached only when our social system is so re-organized that the lag between physiological maturity and economic security is eliminated, and when our moral codes are so reformed that greater personal freedom in sex life is generally accepted. Perhaps eventually an officially and legally sanctioned form of marriage for young people will be developed which will not imply permanence or involve full economic responsibility at the very beginning, and which will be subject to comparatively easy dissolution. We might call it a Junior Marriage. This suggestion is somewhat similar to that of the 'companionate' marriage, so ably advocated by Judge Lindsey, except that I should place more emphasis upon the economic independence of the two during the term of their union, for obviously it is the economic factor which is the greatest deterrent to early marriage. At the expiration of a specified length of time, or at the occurrence of a pregnancy, this union would automatically assume all the aspects of our present form of marriage with full economic responsibility. This might, of course, take place at any previous time, if the couple so desire. Such a relationship among young people, if socially accepted, would add dignity, stability and self-respect to the otherwise furtive associations which are so often resorted to now. This, however, is still a matter for the future. For the present, the sexual conduct of men and women will be determined by their own particular circumstances, by their own ethical and esthetic standards, and by their readiness to abide by or revolt against the prevailing forms of social control. For one thing, however, I should personally speak out strongly against any form of sexual promiscuity. Considerable clinical experience and contact with young people has impressed me with the fact that indiscriminate sexual relations endanger the wholesomeness and balance of one's personal and social life. In spite of our changing values, it seems to me that a lasting union of one man with one woman is still the most ideal form of human sex relationship."

"*What would you consider a happy or ideal marriage?*"

"An ideal marriage, I would say, is one that meets most adequately the essential objects of the marital union. If you will recall I mentioned during our very first session that I consider the main purposes of marriage to be companionship, sexual intimacy and the establishment of a family. In other words, marriage is based upon the instinct for mating or living together, upon the sexual impulse and upon the desire for the begetting of offspring, and an ideal union is one that fulfills most effectively these several requirements.

IDEAL MARRIAGE

"Obviously, a true friendship and companionship can be present only where there is a compatibility of intellect, of temperament, of interests, of tastes, and above all a mutual affection and attraction. Love is, in fact, one of the essential elements in any marriage. 'I would just as soon attempt to bind two stones together without cement,' said John Haynes Holmes once, 'as to bind two lives together without love.' There is some tendency nowadays, it is true, to look upon romantic love as a mere survival of a sentimental era, yet even so realistic a philosopher as Bertrand Russell maintains that there is something of inestimable value in the relations of a man and a woman who love each other with passion, imagination and tenderness, and he adds that to be ignorant of this love 'is a great misfortune to any human being.' Indeed, ideal marriage is hardly possible without such mutual love and affection.

"The importance of a satisfactory sexual adjustment to happiness in marriage we have already discussed on several occasions. Conjugal affection should have a strong element of passion mixed with it. Havelock Ellis defines love as 'a synthesis of lust and friendship,' and both of these are necessary to the establishment of a happy mating. Intelligent sex education during youth and adolescence, an adequate premarital preparation, and the cultivation of an art of sexual love are valuable aids toward marital harmony.

"Lastly, the marriage must eventually grow into a family, and the mates become parents. 'The fullness of love cannot come without children,' says Will Durant, and he stresses the fact that marriage was designed not as much to unite mate with mate as to unite parents with children. While a childless marriage may be quite happy, it is the coming of offspring that brings complete fulfillment to a marriage. This implies, of course, physical and eugenic fitness for procreation on the part of both the husband and the wife.

"There is one other element in marriage that I can hardly refrain from mentioning, although it does not come directly within the scope of our discussions. I have reference to the importance of social and economic security to happiness in marriage. Again and again I come across marital dissensions, discords and maladjustments which are caused not by a lack of affection, by sexual incompatibility or reproductive incapacity, but by a lack of the necessities of life, by poverty, destitution and economic insecurity. One of the severest indictments of our present social system is the very fact that so many young people ready to be married must postpone their union from year to year because of economic uncertainty, and that so many healthy and sound couples, anxious and willing to beget offspring must continually postpone childbearing because they cannot afford the luxury of a child. Under such circumstances it is obviously difficult to realize happiness in wedlock. Perhaps our changing social order will eventually make also for more satisfactory and happy marriages.

"Our story is at an end, but your marriage journey is only at its start. During our many sessions, we have charted the basic problems of the marital relation in the light of our present-day biological knowledge and social attitudes. 'Married travellers,' says Balzac, 'are in need of a pilot and a compass.' Let us hope that our discussions will have served at least to point out the direction toward a happy union and to guide you along the road to an ideal marriage."

BIBLIOGRAPHY

This bibliography includes the books already listed after individual chapters, as well as others which have been mentioned in this volume or which have served as reference works in its preparation.

ACTON, WILLIAM, M.D. "The Functions and Disorders of the Reproductive Organs." Lindsay & Blakiston (1875)

ALLEN, EDGAR (*Editor*). "Sex and Internal Secretions." Williams & Wilkins Co. (1932)

APTEKAR, HERBERT. "Anjea." Wm. Godwin, Inc. (1931)

BALZAC, HONORÉ DE. "The Physiology of Marriage." Liveright, Inc. (1932)

BLACKER, C. P., M. D. "Birth Control and the State." E. P. Dutton & Co. (1926)

BLACKER, C. P., M.D. "The Chances of Morbid Inheritance." William Wood and Co. (1934)

BLOCH, IWAN. "The Sexual Life of Our Time." Allied Book Co. (1908)

BRIFFAULT, ROBERT. "The Mothers." (Three volumes.) The Macmillan Co. (1927)

BROMLEY, DOROTHY DUNBAR. "Birth Control, Its Use and Misuse." Harper & Brothers (1934)

BURTON-OPITZ, RUSSELL, M.D. "Physiology." W. B. Saunders Co. (1926)

BUTTERFIELD, OLIVER M. "Marriage." Privately Printed, LaVerne, Calif. (1929)

CALVERTON, V. E., and SCHMALHAUSEN, S. D. (*Editors*). "Sex and Civilization." The Macaulay Company (1929)

CAPELLMANN, CARL, M.D., and BERGMANN, W., M.D. "Pastoral Medizin." Bonifacius Druckerei (1923)

COUCKE, VALÈRE J. and WALSH, JAMES J., M.D. "The Sterile Period in Family Life." Joseph F. Wagner, Inc. (1932)

CRAWLEY, ERNEST. "The Mystic Rose." (Two volumes.) Boni & Liveright (1927). (New Edition by Besterman, Theodore)

DARWIN, LEONARD MAJOR. "What Is Eugenics?" Galton Publishing Co. (1929)

DAVIS, KATHERINE B. "Factors in the Sex Life of Twenty-Two Hundred Women." Harper & Brothers (1929)

DICKINSON, ROBERT L., M.D. "Human Sex Anatomy." Williams & Wilkins Co. (1933)

DICKINSON, ROBERT L., M.D. "The Control of Conception." (Second Edition) Williams & Wilkins Co. (1938)

DICKINSON, ROBERT L., M.D., and BEAM, LURA. "A Thousand Marriages." Williams & Wilkins Co. (1931)

DUNCAN, J. MATTHEWS, M.D. "Fecundity, Fertility, Sterility and Allied Topics." Edinburgh (1866)

DURANT, WILL. "The Mansions of Philosophy." Simon and Schuster (1929)

ELLIS, HAVELOCK. "Studies in the Psychology of Sex." (Seven volumes.) F. A. Davis Company (1925)

ELLIS, HAVELOCK. "The Psychology of Sex." Long & Smith (1933)

Eugenics, Committee of Publication. "A Decade of Progress in Eugenics." Williams & Wilkins Co. (1934)

EVERETT, MILLARD SPENCER. "The Hygiene of Marriage." Vanguard Press (1932)

EXNER, M. J., M.D. "The Sexual Side of Marriage." W. W. Norton & Company (1932)

FIELDING, MICHAEL, M.D. "Parenthood." Vanguard Press (1935)

FOREL, AUGUST, M.D. "The Sexual Question." Physicians and Surgeons Book Company (1931)

FRANK, ROBERT T., M.D. "The Female Sex Hormone." Bailliere, Tindall & Cox, London

FREUD, SIGMUND. "Three Contributions to the Theory of Sex." Nervous and Mental Disease Publishing Co. (1926)

FREUD, SIGMUND. "Totem and Taboo." Moffat, Yard & Co. (1918)

GENSS, A., M.D. "The Problem of Abortion." (In Russian) Moscow (1929)

GOSNEY, E. S. and POPENOE, PAUL. "Sterilization for Human Betterment." The Macmillan Company (1929)

GOURMONT, RÉMY DE. "The Natural Philosophy of Love." Rarity Press (1931)

GRAY, HENRY, M.D. "Anatomy of the Human Body." Lea and Febiger (1930)

GROVES, ERNEST R. "Marriage." Henry Holt and Company (1933)

GUCHTENEERE, RAOUL DE, M.D. "Judgment on Birth Control." The Macmillan Company (1931)

GUTTMACHER, ALAN FRANK, M.D. "Life in the Making." Viking Press (1933)

GUYON, RENÉ. "The Ethics of Sexual Acts." Alfred A. Knopf (1934)

GUYOT, JULES. "A Ritual for Married Lovers." Waverly Press, Inc. (1931)

HAIRE, NORMAN, M.D. "Hymen, or The Future of Marriage." E. P. Dutton & Co. (1928)

HAIRE, NORMAN, M.D. (*Editor*). "Some More Medical Views on Birth Control." E. P. Dutton & Co. (1928)

HAIRE, NORMAN, M.D. (*Editor*). "Sexual Reform Congress." Kegan-Paul, Trench, Trübner & Co., London (1930)

HALDANE, J. B. S. "Daedalus, or Science and The Future." E. P. Dutton & Co. (1924)

HAMILTON, G. V., M.D. "A Research in Marriage." Albert & Charles Boni (1929)

HARTMAN, CARL G. "Ovulation and the Transport and Viability of Ova and Sperm in the Female Genital Tract." *In* Sex and Internal Secretions. Williams & Wilkins Co. (1932)

HIMES, NORMAN E. "A Medical History of Contraception." Williams & Wilkins Co. (1936)

HIMES, NORMAN E. AND STONE, ABRAHAM, M.D. "Practical Birth Control Methods." Modern Age Books, Inc. (1938)

HIRSCH, EDWIN, W., M.D. "The Power to Love." A. A. Knopf (1934)

HIRSCHFELD, MAGNUS, M.D., and BOHM, EWALD. "Sexual Erziehung." Universitas, Berlin (1930)

HODANN, MAX, M.D. "Geschlecht und Liebe." Givelfenverlag, Berlin (1929)

HOLMES, J. S. "The Eugenic Predicament." Harcourt, Brace & Co. (1933)

HOLMES, JOHN HAYNES. "Marriage and Happiness." The Community Church (1930)

HUHNER, MAX, M.D. "Sterility in the Male and Female." Rebman (1913)

HUHNER, MAX, M.D. "Disorders of the Sexual Function in the Male and Female." F. A. Davis Co. (1920)

HUTTON, ISABEL EMSLEE, M.D. "The Sex Technique in Marriage." Emerson Books (1933)

JACOBSOHN, LUDWIG, M.D. "Sexual Problems." (In Russian) Leningrad (1928)

JARCHO, JULIUS, M.D. "Postures and Practices During Labor among Primitive Peoples." Paul B. Hoeber, Inc. (1934)

JENNINGS, H. S. "The Biological Basis of Human Nature." W. W. Norton & Co. (1930)

KAMMERER, PAUL. "Rejuvenation." Boni & Liveright (1923)

KISCH, E. HEINRICH, M.D. "The Sexual Life of Woman." Allied Book Company, New York (1931)

KNAUS, HERMAN, M.D. "Die Periodische Fruchtbarkeit und Unfruchtbarkeit des Weibes." Wilhelm Maudrich, Vienna (1934)

KNOPF, S. ADOLPHUS, M.D. "Various Aspects of Birth Control—Medical, Social, Economic, Legal, Moral and Religious." American Birth Control League (1928)

KNOWLTON, CHARLES, M.D. "The Fruits of Philosophy." London (1870)

KOPP, MARIE E. "Birth Control in Practice." McBride (1934)

LANDMAN, J. H. "Human Sterilization." The Macmillan Co. (1932)

LATZ, LEO J., M.D. "The Rhythm of Fertility and Sterility in Women." Latz Foundation (1932)

LAUGHLIN, H. H. "Eugenical Sterilization." American Eugenics Society (1926)

LEBEDEVA, VERA, M.D. "The Protection of Motherhood and Childhood in the Land of the Soviets." (In Russian) Moscow (1934)

LINDSEY, JUDGE BEN B. and EVANS, WAINWRIGHT. "The Companionate Marriage." Garden City Publishing Co. (1929)

LOEB, JACQUES. "The Organism as a Whole." G. P. Putnam's Sons (1916)

LONG, H. W., M.D. "Sane Sex Life and Sane Sex Living." Richard G. Badger (1919)

LYDSTON, G. FRANK, M.D. "Impotence and Sterility." The Riverton Press (1917)

MALINOWSKI, BRONISLAW. "The Sexual Life of Savages in Northwestern Melanesia." (Two volumes). Horace Liveright (1929)

MANTEGAZZA, PAOLO. "Sexual Relations of Mankind." Anthropological Press (1932)

MARSHALL, F. H. A. "The Physiology of Reproduction." Longmans, Green & Co. (1922)

MARSHALL, F. H. A. "An Introduction to Sexual Physiology." Longmans, Green & Co. (1923)

MAY, GEOFFREY. "Social Control of Sex Expression." Wm. Morrow & Co. (1930)

MAZER, CHARLES, M.D. and GOLDSTEIN, LEOPOLD, M.D. "Clinical Endocrinology of the Female." Saunders Company (1933)

MEAD, MARGARET. "Coming of Age in Samoa." William Morrow (1928)

MEAKER, SAMUEL R., M.D. "Human Sterility." Williams & Wilkins Co. (1934)

METCHNIKOFF, ELIE. "The Nature of Man." G. P. Putnam's Sons (1903)

MOENCH, GERARD L., M. D. "Studien zur Fertilität." Enke, Stuttgart (1931)

MOLL, ALBERT. "The Sexual Life of the Child." The Macmillan Co. (1923)

MOORE, CARL R. "The Biology of the Testis." *In* Sex and Internal Secretions. Williams & Wilkins Co. (1932)

NAFZAOUI, CHEIK. "The Perfumed Gardens" (Privately Printed)

NOYES, HUMPHREY JOHN. "Male Continence." Oneida (1870)

OGINO, KYUSAKU, M.D. "Conception Period of Women." Medical Arts Publishing Co. (1934)

OVID. "Ars Amatoria" (Privately Printed)

PARSHLEY, H. M. "The Science of Human Reproduction." W. W. Norton & Co. (1933)

PARSHLEY, H. M. "A Biological View of Sex." *In* Biological and Medical Aspects of Contraception. Washington, D. C. (1934)

PAPANICOLAOU, GEORGE N. "The Sexual Cycle in the Human Female as Revealed by Vaginal Smears." *In* The American Journal of Anatomy, May, 1933

PLOSS, HEINRICH, and BARTELS, MAX and PAUL. "Das Weib." Neufeld and Henius Verlag, Berlin (1927). (New Edition by Von Reitzenstein, Ferd.)

POPENOE, PAUL. "The Child's Heredity." Williams & Wilkins Co. (1929)

PELOUZE, P. S., M.D. "Gonorrhea in the Male and Female." W. B. Saunders Co. (1932)

REYNOLDS, EDWARD, M.D., and MACOMBER, DONALD, M.D. "Fertility and Sterility in Human Marriages." W. B. Saunders Co. (1924)

ROBIE, W. F., M.D. "The Art of Love." Rational Life Publishing Co., Ithaca, N. Y. (1925)

ROBINSON, WILLIAM J., M.D. "Birth Control or Limitation of Offspring." Eugenics Publishing Company (1928)

ROBINSON, WILLIAM J., M.D. "The Law Against Abortion." Eugenics Publishing Co. (1933)

ROBINSON, WILLIAM J., M.D. "Sexual Impotence." Eugenics Publishing Co. (1933)

ROBSON, J. M., M.D. "Recent Advances in Sex and Reproductive Physiology." P. Blakiston's Sons & Co., Philadelphia

RONGY, A. J., M.D. "Abortion: Legal or Illegal." The Vanguard Press (1933)

RUSSELL, BERTRAND. "Marriage and Morals." Horace Liveright (1929)

SANGER, MARGARET and STONE, HANNAH M., M.D. (*Editors*). "The Practice of Contraception." Williams & Wilkins (1931)

SANGER, MARGARET. "Motherhood in Bondage." Brentano's (1928)

SANGER, MARGARET. "My Fight for Birth Control." Farrar & Rinehart (1931)

SANGER, MARGARET. "Happiness in Marriage." Brentano's (1926)

SANGER, MARGARET (*Editor*). "Biological and Medical Aspects of Contraception." National Committee on Federal Legislation for Birth Control (1934)

SCHMALHAUSEN, SAMUEL D., and CALVERTON, V. F. (*Editors*). "Woman's Coming of Age." Horace Liveright, Inc. (1931)

SPALLANZANI, LAZARRO. "Dissertations." (Two volumes.) London (1784)

STEINACH, E., M.D. "Verjüngung durch Experimentelle Neubelebung der Altenden Pubertätsdrüse." J. Springer, Berlin (1913)

STEKEL, WILHELM, M.D. "Impotence in the Male." (Two volumes.) Horace Liveright (1927)

STEKEL, WILHELM, M.D. "Frigidity in Woman." (Two volumes.) Horace Liveright (1929)

STOCKHAM, ALICE B., M.D., "Karezza—Ethics of Marriage," R. F. Fenno and Company (1903)

STOKES, JOHN H., M.D. "Modern Clinical Syphilology." W. B. Saunders Co. (1934)

STONE, ABRAHAM, M.D. "Coitus Interruptus." *In* The Practice of Contraception. Williams & Wilkins Co. (1931)

STONE, ABRAHAM, M.D. "The Premarital Consultation." *In* Sexual Reform Congress. London (1930)

STONE, HANNAH M., M.D. "Birth Control as a Factor in the Sex Life of Women." *In* Sexual Reform Congress. London (1930)

STONE, HANNAH M., M.D. "Maternal Health and Contraception." Maternal Health Center, Newark, N. J. (1933)

STONE, HANNAH M., M.D., and STONE, ABRAHAM, M.D. "Genital Spasm as a Cause of Sexual Disharmony." Medical Journal & Record (Nov. 1933)

STOPES, MARIE C. "Married Love." G. P. Putnam's Sons (1929)

STOPES, MARIE C. "Contraception." G. P. Putnam's Sons (1931)

TAUSSIG, FRED J., M.D. "Abortion Control Through Birth Control." *In* Biological and Medical Aspects of Contraception. Washington, D. C. (1934)

TAUSSIG, FRED J., M.D. "Abortion, Spontaneous and Induced." C. V. Mosby Co. (1936)

THOREK, MAX, M.D. "The Human Testis." J. B. Lippincott Co. (1924)

TIMME, WALTER, M.D. "Constitutional Disturbances due to Improper Spacing of Children." *In* Biological and Medical Aspects of Contraception. Washington, D. C. (1934)

TUSHNOV, M. P., M.D. "Spermatoxins." Kazan (1911)

VAN DE VELDE, TH. H., M.D. "Ideal Marriage." Covici, Friede (1931)

VAN DE VELDE, TH. H., M.D. "Fertility and Sterility in Marriage." Covici, Friede (1931)

VATSYAYANA. "The Kama Sutra." (Privately Printed)

VOGE, CECIL I. B. "The Chemistry and Physics of Contraceptives." Jonathan Cape. London (1933)

VORONOFF, SERGE, M.D. "The Conquest of Life." Brentano's (1928)

WALKER, K. M., M.D. "Preparation for Marriage." W. W. Norton & Co. (1933)

WATSON, JOHN. "Behaviorism." W. W. Norton (1930)

WESTERMARCK, EDWARD. "The History of Human Marriage." (Three volumes.) The Macmillan Co. (1922)

WHITNEY, LEON F. "The Case for Sterilization." Fred A. Stokes Co. (1934)

WILLIAMS, J. WHITRIDGE, M.D. "Obstetrics." D. Appleton & Co. (1926)

WILE, IRA S., M.D. (*Editor*). "The Sex Life of the Unmarried Adult." The Vanguard Press (1934)

WOODBURY, ROBERT MORSE. "Causal Factors in Infant Mortality." U. S. Department of Labor, Children's Bureau Publication No. 142 (1925)

WRIGHT, HELENA, M.D. "The Sex Factor in Marriage." The Vanguard Press (1931)

YARROS, RACHELLE S., M.D. "Modern Woman and Sex." The Vanguard Press (1933)

ZUCKERMAN, S. "The Social Life of Monkeys and Apes." Harcourt, Brace & Co. (1932)

INDEX